REPRODUCTION REVISITED

Published by MayflyBooks. Available in paperback and free online at www.mayflybooks.org in 2019.

© Toni Ruuska 2019

Cover photo and design by Risto Musta

ISBN: 978-1-906948-42-9 (Print)
978-1-906948-43-6 (PDF)
978-1-906948-44-3 (ebook)

This work is licensed under the Creative Commons Attribution-Non commercial-No Derivatives 4.0 International (CC BY-NC-ND 4.0). To view a copy of this license, visit http://creativecommons.org/licenses/by-nc-nd/4.0/.

REPRODUCTION REVISITED

Capitalism, Higher Education and Ecological Crisis

TONI RUUSKA

www.mayflybooks.org

CONTENTS

1. INTRODUCTION..1

2. MARX AND MARXISM..14
    Philosophy, ecology, education

3. CAPITALISM AND FINITE PLANET....................56
    The Absolute Contradiction

4. REPRODUCTION OF CAPITALISM......................115

5. CAPITALISM, HIGHER EDUCATION..................156
    AND ECOLOGICAL CRISIS

6. HIGHER EDUCATION AS A FACTORY..............180
    OF COMPETITIVENESS AND INNOVATIONS
    The Finnish Context

7. REPRODUCTION REVISITED.............................240
    Conclusions

8. REFERENCES...256

1
INTRODUCTION

It is warmer now. The climate is changing. Somewhere rains are heavier, somewhere they are non-existent. Storms are more intense. The weather is unstable. Recurring heat waves and floods torment the livelihoods of humans and other earthly beings. Ice melts, and ocean levels are on the rise, as are ocean temperatures. Worse still, climate change is only one part of the ongoing ecological crisis (see e.g. Steffen et al., 2015), although perhaps the most critical part of it together with biodiversity loss. This crisis, for one, is human-induced. With all its inventions, soaring population and societal arrangements, the human race has become a force of nature. However, the Anthropocene epoch (Crutzen, 2002; Crutzen and Steffen, 2003) is not driven forward by humanity as a whole, but rather a relatively small group of wealthy organisations and individuals, as more and more people, cultures and non-human organisms are pushed into the ever-expanding capitalist socio-economic structure as particles of modern industrial civilisation.

When writing this book, the most important question for me has been: *why is the destruction of the natural world happening?* To state the obvious, there are many answers to this question, but the most apparent one is that some parts of the human species

– mostly from the Northern and Western hemispheres – exploit natural resources and destroy non-human life at an unprecedented and unsustainable rate due to various 'economic' reasons. However, within the dominant Western culture, we do not perceive that we destroy life, but rather that our doings are 'economic growth', 'progress' and 'development'.

It is not odd that the general public in the affluent North generally frowns upon environmentalists. For instance, I remember my elders calling the Finnish environmentalists '*hemmetin* (damned) *koijärveläiset!*' denoting a particular event, people and lake (*Koijärvi*) where different streams of Finnish environmental movement were united in 1979. One of the reasons why environmentalists are looked down upon, or even hated and held in disdain is, I feel, because the reproduction of capitalist socio-economic structure – or the 'engine' of industrial civilisation – demands expansive exploitation of natural habitats and resources. Where environmentalists are committed to conservation and protection of natural habitats, the reproduction of capitalism demands the opposite; that is, total exploitation. This claim is for obvious reasons vehemently denied by anyone from the establishment, which argues with more or less one voice that the despotic rule of capital benefits everyone and everything, including ecosystems and the non-human habitants of this planet. In fact, we are rather told that without economic growth, we would not be able to afford to protect the environment in the first place (but make no mistake, this reasoning is analogous to the idea that the only way to save one's life is to commit suicide).

The capitalist socio-economic structure is not only destructive ecologically and naturally, it is also a structure of privilege and social hierarchies – as with any other human civilisation thus far (see Wallerstein, 2003). Through the ages, the majority of 'civilised' human beings have worked hard and somewhat purposelessly for the benefit of the ruling elites (Eagleton, 2012, 84). Our time is no different. '*We are the 99%!*' is a contemporary slogan, but it could easily have been the slogan for any other time.

Nonetheless, I do believe that our time on this planet is unusual. As a prominent Finnish philosopher Georg Henrik von Wright (1995) wrote some twenty years ago: an observer interested in understanding our time could not fail to notice that people increasingly feel they are living in 'the end of times'. This phenomenon, von Wright (ibid) remarks, refers to an instinctive feeling that a particular course of development – which we have been taking for granted – has come to its end and, at the same time, we are approaching a new era beyond our assessment. Concerning what von Wright might have referred to as the end of times, it has become clear that humanity's exploitation of natural resources now exceeds earth's sustainable resource-carrying capacity (Meadows et al., 2002; Jackson, 2009; WWF, 2014). On the one hand, many non-renewable natural resources are at risk of running out, while renewable resources are being consumed at a faster rate than they can be renewed (Lorek and Spangenberg, 2014). On the other hand, some non-renewable resources (such as oil and natural gas) are not running out fast enough, for example, from the perspective of catastrophic climate change (Glade and Ekins, 2015).

Why then do humans, especially in the affluent North (see e.g. Ulvila and Wilén, 2017), over-exploit natural resources? When seeking an answer to this question, could one, for example, claim that the ecological crisis is due to an anthropocentric thinking, based on which humans perceive themselves as superior beings having the right to subordinate other living creatures to human will, or due to other dominant cultural beliefs? (see e.g. Næss, 1989; Bowers, 1993; Heikkurinen et al., 2016). One could also cast the blame of the ecological destruction on the 'sense of progress' that characterises Western thinking (see e.g. Bowers, 1993; Hamilton et al., 2015), based on which social and environmental problems, especially in the modern era, can be – or so it is thought – alleviated by means of technological solutions (see also Heikkurinen, 2016). Another way to answer this question, or rather point the finger, could also be the so-called neoliberal politics and ideology (see e.g. Harvey, 2005; Jones, 2013) that diverts the responsibility of actions, as well as the responsibility of poverty reduction and mitigation of climate change, to an ambiguous 'market' character.[1]

The approach to environmental degradation in this book is explicitly material, because that is what environmental degradation actually is – a material incidence. Just as Soper (1995, 249) has stated, it has not been the discourse of 'global warming' that has produced the conditions about which the discourse is concerned (see also Malm, 2018). Rather than discourses or social constructions, Karl Marx and Friedrich Engels stressed that ecological problems originate from the interaction between humans, society and their natural environments. That is to say, human-caused ecological problems are the outcome of material production processes between humans and their natural environments (Commoner, 1992).

---

[1] Although it seems evident to me that capitalism, with its compulsion for growth and expansion, constitutes the hard core of the current ecological crisis (see Foster, 2009), it also seems apparent that humanity's problems concerning environmental degradation extend far beyond capitalism and even industrial civilisation (see e.g. Bowers, 1993; Jensen, 2006; Jensen and McBay, 2009). As Bowers (1993, 19) notes, 'there is no single cause for any aspect of the ecological crisis, but there are complex and interconnected cultural patterns, beliefs, and values that collectively help to introduce perturbations into ecosystems, causing them to go into decline.' Furthermore, environmental degradation is not only a modern problem, but has also been a problem of the past, as numerous past civilisations have disappeared because of environmental degradation and the exploitation of their habitats (see e.g. Diamond, 2005, Tainter, 2015). Thus, a more profound and philosophical question is whether humans are bound to destroy their habitats, or is this perhaps only a matter linked to human civilisations (Jensen, 2006) or, for example, anthropocentric thinking and misplaced cultural beliefs (Næss, 1989; Bowers, 1993). Nevertheless, these essential questions go beyond the scope of this book.

INTRODUCTION

Despite capitalism's relatively long roots (see e.g. Wood, 2002; Moore, 2007; 2015; Arrighi, 2010) most of its development towards its current industrial form has happened within the past two centuries. During the same period of time, in the era of the Anthropocene (see Crutzen and Stoermer, 2000; Crutzen, 2002), human-caused changes and the degradation of the ecosystem have increased exponentially. Somewhat surprisingly it has been recognised only very recently that industrial civilisation has been and remains to be largely supported and sustained by the use of fossil fuels and the petrol engine (Foster, 2009, 92-99; Moore, 2015, 53-54; Salminen and Vadén, 2015, 1; Malm, 2016). From an ecological perspective, and because we are either living or about to live in the times of peak (cheap) oil (see e.g. Foster, 2009, 92-99; Moore, 2015, 105-109; Salminen and Vadén, 2015, 3-4), it is rather easy to show that this kind of culture and way of living is likely to come to an end somewhat soon (see also Hornborg, 2014). However, in practice, it seems impossible to steer the global economy to a more conservative path ecologically if we are to follow the internal laws and dynamics of (fossil energy fuelled) capitalism (Foster, 2009, 92-99). Hence humanity, with its current path of 'development', has, for now, chosen the same boom and bust road that drives capitalism forward. Of course, where the planet Earth is concerned, after a sufficiently huge bust (for example catastrophic climate change), there will not be another big boom.

If the tide is to be turned, a drastic reorientation in many habitual and societal practices has to take place, and the sooner the better. This call for reorientation asks (if not forces) us to examine the underlying assumptions behind individual action and our way of living, but also the current and prospective economic, social and institutional structures, including education. Meanwhile, we must certainly ask how come, and in spite of all the knowledge and evidence we possess about the ecological crisis, there has not been a turn towards more sustainable futures? However, and tragically the link between capitalism and the ongoing ecological destruction is something that neither mainstream politics nor environmentalism is properly addressing (see e.g. Klein, 2014).

Quite paradoxically, the means offered in mainstream politics, business and civil society to alleviate the ongoing destruction are precisely what have caused it: more consumption, more production, more development, more technology, more education, more material wealth, and so on. In the past thirty years, only the prefixes have changed: words like 'green', 'sustainable' and 'eco-' are attached to products, services and projects, not indicating ecological sustainability, but how profits are now made by using these 'sustainability' labels. Meanwhile, the material throughput of the global economy keeps on increasing, as the hegemony of capital intensifies. Instead of coming across with its own ecological unsustainability, modern industrial gospel is forcibly spread by agents of capital to every corner of the world with structural adjustment programmes, cheap labour, debt and a Western educational curriculum. The last one on the list may surprise some, but contemporary Western (higher) education does not challenge the logic and culture of growth, but is rather keen to participate in it.

The main message of this book is that in the 21st century, one of the main purposes of contemporary higher education is to reproduce capitalism and the dominant capitalist relations of production and ideology. This is not a new claim. Louis Althusser made the same claim half a century ago. But, many things have happened since the late 1960s. The world is no longer bipolar, and capital's rule is global. Sadly, the same is true when it comes to the proportions of the ongoing ecological crisis. At the same time, nation states are struggling with their legitimacy, as global power structures are experiencing changes and geopolitical conflicts seem to be on the rise. Therefore, it is the proper time to update the theory of reproduction of capitalism, and to investigate how the dominant ideologies have shaped the orientation, practices and purpose of higher education, and how these are connected to the ecological crisis.

Personally, I was not aware of the 'hidden curricula' in education when I began my bachelor studies at the Helsinki School of Economics in 2004. As many of my contemporaries, I perceived education naively, as something pure – as some kind of redeemer (see e.g. Allen, 2017). I think similarly to many of my contemporaries, institutional higher education would turn out to be disappointing. Where I had sought knowledge and understanding about the economy, I received no such thing. The first two years of my studies crystallised for me a handful of anecdotes about clever company managers and thriving corporations. The last three years I spent reading management journals and writing about them, which I think only added to my sense of puzzlement over what I was studying or supposed to study. Nevertheless, I did learn two valuable skills: academic reading and writing.

In the end, I can blame only myself for my personal choices. Surely, I was in the wrong place to learn about the economy, above all because the very institutions where I was located were and are, by definition, committed to the reproduction of capitalist economy and ideology. Business schools are schools of business; that is, they educate students about capitalist business, and they educate students to become part of the capitalist business, and the capitalist businesses educate their personnel to conduct capitalist business.

The reader would be right to jump to a conclusion: my political and ecological 'awakening' did not happen in school. Rather it was closely tied to the financial crisis that began in 2008. This might sound odd, but the postfinancialmeltdown confusion (both personal and societal) was a profound wake-up call for me. Most of all I realised how ignorant I had been. For years I had studied in a school of economics, but did not have a clue how various economic and social arrangements contributed to the financial crisis. With hindsight, this was probably the reason I wanted to do a PhD. I desired time to read and think.

In the admission interviews of Aalto University's doctoral programme, it was made clear to me that I was expected to write an article-based doctoral thesis and to publish my work in 'top' academic journals. After I was admitted, I soon became aware of many other trends and developments of the current academia. An insight struck me: the academia I had in mind when I applied to the doctoral programme did not really exist. Rather, what I found was the same competitive logic and instrumental mindset I had become accustomed to during my previous studies and my couple of years working in the private sector. I asked myself, was academia (becoming) a corporation much like the rest of the modern world? As ridiculous as it may sound at first, there certainly is plenty of evidence to support this claim, both from personal experience and from academic literature. Personally, the corporatisation of academia was noticeable to me, not only at the level of national and international higher education policy, but also in Aalto University's mission, strategy and composition of its board members, or in the way the position of PhD students was characterised to me as 'academic entrepreneurs', pointing towards uncertain and discontinuous funding and the precariousness of doctoral studies. Other examples of this change were to me the overall working atmosphere, constant change of personnel in my department, forever changing guidelines for funding PhD students, and also the restructuring of physical working spaces:

INTRODUCTION

I spent the last years working on my PhD thesis in an open-plan office. The evidence is also convincing from the perspective of academic literature. For instance, scholars dealing with the concept of academic capitalism have for the past two decades investigated how higher education and academia have moved closer to capitalist markets (see e.g. Slaughter and Leslie, 1997; Slaughter and Rhoades, 2004; Cantwell and Kauppinen, 2014).

Now the corporatisation of higher education and academia might sound curious enough, but the biggest surprise was yet to come. Certainly, I had already realised when studying at Bachelor's and Master's level at the Helsinki School of Economics that one of the primary purposes of the whole institution was to guide students towards working life, or in other words, to help students to become employees of large national and transnational corporations. However, I had not considered the idea of social and economic reproduction until I read Althusser's essay, *Ideology and Ideological State Apparatus*[2]. In many ways, Althusser's essay changed the way I saw education in the contemporary economic and social setting, but even more how I perceived the nation state and the purpose of institutional education. Ultimately, it was that one piece of text that helped me to see the connections between capitalism, environmental degradation and what seems to be one of the main purposes of higher education in the 21st century – to reproduce and facilitate conditions of capital accumulation, competitiveness and economic growth.

Luckily, policy-making reality is not yet the same reality that academics and faculties face in the institutional level. In academia, there is arguably still some room for questioning and for the Humboldtian academic values and ideas of scientific enquiry. Nevertheless, as transnational and international organisations

---

[2] This essay is included in the collection *On the Reproduction of Capitalism: Ideology and Ideological State Apparatuses* (Althusser, 2014).

(such as the EU and OECD), nation states and differing private interests manage the direction and purpose of higher education in an increasingly instrumental fashion, there is a growing danger and real possibility that we might lose an integral part of higher education and universities, which is, to me, their essential position in facilitating and pursuing free thinking and production of knowledge. Although it is safe to say that the connection between knowledge and power has been noteworthy throughout modern times, it is arguably only within the last couple of decades that we have witnessed a rise of knowledge policy at the very core of national and transnational policy making. If, in the social democratic era of capitalism, the state's interest in higher education was more explicitly in pursuing national competitiveness, the situation is not the same in the neoliberal organisation of capitalism.

While it is still true at national policy-making level that one of the primary purposes of higher education is to contribute to national competitiveness, it is at the same time true that powerful transnational interests are pushing higher education into the direction of transnational academic capitalism. This means that higher education is nowadays steered not only by national, but also transnational interests (see Kauppinen, 2012). Whereas corporations and various lobbying organisations are pursuing efforts to privatise and commercialise knowledge to their benefit, knowledge production and its regulation are, meanwhile, widely stated as an explicit political goal to support various national and transnational agendas. In this sense, higher education is an interesting and important junction, where individuals, practices, the state and various political agendas and trends intermingle.

Education is not a monolith, but neither is it impartial. As Unterhalter and Carpenter (2010, 2) note, *'higher education has the potential to reduce or to increase inequalities depending on the form of policies, institutions, governments, inter-government organizations and transnational associations implement.*' Following Poulantzas' (2000) relational conception of the state, contemporary higher education could thus be considered to be a condensation of class and power struggles, academic tradition, education ideals, and economic ambitions originating from various sources. Which of these elements have the upper hand remains in flux. In this regard, the field of education is also an important mirror to reflect society in general, the issues of which are contested, resisted, and held important in any given period of time. At the same time, I also feel it is important to note that although I criticise capitalism and the structures that support and reproduce it, my purpose is not by any means to argue against or 'attack' education *per se*. Instead, the message is rather that the current outlook and the priorities steering contemporary (higher) education should be questioned, while the condition of planetary ecosystems should frame all future educational reforms (see Bowers, 1993).

To combine capitalism, environmental degradation and higher education, as well as theory development, in a single book requires some time and space. The aim of the theoretical investigation, which takes up the bulk of space in this book, is to argue that capitalism, as it is defined, is ecologically unsustainable, and to update the theory of the reproduction of capitalism, and establish a connection between contemporary higher education and ecological crisis. The task is thus to present what capitalism is, how it functions, and above all, how capitalism is reproduced in general, but especially how higher education contributes to this process and how all this links to ecological questions. The empirical illustration serves to strengthen the theoretical argument, as it highlights how the purpose of higher education is expressed by the Finnish state in the education policy documents of the 21st century. This section of the book concentrates, in particular, on the interplay of state, higher education and socio-economic structures of the contemporary Western industrial social setting. Together these sections form the main argument of this book, which is that:

> One of the primary purposes of 21st century higher education is to reproduce capitalism. Being that higher education is organised in an ecologically unsustainable manner, it exacerbates rather than alleviates the ecological crisis. This is because higher not only is education organised in the framework of capitalist socio-economic structure, but it also directly contributes to the reproduction of capitalism.

Following the outlined plan, in Chapter 2, I first explain the theoretical and philosophical underpinnings of this book, as I briefly summarise the intellectual history of Karl Marx and some of the history of Marxism, as well as Marx and Engels' materialist conception of history. After this, I shortly review the most prominent streams of Marxist studies of education, and literature on education and ecological crisis. In Chapter 3, I define capitalism and outline, again briefly, the historical developments that have given birth to capitalism. I then move on to describe the fundamental logic of capital and capital accumulation, as well as the capitalist market structure, before scrutinising the latest and still ongoing restructuring of the capitalist political economy and its transnationalisation. Following this, I present the most fundamental reasons contributing to the existence of, in my point of view, a serious contradiction between capitalism and ecological sustainability. I then deepen the argument by discussing the Jevons paradox and bottlenecks for further capital accumulation.

In Chapter 4, I present the framework of the updated reproduction theory of capitalism in the 21st century. After briefly highlighting the primary components of the theory, I then discuss them separately starting from the modern nation state and its relation to the reproduction of capitalism. Subsequently, I move on to ground the theory of reproduction, and discuss the works of Antonio Gramsci, Louis Althusser, and Nicos Poulantzas and their insights regarding hegemony and hegemonic state apparatuses, Ideological State Apparatuses, reproduction, and education.

In Chapter 5, the theory of reproduction, contemporary higher education, and ecological crisis are brought together. By going through the neoliberal restructuring of higher education, I attempt to convince the reader that higher education in the 21st century is closely integrated into the capitalist structure in following the logic of capitalism and capital accumulation. By examining some of the contemporary literature concerning, for instance, academic capitalism, I argue that higher education is portrayed in an instrumental fashion, above all because of the overall restructuring of capitalism and the importance of knowledge, knowledge production, and know-how in the global economy. I then argue how these restructurings and developments have had an impact on higher education, and consequently how the current shape of higher education is linked and contributes to the ecological crisis.

In Chapter 6, the insights of Chapter 5 are reflected in the Finnish context. At first, Finnish educational history is outlined very briefly before highlighting the changes of neoliberal restructuring of Finnish higher education. In the empirical illustration, I present how the purpose of higher education is expressed by the Finnish state in the education policy documents and how this is connected to the reproduction of capitalism and to the ecological crisis. In the concluding Chapter 7, I recapitulate the updated reproduction theory of capitalism, before making conclusions concerning the unsustainability of contemporary education.

2

MARX AND MARXISM
Philosophy, ecology, education

The inspiration and essentially all the theories and concepts that are applied in this book originate from Karl Marx, Friedrich Engels and from the Marxist tradition. I have tried to explain to myself many times why Marx and Marxism have 'felt right' to me. The world filled with injustice, oppression and exploitation is part of the answer, but there is more. As Göran Therborn (2007, 67), a prominent Swedish sociologist, explains, Marxism is, at the same time, a historical social science, focused on the operation of capitalism, and more generally, on historical developments defined by the dynamics linked to forces and relations of production. In addition, Marxism is also a philosophical tradition with certain ontological, epistemological and ethical grounds, and, of course, finally, Marxism is a mode of politics, as it has been used historically to overthrow the existing bourgeois order.

Apart from this, it was very difficult to me to comprehend modern economic, social and ecological contexts, before a more close examination of the writings of Marx and his followers. Therefore, it is safe to say that Marx and Marxist tradition has felt right because of its eminent weight of evidence in explaining economic, socio-political and ecological contradictions – especially in the time of global capitalism – as well as because its persuasive combination of the theory of capital(ism) and analysis on power and power structures. To be sure, I do not see scientific inquiry as a mere political project. Rather I perceive it as a way to seek and contemplate the truth. On the one hand, scientific inquiry is, to me, a way to deepen one's understanding about the world we inhabit, but simultaneously, I feel it is a way to express solidarity to fellow beings on this planet. On the other hand, I do have found the claim regarding neutrality of academic social research to be strange. If one sees and feels that there is something wrong or unjust in the world, I strongly perceive that it is one's moral responsibility to act and take a stance. Therefore, scientific inquiry is, to me, also a way to take part in the ongoing societal struggles – a way to change the world for the better, I hope. Nevertheless, by taking a stance, in my mind, I am not giving away my scientific integrity but rather feel that I have become closer to the things that are truly important.

Although Marxists do not speak with one voice, in fact sometimes quite far from it, I believe that fruitful syntheses are out there to be made. That said, many Marxists would perhaps denounce my efforts to bring together Louis Althusser and Antonio Gramsci in certain issues, and in many ways their criticism would be accurate. Nonetheless, I would claim that we need both Althusser and Gramsci to understand the reproduction of capitalism in the 21st century. Gramsci's theory of cultural hegemony and Althusser's theory of Ideological State Apparatuses have both given me inspiration and, more importantly, theoretical grounds to build my argument. However, both of their works were left unfinished. Hence, I try to combine some of their ideas into an updated theory of reproduction with the help of Nicos Poulantzas and William Robinson.

Academic battles between Althusser and Gramsci, and their followers, and 'structuralist' and 'post-structuralist' have left many stones unturned in the Marxist and Neo-Marxist school of thought. I find it strange and without a plausible explanation, that a thesis regarding the reproduction of capitalism had not been thoroughly theorised or developed. Certainly, the capitalist mode of production has been well portrayed and theorised already by Marx, but also by his followers. The case is, however, different in regard to the socio-ideological structures or superstructure(s). There are good reasons for this, I feel. The socio-political sphere is rather messy, and it easily escapes subtle models and theories. At the same time, I would argue that contemporary capitalism, or more precisely global neoliberal capitalism, might be more straightforward as a structure than, for instance, the social democratic phase of capitalism. It seems to me that the hegemony of capital is somehow more exposed in the era of neoliberalism, and so are also, I would argue, the power relations and societal structures penetrated by the logic of capital accumulation and demand of economic growth.

In addition, Althusser's claim that educational apparatus is the dominant 'Ideological State Apparatus' can be considered even more conclusive in the era of neoliberal higher education than it was in the era of social democracy and the welfare state. The same is arguably true in the case of Gramsci's hegemony concept in William Robinson's use, when Robinson studies the transnational capitalist class as a historic bloc and dominant fraction of global capital. In the same sense, an increasingly integrated and homogeneous world economy, although it is in many ways chaotic and complex, might be somewhat less difficult to conceive. But then again, it also seems that transformations within the capitalist socio-economic structure have produced 'hybrid' states, that is, states that are caught in between the welfare state and neoliberal competition and market liberalisation. From my perspective, the Finnish state is one of these hybrid states, because it retains national welfare state functions but at the same time has sought to open up to global capitalist competition and to attract transnational capital by privatising and commodifying public services. Consequently, William Robinson's theory of global capitalism has helped me a great deal in understanding this development, which according to him entails a new kind of understanding of where to locate power and in the global socio-economic order, and thus also invites us to reconsider the role of the nation state (see Robinson, 2014).

It has been particularly rewarding for me to read Marx with certain guidance from more contemporary scholars (such as Terry Eagleton, John Bellamy Foster, Jukka Heiskanen, Jason W. Moore, Jan Rehmann, Peter Thomas and Ellen Meiksins Wood) and to reflect upon the remarks of Marx and classic Marxists in our day. The topicality of Marx in the 21st century seems to me to be undisputed. Environmental degradation, socio-economic inequality, and economic crises are all areas where Marx has a great deal to offer in explaining the fundamental sources of these phenomena. To me, perhaps the most extraordinary account of Marx, which brings together all the main themes of this book, is his assessment of the impact of capital on natural and social environments in *Grundrisse*. In the following passage, the logic of capital, according to Marx, is felt in all corners of life; in the way capital treats its environmental surroundings, and in the way capital influences the social, and for instance science (and education). The passage ends with Marx's impressive take of the final frontier of capital, which is, of course, capital itself always pushing for more and more, until the very end, defying the inevitable collapse of capitalist socio-economic structure as we know it. Marx (1993, 409-410, italics in original) writes that:

> Just as production founded on capital creates universal industriousness on one side – i.e. surplus labour, value-creating labour – so does it create the other side a system of general exploitation of the natural and human qualities, a system of general utility, utilizing science itself just as much as all the physical and mental qualities, while science appears nothing

higher in itself, nothing legitimate for itself, outside this circle of social production and exchange. Thus capital creates the bourgeois society, and the universal appropriation of nature as well as of the social bond itself by the members of society. Hence the great civilizing influence of capital; its production of a stage of society in comparison to which all earlier ones appear as mere *local developments* of humanity and as *nature-idolatry*. For the first time, nature becomes purely an object for humankind, purely a matter of utility; ceases to be recognized as a power for itself; and the theoretical discovery of its autonomous laws appears merely as a ruse so as to subjugate it under human needs, whether as an object of consumption or as means of production. In accord with this tendency, capital drives beyond national barriers and prejudices as much as beyond nature worship, as well as all traditional, confined, complacent, encrusted satisfaction of present needs, and reproduction of old ways of life. It is destructive towards all of this, and constantly revolutionizes it, tearing down all the barriers, which hem in the development of the forces of production, and the exploitation and exchange of natural and mental forces.

But from the fact that capital posits every such limit as a barrier and hence gets *ideally* beyond it, does not by any means follow that it has *really* overcome it, and, since every such barrier contradicts its character, its production moves in contradictions, which are constantly overcome, but just as constantly posited. Furthermore. The universality towards which it irresistibly strives encounters barriers in its own nature, which will, at a certain stage of its development, allow it to be recognized as being itself the greatest barrier to this tendency, and hence will drive towards its own suspension.

I think there is something very telling in this passage for us to be able to understand contemporary capitalism, capitalist societies, as well as ever-worsening environmental degradation. In any case, only this very passage clearly reflects the topicality of Marx's thought and may also further convince the reader of the reasons why I have relied on Marx and Marxists to establish a connection between capitalism, higher education and environmental degradation.

There exists only a few thinkers, if that, who have gone through such steep changes in reading and interpretation of their work as Karl Marx has. On the one hand, as a philosopher and political economist he has repeatedly been declared as 'dead', and as often declared to return (Koivisto and Oittinen, 2011, 7). On the other hand, in the beginning of the 1990s, Marxism in general seemed to be in danger of disappearing completely, as the Soviet Union and state socialism collapsed. Nonetheless, during the past years, there have been clear signs of a new Marx renaissance (ibid). This time, the return of Marx seems to have novel features though, which separate this particular revival from the previous ones. The most important of these is, without a doubt, the progressing MEGA project (*Marx-Engels Gesamtausgabe*), which is committed to publishing the complete works (finished, unfinished and refined manuscripts) of Marx and Engels (ibid, 9). Although the MEGA project is still incomplete – roughly half of the planned publications have been published so far (Heiskanen, 2016, 272) – it is clear at this point that MEGA has already provided an opportunity for a more extensive base to study Marx than ever before (Koivisto and Oittinen, 2011, 9).

It is justifiable to claim that MEGA may entail a new reading and interpretation of Marx, which according to Koivisto and Oittinen (2011, 10) is already the fourth time in history, when the overall reception of Marx may change considerably. The other three periods of different Marx readings and interpretations are: first until the end of 1880s, when the ideas of Marx and Engels begin to gain ground in the workers movement across Europe and especially among German social democrats (Koivisto and Oittinen, 2011, 10; see also McLellan, 2007, Chapter 2). The second period of Marxist interpretations is usually called the Marxism of the Second International (1880-1914) with Karl Kautsky as its leading figure. In this interpretation, the works of Marx were often considered to be positivistic in their treatment of societal development, and the economics of capitalism (Koivisto and Oittinen, 2011, 10), as it was generally perceived in the end of the 19th century that Marxism had no philosophical content (McLellan, 2007, 110).

During the third period, along with the First World War and the breakup of the workers movement, the reading typical to the time of the Second International was gradually replaced, from the 1920s, by a Marxism-Leninist reading of Marx of the Soviet Union era, which was, of course, rivalled by other readings of Marx, but these did not gain similar influence around the world (Koivisto and Oittinen, 2011, 10). Currently, after the collapse of Soviet Union and alongside the progressing MEGA project, the fourth period of Marx interpretation is about to begin, but so far it is too early to say what will be the identifying characteristics of this era (ibid).

Karl Marx was born at Trier, in Prussia, on 5th of May 1818. His family background gave him an opportunity for higher education studies, first at *Gymnasium* in Trier being followed by university studies at Bonn and Berlin (see e.g. Jones, 2016). After a year in the University of Bonn, Marx received his first genuine intellectual stimulus at Berlin University, where he was, along with his law studies, also absorbed by philosophy and history (Kolakowski, 2008, 80).

Likewise in Berlin, Marx went through a serious conversion to Hegel's philosophy. As McLellan (1990, 34) has argued, this conversion was probably the most important intellectual step for

Marx in his life. This was because, as much as Marx later criticised and denounced Hegel's idealism and dialectics[33], he was also first to admit that his methods, as well as some of Marx's critique regarding capitalist ethics, originated from Hegel (ibid). In his PhD thesis, Marx studied the ancient atomists, that is, the natural philosophy of Democritus and Epicurus (Heiskanen, 2010), a thesis he worked on from the beginning of 1839 until April 1841 (Kolakowski, 2008, 83). After completing his dissertation, Marx moved to Bonn after a short stay in Trier. In Bonn, Marx wrote to the Young Hegelian journals. He defended, among other things, the freedom of the press, but also, for the first time, devoted his attention towards economic questions and socio-economic inequality (Kolakowski, 2008, 99; Jones, 2016). According to Kolakowski (2008, 101), Marx's concerns with politics made him to approach Hegel's philosophy of law, which ultimately produced a lengthy critique (*Critique of Hegel's Philosophy of Right*), which was written in 1843 (first published in 1927). Around this time, Marx had moved to Paris with his newly wedded wife Jenny (Kolakowski, 2008, 101). In Paris, Marx met Friedrich Engels. This meeting marked the beginning of forty years of collaboration in politics and academic writing. In Paris Marx attempted, for the first time, to formulate a critique of political economy. This work, as with many others, was never finished. It was first published in 1932, and is generally known as the *Economic and Philosophical Manuscripts of 1844* (ibid, 109). Many scholars consider the Paris manuscripts to be one of the most important sources to trace the evolution of Marx's thought

---

3   Philosopher Herakleitos is famous for his dynamic worldview, in which 'everything flows'. Long after Herakleitos, Hegel, who was greatly influenced by ancient philosophers, claimed to be a dialectic (Heiskanen, 2015). Hegel characterised *dialectics* as flexible operation with concepts, which can also be in contradictory position against each other, but are nevertheless linked to each other, as one contemplates the truth (ibid). Hegel also characterised dialectics as the unity of the opposites. From Hegel this method and ontological stance was first adopted and then criticised as well as developed by Marx and Marxists later on (ibid).

(Heiskanen, 2015), as it can be considered the first experiment of a long intellectual journey, in which *Capital* is the final destination (Kolakowski, 2008, 109).

Marx's and Engels's first joint effort in writing was entitled *The Holy Family* and was published in 1845 (ibid, 121). In the following year, Marx and Engels finished *The German Ideology*, but were not able to publish it (it was first published in its entire version in 1932). In *The German Ideology*, Marx and Engels famously outline the premises of the materialist conception of history (ibid, 126). From this period onwards, Marx went through a reorientation in his work. As Kolakowski (ibid, 150) establishes, from *'1847 onwards Marx occasionally reverted to philosophic speculation of the kind that dominate his early writings.'* Kolakowski explains (ibid) that *'the instance of this are important, as they confirm the essential continuity of his thought and enable us to relate his political and economic ideas to the trends of his earliest thinking.'*

Having joined with German 'true socialism' Marx endeavoured to challenge Proudhon, utopian socialism, Bakunin and Lassalle in *Poverty of Philosophy*, which was written in 1847 in Brussels (ibid, 150). The most widely read work of Marx and Engels saw the light of day in the following year. The publication of *The Communist Manifesto* took place in the immediate aftermath of the political upheavals of 1848. As a result of the events, Marx was deported from Brussels and returned to Paris (ibid, 192). Soon, however, he was forced to leave Paris, and relocated to Cologne, where he started to publish a newspaper and worked for the German revolutionary cause in favour of the Communist League. However, unfortunate political events, from Marx's perspective, took place and he was again expelled, this time from Prussia in 1849. Marx made his way back to Paris, only to be exiled to London with no money, and no source of livelihood (ibid, 192-193). In London, Marx would spend the rest of his days in exile struggling with poverty and various illnesses. Engels settled in Manchester in 1850 and supported Marx financially, drawing income from his father's cotton mill (McLellan, 1990).

It took some time for Marx to take on the topic of political economy, which nevertheless, was Marx's chief occupation at the beginning of the London years (Kolakowski, 2008, 194). The economic crisis of 1857 gave Marx the impetus to draft a revised version of his theories which, however, were not published in his lifetime (ibid). The comprehensive work was titled *Grundrisse der Kritik der politischen Ökonomie (Outline of a Critique of Political Economy)*. *Grundrisse* (written in 1857-1858) is considered to be the first outline of 'later Marx's' approach to political economy, a work he had started in Paris in 1844 (McLellan, 1990, 271). However, when, in 1844, Marx analysed market mechanisms of exchange, in *Grundrisse* Marx grounds his studies in production. Likewise, Marx no longer claims that a worker sells his or her work, but rather his or her workforce (ibid). *Grundrisse* also contains a new version of the theory of alienated labour (Kolakowski, 2008, 194). *Grundrisse* remained unpublished for a long time, until it was published in the Soviet Union during the Second World War. Nevertheless, another of Marx's works regarding economics was published in 1859. It was entitled *A Contribution to the Critique of Political Economy*. In the preface of this work can be found one of the most cited pieces of Marx's texts (ibid, 195), as it contains the most concise and general formulation of the base/superstructure metaphor, that is Marx's conceptualisation of historical formulation and transformation of societies.

After these publications, Marx was absorbed, as one of the leading figures, in the organisation of the First International, which undoubtedly postponed the publication of the first volume of *Capital* (McLellan, 1990, 329). Famously, *Capital*, Marx's *magnum opus*, was not finished in his lifetime, except the first volume, which was published in 1867. Engels edited and ensured that the following two volumes would see the light of day after Marx had died in 1883 (the second volume of *Capital* was published in 1885, and the third in 1894). After Engels had passed away in 1895, Karl Kautsky published the *Theories of Surplus Value* in 1905-1910, which is widely considered to be the fourth volume of *Capital* (Kolakowski, 2008, 211).

Although *Capital* was left unfinished, at least compared to the ambitions Marx had for his work (Heiskanen, 2015, 13), Krätke (2011, 189), for one, has proclaimed that Marx's achievements were nevertheless huge, as *Capital* is clearly distinguished from that superficial economism, to which a great deal of the economic thinking was already sliding towards in Marx's time. Furthermore, Krätke (ibid) confesses that Marx's critique of political economy remains, to date, the only comprehensive critique of political economy and the reductionist thinking of modern economics.

In many parts, Marx's work was left unfinished or it was published much later than originally intended. Marx's work is a rich and manifold collection of remarks of many sorts, which can be well read from different perspectives – a notion which Marxist tradition also professes. At the same time, it is clear historical fact that it can be utilised to a wide variety of political agendas, and thus, it is no wonder that the followers of Marx are and have been diverse, although they are usually categorized broadly as Marxists.

In all its historical inheritance, Marxism can be considered to be, at least, a school of thought (a philosophical tradition, a strand of social sciences), as well as a method to analyse socio-economic structures and historical developments based on the works and method of Karl Marx and Friedrich Engels. Marxism is and has also been a prominent and widespread political project and movement, especially in the 20th century. Communist, socialist, and social democratic parties around the world, as well as various other more or less reformist and revolutionary movements (such as the workers movement) have sought inspiration and collective consciousness from the works of Marx and Engels, and have thus been either labelled Marxists or declared to be Marxist (see e.g. McLellan, 2007; Therborn, 2007; Kolakowski, 2008). In any case, and undoubtedly, Marxism is a rich and multifaceted historical phenomenon, but one which also carries substantial historical baggage. Some of this baggage may be well deserved and some may not, but one can be sure that this historical baggage should not be put on Marx's shoulders. As Kolakowski (2008, 6) has stated:

> There is abundant evidence that all social movements are to be explained by a variety of circumstances and that the ideological sources of which they appeal, and to which they seek to remain faithful, are only one of the factors determining the form they assume and their patterns of thought and action. We may therefore be certain in advance that no political or religious movement is a perfect expression of that movement's 'essence' as laid down in its sacred writings; on the other hand, these writings are not merely passive, but exercise and influence of their own on the course of the movement. What normally happens is that the social forces, which make themselves, the representatives of a given ideology are stronger than that ideology, but are to some extent dependent on its own tradition.

Kolakowski (ibid) continues that every important idea is inevitably subject to division and differentiation, as it becomes recognised and starts to be disseminated. Moreover, and as we already saw, the interpretation of Marx has been in transformation through different times and historical conditions. This is in part, and as McLellan (2007, 1-2) acknowledges, because the passage of time has revealed serious ambiguities in Marx's thought. For a long period of time,

Marx was only known for his rather difficult-to-read *Capital*, and rather simplistic *The Communist Manifesto* (ibid), and thus the publication of Marx's unfinished manuscripts and republication and wider availability of some of his lesser known works, has suggested to many a thorough reassessment of what was thought to be his message (ibid). Another reason for the constant rediscovery and reinterpretation of Marx legacy is that Marx is not easily categorised. Marx was a dialectical thinker, and Marx's dialectics in particular is open-ended, that is, being in itself is considered to be a unity of subjective and objective components, and both theory and practice are constantly in interaction and evolving through history (ibid). Therefore, it is no wonder that Marx shaped and reorganised his ideas and theories throughout his life, although this is not to say that there would not be continuity and consistency in Marx's philosophical assumptions (Heiskanen, 2010, 203). In addition, the interpretation of Marx is also made difficult by the fact that eventually Marxism became the doctrine of a mass movement, and thus, as McLellan (2007, 2) has stated *'the inherited ideas were simplified, ratified and ossified.'*

Similarly, Kolakowski (2008, 8) recognises that it is difficult to outline the chronology of Marxism due to both the changing interpretation and changing bibliography of Marx. But in any sense, he suggests that the years and decades following the death of Marx and Engels, would be called the golden age of Marxism (ibid). This golden age is also known as the era of the Second International (1889-1914). At that time Marxism had reputable defenders such as Karl Kautsky, Rosa Luxemburg, Georgi Plekhanov, Eduard Berstein, Vladimir Lenin, Jean Jaurés, Max Adler, Otto Bauer, Rudolf Hilferding, Antonio Labriola, Antonie Pannekoek, Emile Vandervelde, and Heinrich Cunov, although the influence of Marxism extended beyond 'the believers' to many other disciplines that did not adopt Marxism as a whole but hand-picked and utilised particular ideas and concepts (ibid, 355-356).

The character of Marxism in Europe and in United States was greatly influenced by the collapse of the Second International in 1914, and by the defeats of the working-class movements in Western Europe in the decade following the First World War (McLellan, 2007, 295). In this process, the works of Lukács, Korsch, and Gramsci among others, radically reformulated the systematic take of the Marxism of the Second International, as many central Marxist concepts, such as class struggle and the function of the state, were reconceptualised (ibid, 171). In more broad strokes, the withering away of the workers movement momentum signified that the main body of Marxist thought moved eastwards, only to 'hit another wall', i.e. to be suppressed by the rise of Stalin (ibid, 295). In the Stalinist era, Marxism came to mean, above all, the institutionalisation of power in state apparatus, as Marxism under Stalin cannot be defined by specific ideas or concepts, but the absolute power of authority (Kolakowski, 2008, 791). Stalin himself christened Marxism-Leninism, which was Stalin's own doctrine, in addition to selected dogma from the works of Marx, Engels and Lenin (ibid). In the same sense, Maoist ideology in China, although it relied on Marxist phraseology, seemed in reality to be completely alien to Marx and Marxism (ibid, 1184).

In the following decades, the next generation of Marxist theoreticians brought a serious change in their political orientation. Lukács, Luxemburg, Gramsci, Lenin, to name just a few, were all important figures in political parties, a historical trend that is in sharp contrast to the mid- and post-war years. This is because the next generation of key Marxist theorists would primarily be academics rather than activists, scholars who wrote their work in the period of decline in working-class activity in somewhat political isolation (McLellan, 2007, 297-298). Frankfurt school and its members (such as Horkheimer, Adorno, Benjamin, Fromm, Marcuse, and later Habermas) are probably the clearest example of this change, as Marxism now became an established academic discipline. Another example of this tendency, as well as another influential stream of Marxist thought in the post Second World War era, is the so-called Structural Marxism which arose in France in the mid-1960s (ibid, 348). One of the key figures of this stream of Marxism, Louis Althusser, attempted, among other concerns, to update Marxist thought in accordance with the passive nature of subjects (both bourgeois and working-class) in the advanced industrial society. In following and developing Althusser's conceptualisations, Nicos Poulantzas, for his part, made a significant attempt to apply and to elaborate Althusser's theories into his analysis of state, power and class (McLellan, 2007, 354) as we shall see later[4].

Overall, as the 20th century progressed to its end, state socialism experienced a terminal crisis, and along with this, Marxism went through a shock. As Kolakowski (2008, 1206) wrote *'Marxism has been the greatest fantasy of 20th century'* but to say that Marxism is a fantasy, Kolakowski (ibid) continues *'does not mean that it is nothing else.'* Furthermore, he (ibid) remarks that *'Marxism as an interpretation of past history must distinguished from Marxism as a political ideology.'* To me, this seems to be the proper way to respond to the legacy and historical baggage of Marxism. This is because intellectually, it is apparent that Marx, and Marxism, has and

---

[4] It is worth mentioning that, while I do share many of the premises of Althusser's philosophy, I, at the same time, reject his overly strcturalist takes on subjectivity, and for instance his claim regarding Marx's 'epistemological break' in *For Marx* (2005/1965) and *Reading Capital* (2009/1968). Alongwith these reservations, I wish to note also that I perceive many of Althusser's conceptualisations – especially his ideas on reproduction and Ideological State Apparatuses – to be of great value if one is trying to make sense of the capitalist socio-economic structure in the 21st century.

continues to be greatly influential in various fields of social sciences and beyond (McLellan, 2007, 424).

My reading of Marx and Marxism does not, perhaps, follow the most beaten paths of Marx interpretations. This is because I perceive Marx and Marxism from a position that is critical towards technological progress. Thus, my position stands in contrast to most Marxist and neo-Marxist streams of thought that *'do not reject industry and technology, but only their capitalistic organization'* (Severino, 2016, 6). As Severino (ibid, 6-7) continues:

> The communist revolution simply replaces the capitalistic with a socialist organization of technology, while both forms of organization share that meaning which reality – which the "thing" – assumes within the technology itself. And today it is *within* this meaning – *withing* the project of the production and destruction of all things – that any attempt to render technological civilization less inhuman must be made. Socialist humanism and ecology do not advocate the abolition of this project – they simply affirm that, if rendered more rational, it would become more efficient and more in keeping with the essential values of the day.

Following Severino's argument, in addition to the need to replace the capitalist socio-economic structure, as I also conclude, there exists a demand to push beyond the faith in progress and rationalist techno-scientific solutions (see Hamilton et al., 2015). This seemingly entails that the assumptions that place confidence in human skills and capabilities to master the Earth are questioned (e.g., Bannon, 2014; Hamilton, 2013). In this case, it is also important to make a distinction between the accounts of Karl Marx and those of Friedrich Engels. Although Engels remained sceptical that humans could control nature (see e.g. 1974, 222-223) he nonetheless had faith, as did much of his contemporaries, that humans could overcome the challenges through natural sciences, and at least control the interaction between humans and nature in the future (ibid, 224). In contrast to Engels, Marx's position towards the aim of controlling nature and regarding technological progression was more pessimistic, though it is also clear that Marx was a modern thinker (Eagleton, 2012, 49) who indeed had faith in progress – in particular when it came to developing the means of production, and individual freedom (ibid, see also Heiskanen, 2010, 227). Likewise, the history of Marxist thought testifies that many scholars, politicians, activists represent the so-called 'Promethean' strain of Marxists and/or socialist thought as proponents of modernisation and technological progress (see e.g. Benton, 1989). A Finnish philosopher Pauli Pylkkö (2011) has stated – I would argue correctly – that if ecological Marxists want to overcome some of the pitfalls of the 20th century Marxism, the belief in Western-centric technological progress must be abandoned, as well as the overly deterministic and reductionist conception of history.

Regardless of these reservations, some of the classic Marxist conceptualisations (such as mode of production, class struggle, capitalist state) are utilised in this book to update a theory of reproduction of capitalism more or less in their customary form. With these remarks, I want to explicate that I approach the inheritance of Marx and Marxism with certain convictions and with certain reservations. For instance, I want to separate this work sturdily from 20th century state socialism and the blind belief in industrialisation and (technological) progress. At the same time, I wish to link this work to the continuum of ecological Marxism, and meanwhile to ground the arguments made here to Marx's and Engels's materialist conception of history as an ontological and epistemological frame.

Ontology is, in short, the philosophical study of how the world *is*. An ontological question would be, for example: What is the nature of reality? Or, what is real? Or, as Spash (2012, 37) states in regard to scientific enquiry: *'what exists, and so what are the primary entities of concern in any given field, and what are their most general features and relationships'.* Ontological questions often mix with epistemological questions concerning theory of knowledge, namely, to the basis on which we create understanding of the world or where do the limits of our knowledge lie upon, and to axiological questions, i.e., to questions dealing with values (Heikkurinen et al., 2016).

Marxist social theorists study and analyse historical social structures, along with changes in these structures that have occurred throughout human history. What seem to be immutable laws to an observer in a particular period of time, may in fact, for Marxist scholars, reflect temporary drifts unique to the particular historic moment that have emerged from dialectical interaction of an entirety of social and natural developments (Foster et al., 2010, 27). A notion that social 'laws' vary from one historic era to another, is a notion also known as historicity, which is one of the most basic concepts of the materialist conception of history (ibid). If this notion has, in our time, been lost, Foster (2000, 18) writes, it is partly due to the later narrowing of fields of knowledge, i.e. disciplinary studies, and also partly due to the fact that in the reconstruction of social thought in the post Second World War world there was a trend in several disciplines, such as sociology, to develop primarily constructionist and relational arguments, simultaneously disregarding connections to the natural-physical environment of the social (see also Resch, 1992). Meanwhile, it has also been true in 20th century Marxism that the take on materialist conception of history, and especially regarding natural environment, has been ambivalent. For instance, the Frankfurt School, following Lukács in this respect, did develop an ecological critique (see e.g. Horkheimer and Adorno, 2008), but it remained almost entirely culturalist and lacked attachments to ecological science, or ecological content or materiality for that matter

(Foster, 2000, 245). For Gramsci too, whose writings, along with Lukács and Korsch, founded Western Marxism in the 20th century, ecological questions were not included in his analysis (Foster et al., 2010, 218). Consequently, ecological analyses remained almost completely absent in Marxist social theory from the 1930s to the 1960s (the so-called double death of ecological Marxism, see Foster, 2002; 2009, 155). However, after this slump, the material stream and tradition of Marxists, since the 1960s, has been developing into a prominent stream of environmental social sciences.

In brief, and arguably in contrast to post-modern and post-structuralist streams of social thought, philosophical materialism recognises that thinking is rooted in same material foundations that it attempts to explore. Now this may seem paradoxical, but the aim of materialist ontology is to incorporate itself in reality – into the material world – in which thinking is also embedded, but also some odd ways external to it. This is what Marx is highlighting when he claims that 'societal being' defines consciousness and not the other way around (Eagleton, 1999). According to Marx, what a person says or feels is ultimately the result of one's actions. Thus, historical past and historically shaped practices are the foundation for our 'language games' (Eagleton, 2012, 150). Certainly, it has to be noted as well that what we do as historical beings is, of course, integrally tied to what we think, and to the language that expresses it (Eagleton, 1999), yet human practices are not beyond meaning, aims or imagination, as Marx himself remarked (ibid).

It is often held true that Marxism after Marx and Engels had little to offer concerning ecological analysis – at least before the 1970s (Foster, 2000, 236). Yet, a more truthful account is to claim that the ecological arguments in Marxism were either interpreted in positivistic light or pushed aside since the beginning of the 20th century. Because, in the immediate decades following Marx's death, the ecological arguments Marx and Engels had expressed in their work were, in fact, quite well known (ibid, 236, 244).

While Marx's ecological contributions are now becoming more widely acknowledged, numerous commentators still maintain that his perceptions were not of any importance compared to his more general work, and certainly he did not leave a noteworthy ecological legacy (see Foster, 2000, 9; Heiskanen, 2010, 5-6). Likewise, some environmental commentators continue to claim that Marx believed in the struggle of human beings against nature, and was utterly anthropocentric and unecological, and that the followers of Marx did nothing but reproduce this relation and attitude (see Foster, 2000, 17; Foster, 2009, 160, 219).

However, it seems that most of the accusations concerning Marx and ecology do not match up well with his intellectual history. If one has the patience to look, it is evidently true that the young Marx already criticises the power that capital has had in human alienation from nature, which manifests itself in instrumental relation towards nature (Heiskanen, 2001; 2010). Over twenty years later, Marx writes in *Capital* vol. 1 (1973, 505-507) how agricultural innovations both exploit soil and the worker. In addition, in *Capital* vol. 3 (1981, 949-950) Marx notices how industry and industrial agriculture destroys the workforce that is, in fact, a natural force, and how the latter more directly destroys natural environments. In fact, Marx took a stand in almost every ecological problem of the 19th century, including the pollution of urban surroundings and the health risks it posed, the decline in the fertility of land, deforestation and desertification (Heiskanen, 2001, 8-9). Of course, many of the problems we are now facing did not exist in the time he was living, but this does not mean that Marx's thoughts on environmental degradation would not be relevant in our time.

What then has given birth to all of the misconceptions? First, and maybe the easiest answer, is that Marx wrote about the contradiction relating to nature mostly in his early scientific inquiries. In his later work, ecological arguments are scattered along with everything else, meaning that collecting and interpreting it takes some time and trouble, along with, of course, the fact that older Marx did not compile a specific volume to treat the questions regarding environmental degradation, highlights that these questions were not the primary ones Marx chose to focus upon in his work. As Heiskanen (2010, 225) writes, it is well recognised that, after his doctoral thesis, Marx did not write about nature extensively. As the focus of his thinking shifted from philosophy to political economy, the focus of his remarks concerning nature shifted from nature to human-nature relationship (ibid). However, the latter requires rigorous perception of the former.

In spite of all the controversy and burdens of the past, today, it seems apparent that the work of Marx (and Engels) offer a fruitful foundation to investigate the ecological embeddedness of social theory and the overall human society. Marxist method, as Foster (2000, 19) explains,

> has an enormous potential advantage in dealing with all of these issues precisely because it rests on a theory of society which is materialist not only in the sense of emphasizing the antecedent material-productive conditions of society, and how they served to delimit human possibilities and freedom, but also because, in Marx and in Engels at least, it never lost sight of the necessary relation of these material conditions to natural history.

Heiskanen (2015, 30) argues that Marx seems to have been – already by a young age – a thinker we customarily call a 'monist': one that perceives the reality and its components from a uniform starting point, and thus searches the connections and metamorphoses of those different components. As for consciousness, this entails that, although it does not identify to anything external to it, or anything material *per se*, it is not independent of these entities. This 'external' and 'material' together form an interactive sum of their parts, in which consciousness is also embedded (ibid). This characterisation of Marx's philosophical take on being and consciousness is well in line with his conception of human as well as natural history. For instance, in *The German Ideology* Marx and Engels (1998, 34) state that:

> We know only a single science, the science of history. One can look at history from two sides and divide it into the history of nature and the history of men. The two sides are, however, inseparable; the history of nature and the history of men are dependent on each other so long as men exist.

More generally, Marx's materialist conception of history has been commonly considered to be a philosophical inquiry of the nature of history (Heiskanen, 2015, 23). In addition, the materialist conception of history, or rather historical materialism in this respect, has been perceived to be a general social scientific method. Both of these sides are clearly on display in Marx and Engels' texts (ibid). However, in social sciences, the dual character of such has been proven somewhat of a problem, because it has generated dogmatic interpretations, in which complex and ambiguous philosophical axioms have been reduced to straightforward laws of historical explanation (ibid). Moreover, the phrase 'materialist conception of history' has caused friction in the sense that does it, in fact, represent an accurate interpretation of Marx's on history and philosophy? This is because the phrase does not actually originate from Marx but from Engels, who also used the term historical materialism in his own work (ibid, 22). However, as Heiskanen (ibid) claims, it is difficult to deny that Marx would not have approved these phrases.

In Marx's conception of history, materialist premises orient the actions of human beings, even in the later phases of human history (Heiskanen, 2016, 274). In the *Economic and*

Philosophical Manuscripts of 1844, Marx proposes his non-reductionist approach to materialism. He (Marx, 2011, 105) writes that *'thinking and being are [...] no doubt distinct, but at the same time they are in unity with each other.'* The latter part is predominant, and thus Marx (ibid, 74, italics in orig.) states that:

> Nature is man's *inorganic body* – nature, that is, in so far as it is not itself human body. Man *lives* on nature – means that nature is his *body*, with which he must remain in continuous intercourse if he is not to die. That man's physical and spiritual life is linked to nature means that nature is linked to itself, for man is a part of nature.

Marx (ibid, 111) also recognises that *'history itself is a real part of natural history – of nature's coming to be a man.'* Because humans do not identify with nature *per se*, but are one of nature's most recognisable and distinctive parts, due to the existence of human consciousness, but also empirically, it is possible to search for the most essential characteristic of this being (Heiskanen, 2015, 33). This characteristic is for Marx, labour. In this respect, Marx (2011, 165) gives recognition to Hegel, as he had conceived *'labour as man's act of self-genesis'*. In *Capital*, vol. 1. (1973, 177) Marx characterises labour as follows:

> Labour is, in the first place, a process in which both man and Nature participate, and in which man of his own accord starts, regulates, and controls the material re-actions between himself and Nature. He opposes himself to Nature as one of her own forces, setting in motion arms and legs, head and hands, the natural forces of his body, in order to appropriate Nature's productions in a form adapted to his own wants. By thus acting on the external world and changing it, he at the same time changes his own nature.

Therefore, labour is a process, one which is possible to carry out only with the external nature of a human being which, at the same time, develops human abilities and produces the world of artefacts, through which human abilities can cumulate over the course of history (Heiskanen, 2015, 33). It is also vital to emphasise that, in Marx's conception of history, an ecological community and its environment are seen as a dialectical whole, in which different levels of existence are ontologically significant, but also lacking an overall purpose that guides these communities. This is because even universal human purposes should be open to question for their limited character (ibid). This kind of philosophical interpretation of history does not compete with Darwinism; biological evolution ultimately produced a being, whose gradually developing ability for labour was eminent in many respects, and thus natural selection started to favour the development of this ability (Heiskanen, 2015, 32-34). Moreover, according to Marx we, human beings, transform our relation to the world by transcending our alienation from it, and while doing so, we create our own distinctly *human-natural* relations through material praxis (Foster, 2000, 5). Undeniably, it is also evident that humans remain in interaction with extra-human nature in countless ways other than by simply working.

Generally, Marx's conception of history points to the unity between natural and social sciences, a potential alliance Bhaskar has called 'the possibility of naturalism', despite the significant differences of these fields (Foster, 2000, 7). This is an important notion in the sense that it directs us away from the dualistic division of these two fields of science.

Marx (2011, 156) writes in *Economic & Philosophic Manuscripts of 1844*:

> Man is directly a natural being and as a living natural being he is on the one hand furnished with natural powers of life – he is an active natural being. These forces exist in him as

tendencies and abilities – as impulses. On the other hand, as a natural, corporeal, sensuous, objective being he is suffering, conditioned and limited creature, like animals and plants. This is to say, the objects of his impulses drives exist outside him, as objects independent of him.

Nonetheless, human beings are to be distinguished from other living species in their objects of drive, that is, human needs that are distinct to humans and have developed, and keep on transforming, through natural and social intercourse (Foster, 2000, 77). Thus, the question of material development of a society is always linked to the material development of the human relation to human external nature, which may also indicate that human history is not linear, but rather a complex, contradictory, and dialectical process (ibid, 221).

The contradictions concerning human-nature relationship are clearly also on display in Marx's work (Heiskanen, 2010, 227, 231-232). Marx claims that humans struggle with nature in every social organisation, which of course, does not mean that humans would only struggle with nature (ibid). It is evident that human beings and nature also cooperate, as Marx and Engels remark in *The German Ideology* (1998, 45-46):

> the celebrated 'unity of man with nature' has always existed in industry and has existed in varying forms in every epoch according to the lesser or greater development of industry, just like the 'struggle' of man with nature, right up to the development of his productive powers on a corresponding basis.

This is, for Marx, the eternal duality of the human-nature relationship, which is also one of reasons why Marx also later notes that progress is a contradictory process (Heiskanen, 2010, 227, 231-232). Overall Marx, in various ways, emphasised the paradoxical nature of progress, which is one of the reasons why

Marx can be claimed to be an important ecological thinker (Heiskanen, 2010, 232).

In addition to Marx's ecological observations, there is another layer in Marx's materialist conception of history, one that is linked to the history of human civilisations (Heiskanen, 2016, 277). In this conception, Marx studies the history of civilisations, that is, the last few millennia of human organising into city-states and cultures, by using concepts such as production, mode of production and socio-economic structure (ibid). Production is, of course, based on labour, but in the concept of production, in Marxist thought, also stands out as the results of labour and their relation to other societal components (ibid). Modes of production (such as feudalism or capitalism) are, in contrast, historical formations; they have developed in the course of history, and consist of labour power, upholding human and non-human elements, means of production, and relations of production (ibid). When these components are taken together, they form a socio-economic structure, which Marx divides into base and superstructure (Heiskanen, 2016, 278). Marx wrote in *The Eighteenth Broodmare of Louis Bonaparte,* (1979, 103) that:

> Men make their own history, but they do not make it just as they please; they do not make it under circumstances chosen by themselves, but under the circumstances directly encountered, given and transmitted from the past.

The circumstances Marx refers to are, indeed, the material conditions of production, implying both natural and social history (Foster et al., 2010, 342-343). In other words, humans make use of the legacy of past generations, and especially the material artefacts of these generations. In *The German Ideology* (1998, 61-62), Marx and Engels write that:

> history does not end by being resolved into 'self-consciousness' as 'spirit of the spirit', but that in it at each stage there is found a

> material result: a sum of productive forces, a historically created relation of individuals to nature and to one another, which is handed down to each generation from its predecessor; a mass of productive forces, capital funds and conditions, which, on the one hand, is indeed modified by the new generation, but also on the other prescribes for it its conditions of life and gives it a definite development, a special character. It shows that circumstances make men just as much as men make circumstances.

This statement also means that human beings are not only the result of material reality. If this would be the case, there would be no chance of changing the course of history, as Marx also made clear (Eagleton, 1999). Thus, Marx clearly was not a mechanical materialist, but rather a dialectical materialist, who explained the origins of thought, character, and purpose with historical circumstances (ibid).

Finally, as close fields of knowledge in general, Marx's conception of history and his conception of capitalism are closely intertwined and entangled together. This is observable in Marx's intellectual biography, as the focus of his studies gradually moved from philosophy to political economy. Along with this change of focus, the materialist conception of history came to have more nuanced dimensions as well (Heiskanen, 2015, 48-49). Without a doubt, even the basic characteristics of capitalism cannot be reduced to a materialist conception of history, but notwithstanding, the materialist conception of history is clearly represented in Marx's later studies of capitalism (ibid, 53). First of all, the materialist concept of history has noticeably oriented the theoretical grounds of his theory of capitalism, as well as influenced his method of study (ibid). However, the role of the materialist conception of history does not limit itself to the formulation of hypotheses, but the conception of history is situated in the finished version of Marx's theory of capitalism (Heiskanen, 2015, 53). For instance, *Capital* is filled with concepts that are integral for Marx's materialist conception of history, such as production, labour, division of labour, nature, metabolism, and society; however, it is clear that these concepts are not 'emptied' by the form they have in the capitalist mode of production. Hence, the materialist conception of history can, in this respect, be considered as an integral component of the more abstract part of Marx's theory and conception of capitalism (ibid) (see Chapter 3).

Marxist studies on education

In social sciences nowadays, Marxist studies on education are listed as a part of the so-called critical education studies in textbooks (see e.g. Apple et al., 2009). Critical education studies, according to Apple et al. (2009, 3), seek to establish *'how relations of power and inequality, (social, cultural, economic), […] are manifested and are challenged in the formal and informal education of children and adults'*. However, as Gottesman (2016, 1) argues, it was, in fact, Marxist thought that originally gave birth to critical education studies as a field. To be sure, today critical education studies stretch far beyond the 'borders' of Marxism, to fields such as culture and identity, gender and sexuality, race and ethnicity, ecological crisis, and so on (ibid).

Marx (and Engels) did not write extensively on education, at least not in the modern institutional sense (Cole, 2008, 29-30). This might be due, as Cole (ibid) argues, to the fact that for Marx and Engels the transformation of society is produced through class struggle, instead of the spread of collective consciousness via education. Nonetheless, passages concerning education are to be found from their texts. Marx, for one, stated that the bourgeoisie do not offer a real education, but education is a mere instrument to spread bourgeoisie moral principles (Taylor, 1995, 19). In similar fashion, in *The German Ideology* Marx and Engels (1998, 67) argued that *'the class which has the means of material production at its disposal, consequently also controls the means of mental production, so that the ideas of those who lack the means of mental production are on the whole subject to it.'* In other words, the ideologies of the dominant class are expressed and legitimated in societal institutions such as schools and universities (Anyon, 2011, 12-13). Indeed, the origins of Marxist studies and theories on education can be traced down to these proclamations (ibid), although more explicitly the critical Marxist take on social sciences did not emerge until the period between the two world wars (Gottesman, 2016, 12). Among others, Georg Lukács, Karl Korsch, Ernest Bloch, in the 1920s, and Antonio Gramsci, in the 1930s, as pioneers of critical Marxist scholarship, reacted to the historical determinism and positivist treatment of Marx's thesis by the Second International (ibid). The critical perspective was then carried on, above all, by the members of the Frankfurt School (such as Max Horkheimer, Theodore Adorno, Walter Benjamin, Erich Fromm, and Herbert Marcuse), to materialise *en force* in the 1960s in Western academia (ibid). Subsequently, since the late 1960s and early 1970s, education theorists on the both sides of Atlantic also adopted the critical Marxist perspective.

The critical Marxist take on education can be categorised in two main streams, which are Structuralist Marxist and Neo-Marxist educational theory[5]. On the one hand, in the Structuralist Marxist stream questions regarding ideology, economic, and social reproduction have been of special concern for scholars such as Louis Althusser (1968/2014), Nicos Poulantzas (1975; 2000), and Samuel Bowles and Herbert Gintis (1976). On the other hand, in the Neo-Marxist stream ideology, social reproduction, resistance,

---

[5] This kind of separation can also be considered arbitrary, because scholars in the field of critical education have borrowed and sought inspiration from both of these streams, but I nevertheless consider the separation necessary, especially from the perspective of (education-economic) reproduction theorising.

and culturalist critique of education have been in the spotlight in the work of scholars such as Paolo Freire (1996/1968), Michael Apple (1979; 1982), and Henry Giroux (1983a).

As Gottesman (2016, 45) writes, prominent Marxist analyses began to break into the mainstream of educational scholarship in Anglo-American, continental, and Latin American contexts in the early 1970s. Althusser and Poulantzas in France, Freire in Brazil and Chile, Young and Whitty in Britain, and Bowles and Gintis, and Apple in the United States were among key scholars to pave the way for critical Marxist educational scholarship (ibid).

Unlike in the US, British scholarship had not suffered from an anti-Marxist 'purge', and thus Britain had sustained a Marxist intellectual presence and lively community in the 1940s, 1950s, and 1960s (Gottesman, 2016, 62). The Marxist turn in education, in the UK context, was assisted in particular by the work of Michael Young and Geoff Witty (see e.g. *Society, State and Schooling*, 1977) and the Birmingham Centre for Contemporary Cultural Studies, which came under the direction of a cultural theorist Stuart Hall in 1968 (ibid). To understand the culture and historical and political context in Britain, Young and Whitty stated in *State and Schooling* (1977a, 8) that a more suitable theory of ideology was needed. Like many of their contemporaries, Young and Whitty also leant at first on Althusser and his ideas on Ideological State Apparatuses, but relatively soon discarded his ideas and moved to a more Gramscian position in search for a theoretical 'space' for human agency (Gottesman, 2016, 63). Also, and regarding the turn to Neo-Marxism from more structuralist accounts, a particularly influential reading on Gramsci's thesis on hegemony was Raymond Williams's essay *Base and Superstructure in Marxist theory* (1973).

In the US, the Brazilian Marxist Paolo Freire, with his classic book *Pedagogy of the Oppressed* (first published in 1968), is perhaps most often referred to as the spark that gave rise to critical education as a field (Gottesman, 2016, 9). However, as Gottesman (ibid, 22) has shown, it was Bowles and Gintis's *Schooling in Capitalist America*, published in 1976, that was the first critical Marxist scholarly effort on education to receive a wide audience. Likewise, it is true that Freire does not appear in Michael Apple's classic *Ideology and Curriculum* (1979), which was considered, at the time of its publication, the most sophisticated critical Marxist analysis on the relation between schooling, ideology, and society (ibid, 24). After these publications, a critical Marxist turn in education took hold in the US, as scholars such Jean Anyon (e.g. 1979; 1980) and Henry Giroux (e.g., 1980; 1983a), along with Apple (1979; 1982) took the initiative (Gottesman, 2016, 44). As these foundational pieces in US critical education exhibit, the theoretical influences came from the previous generation of Marxist thinkers, such as Gramsci, and, for instance, from contemporary British cultural Marxists such as Stuart Hall, who were involved in analysis of ideology and social structure in modern capitalist states (ibid, 26; see also Anyon, 2011, 33). In the mid-1980s, however, many of the critical education scholars, who had adopted the language and ideas of the critical Marxists, turned to Freire in thinking about agency and resistance (see e.g. Giroux, 1983a; McLaren, 1988)[6].

Overall, Neo-Marxists in critical education have utilised concepts such as hegemony (Gramsci) and relative autonomy

---

6   Marx and/or Marxism is often accused of downplaying the importance of human agency and the notion of resistance. Personally, I think there is a great deal of truth in this claim, although Marx himself stressed that every component of society has an active role as they interact (see e.g. Heiskanen, 2015, 105; 2016, 278). Nonetheless, I have also experienced the difficulty of combining the so-called macro-sociological level of analysis to agency. Unfortunately, and without a doubt these two approaches have separate narratives in this book. This does not mean, however, that I would think of them as two separate categories. Although this book is, in many ways, about conquering planet Earth, and about world domination, I would never claim that history is made 'behind the backs' of individuals or that capitalism would not, or could not, be contested or resisted.

(Althusser) to analyse, for instance, schools and social reproduction (see, e.g., Apple, 1979; 2006; Apple and Buras, 2006). In addition to social reproduction, resistance is a key concept for Neo-Marxist educational theorists (Au and Apple, 2009, 87). As Apple (1981) has argued, because schools are sites of ideological reproduction, they are contested and struggled over because ideologies are themselves contradictory and continuously contested. Considering resistance in education, along the work of Paolo Freire, the work of Henry Giroux (e.g., 1983; 1983a) is held in prominence. One of the aims of Giroux has been, as Anyon (2011, 35) argues, to understand how student resistance of dominant cultural forms may challenge hegemony.

Apart from social reproduction, ideology, and resistance as areas of interest, Neo-Marxist educational theorists have, since the early 1990s, contributed notably to Latino, black, and feminist scholarship on social class (Anyon, 2011, 40). Antonia Darder (1991), for example, has illustrated in her work how the dominant culture extends to classrooms and strips minority students of their language and cultural beliefs. Also, and although there have been eminent female scholars, such as Jean Anyon (1994) and Kathleen Weiler (1994), the field of education, including the critical turn, was for long mainly the domain of male scholars (Anyon, 2011, 42; Gottesman, 2016, 95). To challenge and reverse this trend, it was especially Kathleen Weiler's writings (1994) in which various strands of feminist literature were brought together with Freire's radical educational methods and through which the Neo-Marxist feminist pedagogy emerged as a field of study (Anyon, 2011, 42). Recently, the rise of 'neoliberal higher education' has sparked the creation of numerous publications in Neo-Marxist studies on education (see e.g. Ross and Gibson, 2007; Green et al., 2007; Giroux, 2014).

Notwithstanding its established and notable role in critical education (see e.g. Apple et al., 2009; Anyon, 2011) certain tensions exist in the Neo-Marxist educational theory (Au and

Apple, 2009). The focus on culture as a unit of analysis separate from the relations of production has provoked serious questions regarding the usefulness of the Neo-Marxist take (see e.g. Kelsh and Hill, 2006). While, Au and Apple (2009, 89), for instance, reject this criticism, they meanwhile recognise that the focus on hegemony, resistance, culture, and ideology *'certainly opens the door for one to adopt a culturalist analysis that denies any role of economy or relations of production have to play regarding power, domination and schooling.'* Similarly, Gottesman (2016, 112) has remarked that whereas the turn to postmodernism and poststructuralism has produced important insights in the field of critical education, it is unclear, as also argued by Anyon (1994, 129), how postmodernist and poststructuralist perception can be utilised to support collective action to deal with concrete and real social and environmental problems.

Considering education and reproduction in particular, Marx and Engels's original notion that ruling ideologies legitimate the power of the bourgeois and affect educational institutions and curriculum was developed by Antonio Gramsci in the 1920s and 1930s (Anyon, 2011, 13). Gramsci used the term hegemony to analyse the history of the bourgeois social formations, and class domination in particular, in the time of the so-called passive revolution (Thomas, 2010, 222). Gramsci's elaboration of hegemony and hegemonic state apparatuses was later picked up by Louis Althusser, Etienne Balibar, and Nicos Poulantzas, leading eventually to a wide international recognition (especially in France, Britain and much of the Spanish-speaking world) of the so-called Structural Marxism (Morrow and Torres, 1995, 141).

In the field of education, it can be argued without exaggeration that Structural Marxism inspired a renewal of a Marxist theory of education, as it generated debates surrounding the concept of 'reproduction', though in retrospect it is clear that Pierre Bourdieu's alternative take on the term popularised the concept

(Morrow and Torres, 1995, 141). Structural Marxism is a peculiar example of an academic trend that emerges with force but disappears as fast as it arrived. Indeed, as Wright (1987, 14) has written:

> By the late 1960s, he [Althusser] was a powerful intellectual force within the French left, and by the early 1970s, as translations of his work and that of his followers became readily available, Althusserian Marxism was one of the leading tendencies on the left in the English-speaking world. By the mid-1980s that influence – at least explicitly – had almost entirely disappeared.

Following the general rejection of Althusser's thesis within academia, his remarks concerning education were also devalued (Morrow and Torres, 142). However, as the socio-political context has changed over the past decades, there has arguably been a call for a revival of many 'once forgotten' Marxist scholars and streams of research such as Althusser and Structural Marxism (Resch, 1992). As Resch (1992, 5) wrote already 25 years ago, the restructuring of the capitalist political economy invites us to revisit Althusser and to remove the 'quarantine' from Structural Marxism. In his own words, Resch (ibid), argued that to explain *the dramatic shift from prosperity to austerity in the capitalist heartlands, we have little choice but to admit the theoretical failures of post-Marxist and postmodern social theory and to revive Marxist principles of economic determination and class struggle.*

Reproduction theories in the field of education were particularly popular in the 1970s and 1980s in Britain and continental Europe, because of the influence of Antonio Gramsci, Louis Althusser and Nicos Poulantzas, and in US in the late 1970s and 1980s, especially because of the impact of Bowles's and Gintis's *Schooling in Capitalist America* (see Giroux, 1983; Gottesman, 2016). In general, theorists in this field have argued that the main functions of schools are the reproduction of dominant ideology and relations of production (Althusser, 2014), or work-force and its forms of knowledge (Bowles and Gintis, 1976), or the distribution of skills needed to reproduce the prevailing social hierarchy (Bourdieu and Passeron, 1990).

A definitive idea in this stream of research is that schools, as state institutions, could only be understood through their wider relationship to other societal structures, namely to state and economy (Giroux, 1983). Moreover, reproduction scholars claimed that the 'deep structure' of schooling would remain hidden without an analysis of how schools function as agencies of social and cultural reproduction (see Bourdieu and Passeron, 1990), or in other words, legitimate capitalist 'rationality' and sustain dominant social practices (Giroux, 1983; Khalanyane, 2010). Indeed, in this field of research, schools and education are often considered central agencies in the politics and processes of domination (Giroux, 1983). Whereas the liberal view has perceived education as the great equalizer, reproduction theorist have made a claim (Willis, 1983, 110) that '*education is not about equality but inequality*', that is:

> education's main purpose of the social integration of a class society could be achieved only by preparing most kids for an unequal future, and by insuring their personal underdevelopment. Far from productive roles in the economy simply waiting to be 'fairly' filled by the products of education, the 'Reproduction' perspective reserved this to suggest that capitalist production and its roles required certain educational outcomes.

In addition, reproduction theorists in the field of education have examined, in particular, class-specific experiences in the field of education (Anyon, 1980, 1997, 2005), the culture of schools and class-defined relations of students who attend to these schools (Bourdieu and Passeron, 1990), and how the economic, ideological, and repressive functions of the state affect school policies and practices (Poulantzas, 1975).

According to Giroux (1983), critical educational theorists and theories regarding schooling and reproduction can be broadly categorized into three reproductive models, which are the *economic* (e.g. Bowles and Gintis, 1976; Poulantzas, 2000; Althusser 2014), *cultural* (e.g. Bourdieu and Passeron, 1990; Bourdieu, 1996), and *hegemonic-state* (e.g. Gramsci, 1971; Poulantzas, 1975; Apple, 1979) reproductive models.

At the core of the economic-reproductive model are two questions: first, how does the educational system function within society? Second, how do schools fundamentally influence the ideologies, personalities, and needs of students? From this perspective, reproduction theorists perceive that the dominant groups in a given society utilise their power and influence to reproduce the kind of educational system and educational outcomes that function in the interests of the accumulation and expansion of capital (Giroux, 1983). In this view, the underlying experience and relations of schooling are managed by the interests of capital, that is, the need to provide certain ideology, skills, attitudes, and values to students (Althusser, 2014). Important theoretical constructs that highlight the structural and ideological connection between schools and workplace are the notions of 'hidden curriculum' (Bowles and Gintis, 1976) and correspondence (Bowles and Gintis, 1976; Althusser and Balibar, 2009). The concept of hidden curriculum refers here to a certain classroom social relations that legitimise particular views of work, authority, social rules, and values that sustain capitalist logic and rationality particular manifested in the workplace (Giroux, 1983). Althusser's notion that ideology has a material basis (2014) is to some extent connected to the idea of Bowles and Gintis' hidden curriculum concept. Ideology has a material basis in Althusser's (2014) view in the rituals, routines, and social practices that both structure and mediate the day-to-day workings of schools. Similarly, the theory of correspondence (Bowles and Gintis, 1976) indicates that there is an intentional correspondence between the capitalist structure and its wage labouring needs and the outcomes of the school system. Less rigidly, Althusser and Balibar (2009, 301-302) have argued that from the perspective of economic and social reproduction certain forms of correspondence exist between various instances of the social structure.

Regarding his theory of cultural reproduction, Bourdieu argues that the logic of domination must be analysed within a theoretical framework that is capable of linking together human agents and dominant structures in a dialectical manner (Giroux, 1983). He argues against the notion that schools would simply mirror the rest of the society, as they have a relative autonomy that is influenced only indirectly by more powerful and political institutions. In this respect, the concept of symbolic violence is, for Bourdieu and Passeron (1990), in essence, as it denotes that class control is reproduced through subtle means of symbolic power waged by the ruling classes to impose their definition of the dominant culture in line with their interests. Thus, education is seen in Bourdieu and Passeron's conception as an important social and political force in the reproduction of classes and class hierarchies, because schools, on the surface, appear impartial and neutral mediums of the valued culture, but in fact promote inequality and class division in the name of justice and objectivity (Giroux, 1983). Hence, schools play a significant role in legitimating and reproducing dominant culture and cultural capital (Bourdieu and Passeron, 1990).

State and domination have been major concerns for educational theorists concerned with the hegemonic-state reproductive model, which especially deals with questions of how the state intervenes and influences the educational system (Giroux, 1983). Theorists in this field (such as Poulantzas, 1975; Apple, 1979) perceive that educational change cannot only be explained through economic or cultural reproduction, but what needs to be reconciled is how political factors lead to interventionist policies of the state and shape the reproductive functions of education (Giroux, 1983). In particular, scholars have argued that as part of the state apparatus, schools and universities play, among other things, an essential role in furthering the economic interests of the dominant classes (Carnoy, 1982; Dale; 1989), by providing students with certain ideology, skills, attitudes, and values (Althusser, 2014). To be sure, this does not imply that the dominant state ideology would be disseminated or indoctrinated successfully, especially because the state does not have a clear 'voice', but rather various contradictory voices (see Carnoy and Levin, 1985; Poulantzas, 2000), or that the 'hidden curriculum' – especially benefitting the dominant classes – would not be resisted among teachers, students and university faculty.

Even though, for example, Bourdieu's theory is in many respects useful and perceptive, he is mostly applying it, as have many others after him, to explain cultural and social reproduction, and especially social inequality. The situation is much the same concerning the majority of the reproduction theory research in the field of education since the early 1980s (see Collins, 2009; Khalanyane, 2010). Almost without exception, scholars and theorists have been dealing with 'social reproduction' and trying to explain how education contributes to social inequality, but at the same time neglecting explicit economic accounts regarding reproduction. Furthermore, and somewhat puzzlingly, since the early 1990s, academic work even regarding social reproduction has decreased remarkably (Collins, 2009).

There are many reasons for this phenomenon, which can, for one, be seen to be linked to a bigger trend in social sciences, the so-called cultural turn (see e.g. Ray and Sayer, 1999). As Gottesman (2016, 46) notes, the rise of neoconservatism, the continuing attacks on the working class, and the withering away of civil rights gains by the end of the 1970s and early 1980s shifted the political tone and radical vision of the left. Similarly, as the 1980s progressed, critical education scholars shifted their political position from revolution to reform, and their theoretical focus to cultural critique and strategic resistance in schools, instead of favouring radical social reconstruction, macro-level critiques on capital, and building mass movements (ibid, 47). In Gottesman's (2016, 47) own words:

> Educational scholars thus increasingly preferred a cultural Marxist lens that looked at the ideological structure and content of schooling as opposed to the political economic Marxist lens that theorized capital and assessed quantifiable inputs and outcomes of schooling's reproductive tendencies.

Like the rest of the academia, the field of education is no exception considering the cultural turn in the late 1970s and early 1980s, which entailed that economic reproduction theorising, such as Bowles and Gintis's theory of correspondence and Althusser's Ideological State Apparatuses (1968/2014) were to be considered crudely mechanistic and overlooking agency (ibid, 47-48)[7].

Consequently, the streams of research done under the 'economic reproduction' banner slowed down in the field of education. However, it seems to me that academic research, especially in

---

[7] In addition to structural determinism, a common criticism of Althusserian Structural Marxism has been the absence of empirical research. However, education as a field of study is an exception in this case (Morrow and Torres, 1995, 156). For instance, Baudelot and Establet, in their *L'Ecole capitaliste en France* (1971), base their arguments on Althusser's theory of Ideological State Apparatuses (ibid, 151). Another application of structuralist Marxism in empirical research is the work done by Tomás A. Vasconi in the Latin American context (ibid, 156).

social sciences, is in many ways cyclical. Discourses, research topics, traditions, even disciplines, and research trends come and go, only to appear again later as societal context changes. Indeed, along the rise of 'neoliberal higher education' there has been recent reheating and recapitulations of reproduction theorising (see e.g. Anyon, 2005; Kumar, 2012; Sotiris, 2012; 2013); meanwhile other streams of critical education studies have emerged to analyse the connections between education and capitalism (see Slaughter and Leslie, 1997; Slaughter and Rhoades, 2004; Cole, 2008; Au and Apple, 2009; Anyon, 2011). Particularly in conjunction with the rise of neoliberalism, a countless number of academic publications have sprung up to express concerns for the future of higher education (see Chapter 5 for a short review of academic capitalism). Notwithstanding, it seems clear to me that crucial connections between contemporary higher education and reproduction of capitalism, and their wider repercussions, in particular from an ecological perspective, are left unaddressed in the current educational scholarship.

Although education's connection to politics and power is somewhat explicit, as is also well established in the field of critical education studies (see, e.g., Apple et al., 2009; Gottesman, 2016), the link between education and environmental degradation is perhaps not so clear. Already, the near non-existence of academic inquiries, especially before the new millennium, seeking to discuss the connections between education and environmental degradation or ecological crisis could be considered a demonstration of this claim. However, a notable exception to the silence of the 1980s and 1990s is the work done by C. A. Bowers (see, e.g., *Education, Cultural Myths and Ecological Crisis*, 1993). Bowers has already for many decades argued '*how cultural beliefs contribute to the accelerating degradation of the environment*' (Bowers, 1993, 1). In examining cultural beliefs and ecological crisis, Bowers, building on the ideas of Gregory Bateson (e.g. 1972; 2002), has studied education in particular and, while doing so, made a convincing contribution to academic scholarship by illustrating how modern Western education and its underlying assumptions are connected to the ecological crisis (see Bowers, 1993; 2011). While Bowers' take on education and ecological crisis is, in essence, in understanding how, for instance, culture-bound belief in progress, individualism, and rationality contribute to modern ecological devastation, his analysis does not extend to economic or social reproduction of the capitalist workforce or relations of production, for instance.

Along the work of Bowers, arguably the most viable stream of research on education and ecological crisis is the literature on ecopedagogy (see e.g. Kahn, 2010; Fassbinder et al., 2012; Grigorov, 2012). Ecopedagogy is, above all, a field of study and a project concerned with mitigating the ecological and social crisis via pedagogical means (Grigorov, 2012, 14). Generally, ecopedagogy follows the postmodernist theoretical and methodological tradition in its analysis, and thus the focus is more in ways of knowing, discourses, and cultural constructs than in an explicit material analysis on education and its ecological consequences. To be sure, it is to be noted as well that in ecopedagogy there are to be found accounts that attempt to criticise the dominance of the capitalist take on education (e.g. Fassbinder, 2008). However, these analyses do not point out exactly how 'capitalist education' contributes to the ongoing ecological crisis.

Although it is true that some Marxist educational scholars such as Cole (2008, Chapter 7) have dealt with questions regarding education and environmental degradation, from a Marxist perspective, the analysis is rather focused on exhibiting the fundamental reasons behind the ecological crisis (such as how capitalism contributes to it) rather than trying to understand what is the role of contemporary higher education in it. Similarly, McLaren and Houston (2005) do not seek to explain this connection, although they recognise, in a noteworthy manner, the importance of tackling ecological questions and analysing in classrooms the reasons behind the ecological crisis, as they propose reforms to alleviate various social and environmental problems. The structure of the argument is the same also in McLaren's (2013) later treatment of capitalism and ecological catastrophe wherein he proposes ecopedagogy as a means to resist and alleviate social and environmental problems. Whereas McLaren (ibid) again acknowledges capitalism as being one of the primary concerns, both in education and from the perspective of ecological crisis, he does not explain how capitalist education and environmental degradation relate to one another.

3

CAPITALISM AND FINITE PLANET
The Absolute Contradiction

Ever since the late 18th century, expanding industrialisation, led by the capitalist mode of production and its diverse social formations, has shifted the emphasis of organised human action from delivering utility and use values to providing quantity and exchange values is search for continuous accumulation of capital. Capitalist way of organising production and society is only one of many possibilities, and one of many simultaneously existing modes of production – although it is, without a doubt, the dominant one. Louis Althusser (2014, 22) contends that a mode of production is a way or a manner of production, of producing the required goods for the material existence of human beings living in a given social structure. Althusser continues (ibid) that:

> a way of 'producing' is a way of 'tackling nature', since it is nature and nature alone that all social formations which do not live on thin air or the Word of God, extract the material goods necessary for their subsistence (food, clothing, shelter, and so on), that is for their stagnation or 'development'.

Humans 'tackle' their external nature in order to extract the required goods for their subsistence (by hunting, gathering, fishing, lumbering, and so on) or use up their external nature to produce for them (agriculture, cattle farming). These various labour processes together constitute the production forces of a particular mode of production. Althusser (2014, 19-21) claims that every concrete social structure is based on a *dominant* mode of production, which, in principle, means that in every social structure there exists more than one mode of production. However, one of those is the dominant one, while others are dominated by it. Thereafter, Althusser asks, what constitutes a mode of production? He responds by noting deploying Marx's conceptualisation, which states that it is the 'unity' between productive forces and relations of production (ibid). However, these productive forces are nothing by themselves if they are not 'tendered operational', as Althusser (ibid) notes, and thus, can only operate in and under the 'guidance' of the relations of production.

Relations of production are, on the one hand, quite simply the relations between the agents of production, which in a classless society, means all the members of a social structure, or in the capitalist social structure, relations between agents of production, and on the other hand, a group of people who are not directly agents of production although they intervene in the production processes (Althusser, 2014, 27). Furthermore, every production process in a mode of production includes several different labour processes, which necessarily indicates a division of labour, even in the most rudimentary forms of labour processes (ibid, 24). In every labour process, the agents of production must possess the needed skills and techniques, in other words, they must be qualified to do their tasks. This means that they must have some kind of technical experience and knowledge of the task (ibid, 22).

Accordingly, Althusser (2014, 25) claims that the productive forces of a mode of production are constituted by the unity of complex interplay of elements. The first element is the objects of labour, i.e., human external nature in various forms such as natural energy (for instance, a stream of water) and raw materials (e.g. minerals or trees). However, they have to be first harnessed so they can be utilised in the production process. The second element is the instruments of production, which are, for example tools, machines, factories and other devices and technologies. The third element is the agents of production (or labour power). Althusser (ibid, 23) reminds that Marx used the term 'means of production' to include both objects of labour and instruments of labour (or production), and 'labour power' to include various activities set up by agents of the labour process, who possess technical skills to utilise the existing means of production. Thus, productive forces = (unity of) means of production + labour power.

In much similar fashion, Marx writes that the basis of any given culture is labour. Before we can do much more, we humans have to eat, drink, keep warm and have some kind of shelter from forces of nature (Eagleton, 2012, 116). Therefore, human culture cannot exist without a material production of some kind (ibid). Nonetheless, Marx and Marxism want to argue further: that material production is fundamental to the existence of human cultures and not merely as a (basic) need provider. One of the claims in Marxist tradition is that the material production, 'in the last instance', defines the character of human culture (Althusser, 2014, 237). However, this does not say that economic factors or productive forces are the *only* aspects that determine the course of history or human condition.

Marx was the first to recognise the 'historical object', which we today recognise as capitalism[8]. In his detailed analysis, he showed

---

[8] Capitalism is defined and conceptualized here and more generally in this book based on the works of Karl Marx and Marxist scholars. There are, of course, other ways and traditions to investigate capitalism. One of the most prominent alternatives to the analyses of Marx can be found, for instance, in Max Weber's *Protestant Ethic and the Spirit of Capitalism*.

how it came to be, how it functions and how we could get rid of it (Eagleton, 2012, 9). As centuries have past, it has become clear that capitalism, as a mode of production and as a socio-economic structure[9], is remarkably flexible in adopting various forms (see e.g. Boltanski and Chiapello, 2005; Arrighi, 2010; Moore, 2015). Hence, the task of defining capitalism remains difficult, and consequently it is no wonder there is a lack of consensus regarding what it is ultimately composed of (Graeber, 2014). Nonetheless, in order to understand or critically analyse the phenomenon, it seems clear that there needs to be some kind of definition. Although there has existed and still exist various versions of capitalist socio-economic structure all around the world, ranging from liberal to authoritarian, or from democratic to fascist, I argue, while leaning on the classic analysis of Karl Polanyi (1968), that each version shares some fundamental similarities. With these similarities, it is implied that the basic institutions and practices that characterise capitalism are in place, though intertwined with the local relations of production and also to the natural and socio-cultural history.

Either way, there are quite a few identifying characteristics of capitalism. The first is the production of commodities for an external body (typically to a 'market'). A second is the production of commodities in order to produce a, most often private, surplus, which also entails the existence of an institution and abstraction called private property. The third characteristic of capitalism, one found everywhere around the planet, is wage-labour. Nonetheless, these kinds of general manifestation clearly are not enough to

---

[9] On the one hand, capitalist mode of production is referred to predominately when I'm speaking about capitalist forces, means and relations of production. On the other hand, when I'm using the word capitalism in general, I'm referring to capitalist socio-economic structure (which includes the capitalist mode of production and its forces, means and relations of production) meaning a wider social formation, in which institutions, social practices and norms, which are not necessarily linked to material production, reproduce and support the functioning of the capitalist mode of production.

really understand or even analyse capitalism. As Wallerstein (2013, 10-11) claims, an exercise that simply seeks to identify the different characteristics of capitalism is insufficient if one is trying to understand it. Moreover, Wallerstein (ibid) argues that many scholars focus on a single institution that they consider crucial, for example the abovementioned. Alternatively, many scholars claim that the most signifying characteristic of capitalism is the class struggle between capitalists (those who own the means of production) and wage-labourers (those who do not). While these are certainly some of the defining characteristics of capitalism (but not necessarily original or exceptional characteristics of a particular socio-economic structure), Wallerstein claims that many scholars appear to miss the most critical aspect of capitalism, which is the endless accumulation of capital, or in his own (Wallerstein, 2013, 10-11) words: *'the accumulation of capital in order to accumulate more capital.'*

As the name suggests, in capitalism economic actors (such as companies, venture capitalists, investors, states, or other economic organisations) organise economic activity through the fluid deployment of wealth – capital – by means of investments in different kinds of surplus-making operations. Finance, including debt and its interests, but also various tradable financial instruments, are *'crucial to the liquidity and mobility of capital as well as to expansion and spreading costs over time'* (Calhoun, 2013, 136). However, as Harvey (2011, 40) argues, capital is not just a *thing* but also a *process* in which capital is constantly sent to circulate or spent in search of more capital by capital accumulators who own the means of production, i.e. the capitalists. Harvey (ibid, 40-41) explains:

> Capitalists – those who set this process in motion – take on many different personae. Finance capitalists look to make money by lending to others in return for interest.

Merchant capitalists buy cheap and sell dear. Landlords collect rent because the land and properties they own are scarce resources. Rentiers make money from royalties and intellectual property rights. Asset traders swap titles (to stocks and shares for example), debts and contracts (including insurance) for profit. Even the state can act like a capitalist, for example, when it uses tax revenues to invest in infrastructures that stimulate growth and generate even more tax revenues. But the form of capital circulation that has come to dominate from the mid-eighteenth century onwards is that of industrial or production of capital. In this case, the capitalist starts the day with a certain amount of money. And, having selected a technology and organisational form, goes into the market place and buys the requisite amounts of labour power and means of production (raw material, physical plant, intermediate products, machinery, energy and the like). The labour power is combined with the means of production through an active labour process conducted under the supervision of the capitalist. The result is a commodity that is sold by its owner, the capitalist, in the market place for a profit.

To move beyond mere characteristics, capitalism is, as Harvey (2014, 6-7) puts it, a social formation (socio-economic structure) *'in which processes of capital circulation and accumulation are hegemonic and dominant in providing and shaping the material, social and intellectual bases for social life'*. Furthermore, and in this respect, capitalism is a historical formation (a historical socio-economic structure) (Heiskanen, 2016), supported by a set of power networks such as ideological, economic, military and political (Calhoun, 2013, 134). Capitalist socio-economic structure is also a hierarchical and unequally integrated material organisation (ibid), embedded in nature (Moore, 2015), in which economic actors are vitally dependent on the conditions provided by political power (Calhoun, 2013, 134), such as, nation states, state institutions, and various transnational organisations (Robinson, 2014).

Rather than a unified and concentrated system of power, capitalism is rather a set or a grouping of economic and social structures and practices dispersed over a landscape (Gibson-Graham, 2006). Although it is true that the accumulation of capital produces a concentration of wealth (Piketty, 2014) and arguably along with it also concentration of power (Robinson, 2014), what I intend to say is that capitalism is not a structure managed by some specific power bloc, but rather the capitalist structure remains in change while scattered groups and organisations of power try to steer and reshape it in their favour with more or less joint interests while at the same time securing the reproduction of capitalism.

To conclude (see also Table 1 below) and elaborate further, capitalism is a historical socio-economic structure[10] in constant and endless pursuit to accumulate capital. The key characteristics of, in particular, 20th and 21st century capitalism are advanced (material and 'immaterial') commodity production within a competitive capitalist market structure. Another key characteristic of capitalism is a class structure in which a group of individuals – capitalists – own the means of production, and appropriate economic surplus value from the use of raw materials and labour-power (conducted by wage-labouring class, non-human labour and machines), or apply other means to extract surpluses (for

---

[10] As the reader may have already noticed, I frequently use the concept (social) *structure* to refer to existing material, social, and historical societal relations (institutions), as well as social contracts, norms, values, and artefacts, which are, on the one hand, (at least somewhat) durable but, on the other hand, open to change and transformations. The term Social structure is conceptualised according to the Structural Marxist tradition. As Resch (1992, 23-24) explains in his discussion of Structural Marxism, the socio-economic structure is an outcome of economic, political, and ideological forces. Whereas, the economic function is held primary, political and ideological functions have their own distinct character and influence, and thus all determinate structures and relations, if in unequal manner, as a whole (ibid).

example from buying cheap and selling dear, rents, fees, interests, or from financial investments and speculation). In capitalism, the aim of a single capitalist or a single corporation (or other economic actors, such as states) is, in principle, to accumulate capital from various economic activities and then invest part of the profit back to the production in order to expand production, enhance productivity, and increase market share, or find other profitable ways to reinvest capital (e.g. infrastructure or education), in order to be able to accumulate more capital in the future (and so forth).

Some of the key institutions supporting the reproduction of the capitalist historical socio-economic structure are nation states and their repressive (military, police, judiciary) and ideological (education, church, media) institutions (Althusser, 2014), and various international organisations (such OECD, IMF, World Bank, WTO, EU, UN) (Robinson, 2014). Also many abstractions and social constructions generally protected by law (Poulantzas, 2000), including private property and the joint-stock company (or limited liability company) are in key role to secure the reproduction and legitimacy of capitalism. The history of capitalism has also shown that a particular alliance of class interests have come together to form a hegemonic historic bloc or a dominant class (Thomas, 2010) that seeks to secure and reproduce its dominant position in control of the means of production, as well as to influence societal conditions in their favour (Robinson, 2014).

Table 1. Capitalism summarised

CHARACTERISTICS	INSTITUTIONS	SUBJECTS	OBJECTS
Commodity production	Nation states and state institutions	Capitalists (owners of the means of production)	Biosphere and ecosystems
Surplus creation	Financial apparatus	Wage labourers and consumers	Human labour
Capital accumulation	International organisations	Companies, and self-employers	Non-human labour
Market exchange and competition	Private property	Other agents of capital	Raw materials and technology
Class society and social hierarchy	Limited liability company	Non-profit organisations	Other means of production

What then is *not* included in the capitalist socio-economic structure? In other words, are there social structures, practices and norms that a not capitalist? On the next page is a table by Gibson-Graham (2006, 71) representing what they call as diverse economy, a table, which, in an informative way, draws boundaries between capitalism and '*not* capitalism'. Following Gibson-Graham, the boundaries of capitalism and not capitalism are indeed quite easily recognisable, because the 'sphere of capitalism' can be traced based on capital (capitalist money) circulation.

One of the key issues in capitalism is money, or more precisely capital circulation in the shape of capitalist money to be used in a certain way[11]. While it is true that many individuals, organisations or institutions do not partake directly in capitalist processes, that is, they do not directly make efforts to accumulate capital, they do take

---

11 Particularly since the 1970s (in the post-Bretton Woods era), it has become apparent that money is a symbol (most often an abstract number, a paper note, or a metal coin) to value debt relations, and a symbol to signify economic value of things, as well as a legitimate (based on social contract and trust) item used to pay for things (see Iivarinen, 2015; Järvensivu, 2016). In any sense modern money is 'invented', as it is basically created out of thin air, by pushing a button, by institutions who have the societal legitimacy to add its quantity (banks, and central banks in capitalism). However, the capitalist money (dollars, euros, yuan, numbers in a bank account) is only one type of money available. In parallel, there exists also local monies, bit money, and other things used as money, such as gold, jewellery, diamonds, and others. Irrespective of this, the overall existence of money is, in itself, not a problem but rather the potential skewed social contracts and structures a certain type of money symbolises and represents. In the capitalist socio-economic structure there does exist a problem concerning money, namely because exchange value dominates use value due to the imperative of capital accumulation, and thus the capitalist money has been elevated in god-like position, as Marx noted in Grundrisse (1993, 221). However, again in this respect, money in itself as a thing, or as a social relation is not to blame, but the social relations and structures that the capitalist money represents. Nonetheless, it is peculiar that, in capitalism, money is often understood as scarce, although it is rather clear that actually the opposite is true (Järvensivu, 2016). In contrast, scarcity in capitalism, or in any other structure concerning material production, is linked to the means of production, namely, work, energy, and natural resources (see e.g. Moore, 2015; Järvensivu, 2016).

part in the circulation of capital by buying commodities, paying rents, spending their salaries they have received from working in an university, or by donating to a non-profit organisation campaigning for human rights. This is to say that, from the point of view of capitalism, it does not matter where to one spends his or her money as long as one keeps on spending it and thus keeps capital circulating.

TRANSACTIONS	LABOUR	ENTERPRISE
Alternative Market • Sale of public goods • Ethical 'fair trade' markets • Local trading systems • Alternative currencies Underground market • Co-op exchange • Barter • Informal market	**Alternative Paid** • Self-employed • Cooperative • Indentured • Reciprocal labour • In-kind • Work for welfare	**Alternative Capitalist** • State enterprise • Green capitalist • Socially responsible firm • Non-profit
Non-market • Household flows • Gift giving • Indigenous exchange • State allocations • State appropriations • Gleaning • Hunting, fishing, gathering • Theft, poaching	**Unpaid** • Housework • Family care • Neighbourhood work • Volunteer • Self-provisioning labour • Slave labour	**Noncapitalist** • Communal • Independent • Feudal • Slave

Table 2. Diverse economy (Gibson-Graham, 2006, 71)

As long as capital circulates, and keeps on circulating in an expansive manner, capitalist structure is alive and well. From capitalism's point of view, it does not matter whether one buys a hybrid car or a SUV, or whether one buys organic apples rather than GMO apples, or if one supports financially the local football team or Greenpeace, or whether one invests in Arctic oil or solar panels, the most important thing is that capital keeps on circulating through incurring consumption, investments and debts (we will came back to this later in this chapter, as Jevons paradox is discussed).

Therefore, the sphere of capitalism has to be framed accordingly. This implies that all actions, practices and structures beyond the scope of capitalist accumulation processes and circulation of capital can be considered *not* capitalist. For example, time banks are not capitalist (as ways to organise exchange, where actors exchange services for time, and thus time is the object of exchange). Another example is all the care work (children, the elderly, community etc.) that is beyond the capitalist monetary exchange. In contrast, all actions, practices, structures that do partake in accumulation of capital and circulation of capital one way or another are to be considered capitalist, disregarding their motivations, or whether they take part in capitalist accumulation and circulation processes directly, indirectly, intentionally or unintentionally.

Historical origins

Civilisations have transformed their surroundings on a large scale long before capitalism came along: clusters of commercial activity, commodity production, as well as huge imperial projects, such as the Pyramids, have been found in the ruins of past empires (Moore, 2015, 59). What has changed along with capitalism are the relevant units and organisation of time and place: while it took centuries for pre-modern civilisations to transform their environments, in capitalism, regional landscapes have been transformed only in decades (ibid).

Wood (2002, 34) argues that the way we understand the history of capitalism has a great effect on how we understand capitalism in the first place. In the *The Origin of Capitalism* Wood (2002) argues that capitalism, with all its very specific tendencies towards accumulation and profit, originates from the countryside, and not from the city, and quite late (but still a couple of centuries before the Industrial Revolution) in terms of human history. Moreover, and unlike how some of the classic political economists such as Adam Smith might argue, the birth of capitalism did not occur 'organically' (see Perelman, 2000) nor does it continue to spread organically (see Moore, 2015). On the contrary, the birth and spread of capitalism has required a comprehensive transformation of the most basic human relations and practices, and on top of it all, a rupture the in age-old pattern of interaction between humans and their external nature (Wood, 2002; Perelman, 2000).

As Perelman (2000, 25) points out, what is, in our day, apparently Marxian expression – primitive accumulation – comes from Adam Smith's proclamation (1976, 277) that *'the accumulation of stock must, in the nature of things, be previous to the division of labour.'* In any case, it is clear that Marx's treatment of previous accumulation is striking compared to Smith's historical explanation of how original accumulation occurred (Perelman, 2000, 26). In the end of *Capital* vol. 1 (1973) Marx portrays the several centuries-long process, in which small groups of people pitilessly exploited, ripped and stole resources from indigenous and other people inhabiting pre-capitalist societies around the world. Marx famously wrote (ibid, 751):

> The discovery of gold and silver in America, the extirpation, enslavement and entombment in mines of the aboriginal population, the beginning of the conquest and looting of the East Indies, the turning of Africa into a warren for the commercial hunting of black-skins, signalised the rosy dawn of the era of capitalist production. These idyllic proceedings

are the chief momenta of primitive accumulation. On their heels treads the commercial war of the European nations, with the globe for a theatre. It begins with the revolt of the Netherlands from Spain, assumes giant dimensions in England's Anti-Jacobin War, and is still going on in the opium wars against China, &c.

According to Adam Smith, the economic development progressed through the voluntary acts of the parties involved (Perelman, 2000, 26). Marx, on the contrary, argued (1973, 760) that *'capital comes dripping from head to foot, from every pore, with blood and dirt'*. He claimed that the workers, in general, did not really have a choice, but were forced to accept wage-labour. Moreover, Harvey (2011, 47) notes that the original (or primitive) accumulation of capital during the late medieval times in Europe caused violence, predation, thievery, fraud and robbery. By these means merchants, priests, pirates and, I might add, the aristocracy accumulated, with the help of usurers, enough initial monetary funds to begin the circulation of money systematically as capital. The conquistadors robbing the Inca gold are one of the most prominent examples of these activities, as Marx noted in the end of *Capital* vol. 1 (1973).

Taking the British context as a classical case, Marx saw primitive accumulation as having three aspects (Foster, 2009, 235). First, with the removal of peasants from rural lands by enclosures conducted by the authorities and the abolition of customary, common rights, the peasants no longer had direct access to or control over the means of production (see also Perelman, 2000). Second, and a direct consequence of the first, a creation of pauperised groups of landless labourers that eventually became wage labourers under capitalism through flocking into the towns and eventually forming the industrial proletariat (Foster, 2009, 235). Third, a concentration and centralisation of wealth as the means of production – initially through the control of the land – came to be monopolised by fewer and fewer individuals, as the surplus made available poured to the newly formed industrial hubs such as London (ibid).

Wood (2002, 36-37) concludes that Marx, in his critique of the 'so-called primitive accumulation', departed radically from the classical political economist and the so-called commercialisation model. Marx, for one, insisted that capital is a specific social relation not by itself wealth. The 'primitive accumulation' of classical political economy is 'so-called' because capital, as Marx defines it, is a social relation and not just any kind of wealth or profit, and moreover the accumulation of wealth as such is not what brings about capitalism (ibid). What transformed wealth into capital was, according to Marx, the transformation of social property relations. The history of capitalism is a history of enclosures and privatisation of commons to transform them into commodities and resources for production (Moore, 2015, 237). Marx and Marxist literature (e.g. Marx, 1973; Perelman, 2000; Wood, 2002; Moore, 2015) clearly argues that capitalism did not just occur, but it was a result of certain historical circumstances, partly conscious and partly unconscious social, and societal transformation and oppression.

Along with Marx and perceptive Marxist social scientists and historians, Karl Polanyi's classic book *The Great Transformation* offers a complelling description of the so-called 'fictitious commodities'. In Polanyi (1968) points out that the markets for labour, land and money are essential for the functioning of capital and the production of value. But, before labour and land can be part of the creation of surplus value in the markets, they have to be commodified. Polanyi argues (1968, 72) that:

> labour, land, and money are obviously not commodities [...]. Labour is only another name for a human activity which goes with life itself, which in turn is not produced for sale but for entirely different reasons, nor can that activity be detached from the rest of life, be stored or mobilized; land is only another name for nature, which is

not produced by man; actual money, finally, is merely a token of purchasing power which as a rule, is not produced at all, but comes into being through the mechanism of banking or state finance. None of them is produced for sale. The commodity description of labour, land, and money is entirely fictitious.

Polanyi (1968) complements the arguments of Wood (2002) and Perelman (2000), claiming that capitalism, as a structure of accumulation, would not be complete if the labour market would not be part of it. Consequently, the foundation of wage-labouring class meant that the traditional customs and structures were to be abolished, for example, in rural England. Nevertheless, and perhaps the most important aspect of Polanyi's analysis is his realisation that the more complicated the industrial production processes become, the more of its components have to be secured institutionally for industrial demand (often by force). In this case, three components are more crucial than others: labour, land and money. In capitalism, their demand could be guaranteed only by making them available for buying and selling. Thus, they are to be organised accordingly, that is, in a commodity form (Polanyi, 1968), which entails that conditions for their buying and selling, in practice, are conducted and guaranteed by the state.

But when precisely did these changes start to take place? Over hundred years ago R.H. Tawney (1912, 189) wrote that the 16th century marks a turning point from the medieval, in which land was the foundation of deeds and duties, towards the modern, where land is perceived as a productive investment. Wallerstein (2003, 19) argues, that the change from feudalism towards capitalism might have started to happen even earlier, in the late 15th century Europe. Moore (2007; 2015) places the origins of capitalism to the long 16th century (ca. 1450-1640) driven by the Dutch and later the English ascendant hegemonic powers of the time. Wood (2002, 100-101), in turn, places the origin of capitalism in the

16th century English countryside.

What needs to be taken under consideration, of course, is that feudalism existed parallel to capitalism for centuries before feudalism was gradually consumed by the newly dominant mode of production and societal structure (Calhoun, 2013, 135-136). As Wood (2002, 78) observes:

> Even later than the 17th century, most of the world, including Europe, was free of market imperatives. A vast system of trade certainly existed, extending across the globe. But nowhere, neither in the great trading centres of Europe nor in the vast commercial networks of the non-European world, was economic activity and production in particular driven by the imperatives of competition and accumulation.

Calhoun (2013, 135-136) points to a crucial difference between the two modes of production. He argues that feudalism was not 'systemic' in the sense of modern capitalism. In addition, he (ibid) argues that the long decline in feudal relations came in the era of state building and war, of agricultural innovations, religious revitalisation and Reformation and eventually Industrial Revolution, leading to growing global commerce. This decline, he believes, lasted over 300 years. Along the same lines, Wood (2002, 73) argues that feudalism in Europe was internally diverse, and it produced various outcomes, of which only one was capitalism.

As Moore (2015, 189) remarks, although it took centuries for capitalism to take its late industrial form, already the immediate consequences were dramatic. He (ibid) points out how, in particular, the human-nature relation was transformed along with the property relations by stating that *'there was a transition from control of land for advancing labour productivity within commodity production'*. Retrospectively, according to Moore (ibid, 95), these transformations represent an early modern revolution in labour productivity within commodity production and exchange with specific priority: accumulation by appropriation.

Finally, when locating the origins of capitalism to the 15th or 16th century (Wood, 2002; Moore, 2015), it is no surprise that capitalism originated in the countryside rather than in urban setting, especially if we were to look at the historical relations between agriculture and capitalism. As Burkett (2003, 150) argues, Marx recognised that *'without an agricultural surplus, there can be no surplus labor in agriculture and no means of subsistence for nonagricultural workers, hence no surplus value in the economy as a whole.'* Unlike pre-capitalist civilisations, capitalism has expanded by creating vast agricultural surpluses originating from rising labour productivity, imposed by social order and class relations created and legitimised by states (Wood, 2002, 175). The history of capitalism also tells us that ascendant hegemonic powers (the Dutch in the 16th and 17th, the English 17th and 18th, the Americans in the 19th and 20th centuries) have likewise been leading agricultural innovators and locus of knowledge (Moore, 2015, 242-243).

Wood (2002, 100) states that property and class relations, for instance, in rural England in the 16th century destined that the agrarian landlords had incentives to reduce costs and to enhance their productivity to gain better yields (Wood, 2002, 100). As for the tenants, they were gradually exposed to systemic imperatives of the market competition that compelled them to make more efficient use of their means of production. In course of time, more and more land came under this economic organisation, and an advantage in access to the land would go to those who had succeeded in the competition and were able to pay good rents by increasing their crops and productivity (ibid).

In short, capitalist social and class relations emerged from the early capitalism's primitive accumulation (Perelman, 2000; Wood,

2002; Moore, 2015), starting from the Middle Ages, and have spread onwards in various shapes of imperialism (colonial, cultural and economic) ever since (Marx, 1973; Wood, 2002; Moore, 2015). Evolving capitalist relations of production gradually created increasing agricultural surpluses that were able to sustain larger human populations (Wood, 2002; Herrmann, 2013), but at the same time dispossessed countless people from their lands (Foster, 2009), including those who could not measure up in the competition (Wood, 2002). These masses of people were eventually to constitute a large wage-labouring industrial proletariat but also demand for cheap consumer goods (Foster, 2009), while nations across the globe would be forced to become colonies to feed raw materials and labour power to foster industrialisation and advance imperialist projects of emerging imperialist European nation states (Moore, 2015).

Capitalism of the real: *'Accumulate, Accumulate!'*

Marx and Engels remarked in *The Communist Manifesto* (2002, 223) in 1848 that capitalism – at the time in the early stages of modern industrialisation – is in constant need of expansion: *'The need of a constantly expanding market for its products chases the bourgeoisie over the whole surface of the globe. It must nestle everywhere, settle everywhere, establish connexions everywhere'*. Marx and Engels (ibid) continue in the *Manifesto* that:

> All old established national industries have been destroyed or are daily being destroyed. They are dislodged by new industries, whose introduction becomes a life and death question for all civilised nations, by industries that no longer work up indigenous raw material but raw material drawn from the remotest zones; industries whose products are consumed, not only at home, but in every quarter of the globe. In place of the old wants, satisfied by the productions of the country, we find new wants, requiring for their

satisfaction the products of distant lands and climes.

Another famous quote (ibid, 224) suggests that:

> The bourgeoisie, by the rapid improvement of all instruments of production, by the immensely facilitated means of communication, draws all, even the most barbarian, nations into civilisation. The cheap prices of its commodities are the heavy artillery with which it batter down all Chinese walls [...]. It compels all nations, on pain of extinction, to adopt the bourgeois mode of production; it compels them to introduce what it calls civilisation into their minds, i.e. to become bourgeois themselves. In one word, it creates a world after its own image.

Overlooking the ethnocentristic tone of the latter quote, it is clear that for Marx, and many others after him, including myself, capital is the key element in, but also to understand, capitalism. But what is capital? For one, capital is invested or investable wealth (Calhoun, 2013, 136) meaning money, bonds, jewelry, gold, etc. And yes, capital is also accumulated wealth (money, gold, buildings, machinery, forests, fields, etc). Yet, when capital is analysed in a more specific historical context it has more elaborate definition. As Wallerstein (2003, 13-14) argues:

> It (capital) is not just the stock of consumable goods, machinery, or authorized claims, or material things in the form of money. [...] What distinguishes the historical social system we are calling historical capitalism is that in this historical system capital came to be used (invested) in a very special way. It came to be used with the primary objective or intent of self-expansion. In this system, past accumulations were 'capital' only to the extent they were used to accumulate more of the same. [...] it was this relentless and curiously self-regarding goal of the holder of capital, the accumulation of still more capital, and the relations this holder of capital had therefore to establish with other persons in order to

achieve this goal, which we denominate as capitalist.

Capital is then accumulated wealth to be invested in order to accumulate more capital and so forth. The drive to expansive, unlimited accumulation, the never-ending revolutionising of the means of production, as Marx already argued, is an integral part of the juggernaut of capital (Foster, 2009, 230). Capital is for Marx is, as he argues in *Grundrisse* (1993, 408-410) the final frontier of capitalism. Its constant reproduction represents a line that capitalism cannot cross (ibid). Therefore, the capitalist structure, which is by far the most dynamic that humanity has ever witnessed, is at the same time, peculiarly static and repetitious (Eagleton, 2012, 22). It is precisely for this reason, that Marx's critical analysis of capital and capitalism can still be considered to be valid and up-to-date in the 21st century.

Nonetheless, it might, for instance, seem peculiar why a single capitalist drives towards ever further accumulation and expansion rather than using the profits for personal pleasure. One reason for this is the so-called 'coercive law of competition' and its pivotal role in capitalism (Harvey, 2011, 43). If a capitalist (or an economic organisation within capitalism) for some reason or another decides not to invest in expansion, or not to come up with new products and services, or not to improve productivity, and one of his/her rivals does, the one who decided not to, will likely be driven out of business eventually (ibid). Thus, capitalists and all the other economic actors (including wage-labourers, but also other actors such as nation states) within the capitalist socio-economic structure are practically compelled to follow suit, that is, to stimulate the capitalist economy, to maximise profits and market share, if they want to stay within and succeed in the capitalist market competition. This, of course, means that the requirements of market share competition and profit maximisation, alongside never-ending capital accumulation, are one of the fundamental principles of the capitalist socio-economic structure.

What is true to a single capitalist is also true at a more systemic level. Capital accumulation has to continue in an expansive manner or the overall reproduction of capitalism is in danger. Consequently, as Harvey (2014, 222) claims '*capital is always about growth and it necessarily grows at compound rate.*' Similarly, Magdoff and Foster (2011, 42) state that no-growth capitalism does not exist, or is by no means desirable, because when capital accumulation ceases, or even slows down, a systemic crisis ensues. One of the significant reasons why this is so, is a factor called return on investment, as well as interest and interest of interest. David Graeber (2014, 332) writes in *Debt: The First 5000 Years* that '*what is 'interest' but the demand that that money never ceases to grow?*' The same is true, Graeber continues, for investments, which are, in principle, capital placed in the continual pursuit for profit.

Money, finance and banking are, and have been, at the heart of the functioning of capitalism, even before the Industrial Revolution (Graeber, 2014, 345-346). But especially since the 18th century, the world has witnessed a rise of a gigantic financial structure of credit and debt (ibid). Credit, interest, and economic growth are, and have been, deeply intertwined in capitalism for systemic reasons. For instance, when a finance capitalist lends money capital to states, companies, or individuals, he expects a return for their investment to compensate the risk he/she is taking by lending the money capital (Harvey, 2011, 41). This means that the individual who has taken the loan in order to build a factory, or buy bonds, or a wedding ring for instance, has to pay back more money (interest) than he/she borrowed from the creditor. At the systemic level, this signifies that, for most people to be able to repay their debt and not to default, there has to be growth in the overall economy (see Herrmann, 2013). Of course, this means that capital has, in principle, to circulate endlessly, which means, again, a never-ending cycle of consumption, new loans, new investments, and constantly expanding requirements for supply and demand for goods. On top of all, transactions, circulation, and accumulation need to happen in an accelerating fashion, because of interest of interest (or growth of growth). Ultimately, and because of return on investment, interest of interest and the necessity of continuous capital accumulation, capitalist economy is forced to grow at a compound rate, that is, exponentially, to be able reproduce itself without crises. As Harvey (ibid, 112-113) explains: *'capitalism […] must generate and internalize its own effective demand',* which means that the circulation and accumulation of capital cannot stop but must accelerate and grow, or else a systemic crisis follows in the shape of a depression.

It is also vital to mention, that credit and interest alone do not necessary bring about economic growth, not to mention capitalism (Herrmann, 2013). The same goes for money, the market economy and even profit orientation in production. None of these arrangements have, historically, given way to economic growth in such a way as they have done in the era of capitalism (ibid). Consequently, it is and was only when credit, interest, money and profit orientation were coupled with other capitalist relations of production, namely, market competition and profit maximisation, that the era of economic growth began, as did the era of capital accumulation through productivity gains and capital investments (ibid). Indeed, it seems that the 'secret of growth' in capitalism is the combination of credit, interest, and market competition with capitalist relations of production, which ultimately produce surpluses, as well as the necessity to accumulate capital through productivity enhancements, innovations, and new products and services, by adding more energy and labour into the production (Herrmann, 2013; Moore, 2015).

Because of market competition, economic actors are constantly trying to outdo their competitors and to come up with means to expand their production and grow their share of the market. In other words, in capitalism, economic actors are compelled to take loans and to invest some of their profits to expand production, and to improve the productivity of the means of production to produce surpluses. This is in order to accumulate capital to be able to succeed in the competition, but also to be able pay back their debts (the so-called treadmill of accumulation, see Foster, 2009, 23; Foster et al. 2010, 201). The 'treadmill of accumulation' keeps on turning because of capitalism necessitates growth, but also because the coercive laws of competition position all capital accumulators against each other. Therefore, the reality is that no individual capitalist, or economic organisation within capitalism, could ever be more than a volatile ally of any other capitalist (Wallerstein, 2003, 62). Wallerstein (2003, 33-34) states that acute competition among capitalists is, and has been, one of the significant features of capitalism, and because of this, it is evident that no specific pattern linking the productive forces could be stable. On the contrary, it would always be in the interests of a large number of competitive economic actors to try to change the rules of the game to their advantage. Hence, Adam Smith's 'invisible hand' has functioned in the sense that the 'market' has set constraints on individual behaviour, but it would be utterly wrong to assert that the outcome has been any kind of harmony (ibid). Instead of harmony, the outcome has been an alternating cycle of expansions and stagnations.

The continuity of the flow of capital is also very important, because the process of circulation cannot be interrupted without the economic actors suffering losses (Harvey, 2011, 41). There are also strong incentives to accelerate the speed of circulation, due to the potential competition advantage it might impede, because those who can move faster through the phases of capital circulation are likely to gain higher profits than their competitors (ibid). In this harsh reality, bankruptcy has served as the internal cleaner of capitalism, persistently forcing all economic actors (from companies to states) to stay in line, while pressuring them to act in such a way that, through time, has reproduced it and expanded the accumulation process of capital (Wallerstein, 2003, 18).

Furthermore, one has to consider that economic actors within capitalism are all depended on the 'market' (see e.g. 2002; 2005). However, there are important distinctions to be made, when conceptualising a thing called *market*. The word 'market', is nowadays widely and loosely used in political and economic debates and in mundane communication to describe a physical 'marketplace', or a cyber-spatial space in the age of the Internet, to buy and sell products and services. An expression 'to search for new markets' is similarly used to imply to a place or region or cohort of potential new customers/buyers for products and services. More importantly, the word 'market' is also commonly used to describe a thing that organises the current economic structure ('*market*' sets prices, '*market*' regulates supply and demand, '*market*' allocates resources, etc.). Curiously, the latter way of talking about '*market*' gives it, and I argue falsely, a subject-like form, and while doing so, it is forgotten that a market, or more precisely a *market structure*, is always constructed of various social structures and relations.

Therefore, it makes more sense to speak for instance of the *capitalist market structure* (apart from other market structures, or market-based economies in the past) that is constructed of specific social relations (such as private property, class division, limited liability company) and employed in the capitalist socio-economic structure as means to allocate and distribute resources and division of labour, and thus, it forms an integral part of the modern capitalist structure. However, a structure of markets is only one way to organise an economy that is based on accumulation and growth, as state socialism in the Soviet Union was also an economy based on accumulation and economic growth, although it, in many respects, lacked markets in the form that is now considered conventional in capitalism.

With these distinctions, I want to argue that a market or the capitalist market itself is not an autonomous or independent entity (thing-for-itself), but a specific and context-dependent historical social relation, which reflects certain societal structures, practices, ideologies, and relations of production and their interaction. In other words, the capitalist market structure is constructed by certain context-dependent social relations and structures, which can, and have, been negotiated over and over in the course of history.

Similarly, as Wood (2005, 30-31) I also want to make a claim that the capitalistic market structure differs from other historical economic arrangements. In particular, this is true when comparing capitalism to pre-capitalist societies not based on market exchange, in which direct producers were able to use and utilise the means of production, especially land, for their personal or community's use (and to sell/trade the possible surplus to an external body), instead of primarily producing commodities for external bodies or, in other words, for the market, while organising the economic activity in specific economic organisations (companies) (ibid). In this regard, it is also vital to make a separation in use and exchange value, as well as to explore Marx's fetishism conception.

Behind Marx's concept, *commodity fetishism* is a question of how extensively the exchange of goods affects people (Heiskanen, 2015, 86-87). Heiskanen (ibid) states that Marx explains this with his famous use-value exchange-value dichotomy. Use-values are, by definition, the useful features of things that satisfy human needs. In contrast, exchange-values are quantitative relations that manifest themselves in money as use-values are exchanged (ibid). It would, of course, make sense that use-values would steer the production processes, but in capitalism, exchange-value tends to dominate over use-value (ibid). Kolakowski (2008, 239) writes that, by favouring exchange-value over use-value, in order to guarantee accumulation and expansion, capital is actually indifferent to the nature of the goods that are produced. In fact, from the perspective of capital accumulation, the agents of capital are interested in use-values if they serve to increase their exchange-value. From the point of view of capitalists, it does not really matter what they produce, as long as they succeed in the competition and are able to accumulate capital. In other words, use-value, i.e. the actual product and its usefulness, is secondary to its potential monetary exchange value in capitalism. Marx writes in *Capital* vol. 1 (1973, 151-153) that:

> The circulation of money as capital is, on the contrary, an end in itself, for the expansion of value takes place only within this constantly renewed movement. The circulation of capital has therefore no limits. As the conscious representative of this movement, the possessor of money becomes a capitalist. [...] The expansion of value, which is the objective basis or main spring of the circulation M-C-M, becomes his subjective aim; and it is only in so far as the appropriation of ever more and more wealth in the abstract becomes the sole motive of his operations, that he functions as a capitalist, that is, as capital personified and endowed with consciousness and a will. Use-values must therefore never be looked upon as the real aim of the capitalist; neither must the profit on any single transaction. The restless never-ending process of profit-making alone is what he aims at. This boundless greed after riches, this passionate chase after exchange-value, is common to the capitalist and the miser; but while the miser

is merely a capitalist gone mad, the capitalist is a rational miser. The never-ending augmentation of exchange-value, which the miser strives after, by seeking to save his money from circulation, is attained by the more acute capitalist, by constantly throwing it afresh into circulation.

Heiskanen (2015, 87) states that every supplier in capitalism attempts to respond to the needs of their customers; however, suppliers are secluded from each other and constantly seek to succeed in the competition. In this kind of circumstance, each supplier seeks to minimise risks, and thus focus more and more into the operations of the 'market', as well as to market their own products. This does not, of course, remove the problem, but makes it worse, and as the market requires more and more attention, it gradually becomes to be perceived as an absolute value (ibid). As Kolakowski (2008, 242) proclaims the capitalist market *'is a race to turn goods into money, in conditions where demand and supply are never exactly matched and consequently prices are never the same as values.'* Generally, this situation signifies that abstract and quantitative matters dominate the capitalist society in contrast to concrete things, and while doing so, it generates conditions for commodity fetishism, which governs the consciousness and actions of individuals (Heiskanen, 2015, 87-88).

Commodity fetishism entails that human relationships manifest in the relationships of things, that is, individuals perceive that exchange value and the price of a commodity directly consist of the features of that commodity, although commodities are produced in complex processes and are simultaneously affected by the prevailing relations of production, the rules of the market, as well as overall societal circumstances (ibid). A person may think that the cheapness of a particular commodity is due to the features of that commodity, rather than perceiving that the commodity has been produced by, for instance, exploiting cheap temporary workers (ibid). Hence,

Kolakowski (2008, 227) writes that these processes in which *'social relations masquerade as things or relations between things is the cause of human failure to understand the society in which we live.'* Indeed, the 'market' neither exists as it is nor is a thing-for-itself, but is instead constructed of various interests, power structures, social contracts and bonds, which affect and influence the behaviour of individuals and overall society, and remain negotiated and contested over time.

The inequality of capital accumulation

Capitalism is perhaps most often defended when it comes to material affluence. It is of course true that material wealth and affluence in the modern industrial era is something previously unseen in human history. However, and regardless of all the wealth and affluence, majority of the people have still been left hungry, poor and exploited (Wallerstein, 2003, 136-137). This is because of what Marx called the *'general law of capital accumulation': 'the accumulation of capital in hands of the few, the accumulation of poverty in the hands of the many'* (Moore, 2015, 91).

Palpably, the question to ask is how real have the benefits of capitalism been in the course of history? Moreover, the rather self-evident follow-up question is in whose interests? As is very well established, capitalism has involved a monumental creation of material and immaterial goods, but at the same time, also a monumental polarisation of reward (Jackson, 2009). Perhaps a most compelling single piece of evidence of this is an Oxfam briefing paper, which concludes that just 8 richest men (Bill Gates, Amancio Ortega, Warren Buffet, Carlos Slim Helu, Jeff Bezos, Mark Zuckenberg, Larry Ellison and Michael Bloomberg) own as much as the bottom half of the entire human population, this is, 3,6 billion individuals (Oxfam, 2017). In a similar vein, Rothkopf (2008, 37) has observed that 85% of the world's wealth has been monopolised by just 10% of the world's human population, while the bottom half of the adult population owns barely 1% of the total wealth. Thomas Piketty, in his part, (2014) has convincingly shown how the real income gap has increased steadily since the Industrial Revolution (disregarding a short social democratic era after the Second World War). Also Vitali et al., (2011) have shown in their study how centralised is the ownership of global means of production and the flow of capital, or in other words, who benefits the most from the status quo or from the reproduction of the business-as-usual (in addition to those eight business men that were already mentioned). From altogether 43 000 transnational corporations, Vitali et al. (2011) identified a core of 1318 transnational corporations with interlocking ownership. Collectively they were responsible of 80% of total global operating revenues. As the researchers furthered their analysis, they ultimately came across with a 'super-entity' of 147 companies that controlled 40% of the total wealth of the whole network. Tellingly, the top 50 of these 147 corporations principally represented global financial institutions and insurance companies, among them Goldman Sachs, Citigroup, JP Morgan Chase, AIG, Barclay's Bank, Bank of America, Deutsche Bank (ibid).

Capitalism does not vary from any other historical socio-economic structure; it is also a structure of hierarchies and privilege (Wallerstein, 2003, 136-137). There has never been a golden era in human recorded history, as Wallerstein (ibid) bluntly puts it, and as Piketty (2014) has shown in terms of wealth distribution in the modern era. On the contrary, the trend has been towards the centralisation of ownership of the means of production (Piketty, 2014). Wallerstein et al. (2013, 171-172) similarly note that the redistribution of income has been running in the upward direction since the 1970s, to those located in more powerful nation states, and to elites making political and financial decisions. Meanwihle, cuts in social redistribution, as the public sector has been in many ways opened up to capital accumulation, have made sure that capital has accumulated ever more steeply to a small economic-financial elite while the rest – states and citizens alike – have become indebted (ibid).

Likewise, competition, dominated by semi-monopolistic transnational corporations (Graeber, 2015), as well as capitalist class relations and hierarchies, are bound to create socio-economic inequality. As Shaikh (2005, 43) accurately writes: *'it is not the absence of competition that produces development alongside underdevelopment, wealth alongside poverty, employment alongside unemployment. It is the competition itself.'* In fact, what is usually left untold alongside all the success stories of hard-working entrepreneurs, are the negative impacts of competition (Kohn, 1992) to the social fabric, including rising economic uncertainty (Standing, 2011), inequality (Stiglitz, 2012) and isolation (Sennett, 1998) of those who are unable to measure up (see also du Gay, 2000).

In particular, what has made the situation far more uncertain and precarious for countless number of people is the increasingly global nature of capitalism (Harvey, 2014, 148-150). Robinson (2014, 52) argues that, during the past decades, proletarisation has accelerated worldwide through new waves of primitive accumulation, as billions of people have been dispossessed from their lands and shunted into the global capitalist structure. The numbers of the global labour force doubled between 1980 and 2006 from 1.5 billion to 3 billion, as workers from China, India and the former Soviet Bloc became part of the global labour supply (ibid). In China alone, 200 million people have moved from rural areas to cities (Davis, 2007). While these people had, of course, existed before, the difference was that their national economies were suddenly attached to the global system of production and consumption (Freeman, 2006). As Moore (2015, 237) remarks, the 'global factory' depended upon the 'great global enclosure' that began in the early 1980s. The great enclosure, entailing the dispossession hundreds of millions of peasants from their lands, was realised, among other elements, through structural adjustment programmes and market liberalisation policies, which have restructured agrarian class relations worldwide (ibid, 301-302).

In the era of global capitalism, lower costs in transport and communications facilitate dispersal and the decentralisation of economic activity across the planet – to a larger and larger geographical space (Harvey, 2014, 148). From the point of view of the global workforce, the problem is the 'runaway factory' (Wallerstein, 2013, 22). The constant geographical restructuring of capitalism (Wallerstein, 2003, 35), arguably means increasingly uncertain and precarious jobs and job opportunities for the growing global workforce (Standing, 2011; Moore, 2015), which is, at the same time, increasingly more urban in nature (Davis, 2007). Again, a plausible explanation for the constant relocation is the logic of capital and its continuous search for lower production costs, i.e. low-cost labour force (Wallerstein, 2003, 38-39). When local labour costs are on the rise, investors and corporate leaders look for other possibilities, in this case, other geographical spaces to relocate production (Harvey, 2014, 150-152).

Such geographical expansion and relocation generally threaten the established conditions of production. This contradiction, as Harvey (2014, 152) argues, is inescapable in capitalism: *'either capital moves out and leaves behind a trail of devastation and devaluation (for example, Detroit). Or it stays put only to drown in the capital surpluses it inevitably produces but cannot find profitable outlets for.'* The most peculiar part of this process is, Harvey (2014, 154) continues, that in capitalism, this systemic failure is never addressed because capital moves around in time and space. The geographic landscape of capitalism, as opposed to that of capital, is shaped by an assembly of interests (individuals, organisations, institutions, nation states) seeking to define spaces and places for their favour. More importantly, as Harvey (ibid, 161) suggests:

> Without uneven geographical development, capital would surely have stagnated, succumbed to its sclerotic, monopolistic and autocratic tendencies and totally lost legitimacy as the dynamic engine of a society that has pretences to being civilized even as it is in danger of heading towards barbarism. Unleashing interurban, interregional and international competition is not only a primary means whereby the new comes to supplant the old, a context in which the search for the new, billed as the search for competitive advantage, becomes critical to capital's capacity to reproduce itself.

Because of many internal contradictions the capitalist structure is in constant motion – an argument that is widely acknowledged in Marxist literature (see e.g. Marx, 1973; Arrighi, 2010; Harvey, 2014). This restlessness does not only limit to tomorrow's uncertainty and unending competition, but ultimately generate socio-economic crises that often lead to significant restructurings of key institutions, as well as social and power relations within capitalism (Harvey, 2014).

Neoliberal restructuring of global capitalism

> [...] capitalism is vulnerable not just to market upheavals, excessive risk-taking, or poorly managed banks but also to wars, environmental degradation and climate change, and crises of social solidarity and welfare. (Calhoun, 2013, 132)

David Harvey states in his book *Seventeen Contradictions and the End of Capitalism* (2014) that crises are essential to the reproduction of capitalism. Harvey (ibid, ix) argues that through crises the instabilities of capitalism are confronted, reshaped and re-engineered to create a novel version of what capitalism is about.

Before the economic crisis in the 1970s, extensive influence of state socialism, over social policies in the capitalist countries, meant that capitalist states were pressured to share the fruits of economic growth among a wider share of the general population (Harvey, 2014, 165). The welfare states that resulted from the social democratic 'class compromise' were, nevertheless, far from being socialist. For instance, strong elements of gender bias and paternalistic mind-set persisted along with pro-capitalist mentality to an extent that the state became demeaning, punitive and bureaucratic in its approach to its own citizens (ibid). Regardless, the welfare state benefits (like social security and pension system) brought security to most citizens of these countries (ibid) and levelled socio-economic inequality especially in the Nordic countries (see Piketty, 2014).

Yet, the lifespan of the social democratic welfare state would be relatively short, although one could also argue that the welfare state has survived up until our day in one form or another. The economic crises of the 1970s along with the Thatcherite neoliberal counter-revolution of the 1980s (Harvey, 2005; 2014; Jones, 2013) and ultimately the collapse of state socialism, removed the external pressure to commit to equality and eventually wiped out strong political opposition (Harvey, 2014, 165).

Peculiarly, as Eagleton (2012, 15-16) proclaims, in 1976 many Western people thought that many Marxist ideas held ground, but did not any more by 1986. We have to ask, what, on the one hand, explains the crisis of capitalism in the 1970s and on the other hand the changing opinions of the general public? As Eagleton (ibid) highlights, during that period of time vital changes started to occur in the Western way of living. Since the mid-1970s industrial manufacturing has been replaced by 'post-industrialism', i.e., communications, information technology and service industries. At the same time, national economies were gradually liberated and re-regulated, as well as workers movements being targeted both legally and politically. Eagleton (2012, 17) continues that none of these things happened because capitalism was thriving. Quite on the contrary, aggressive economic counter policies were due to the internal crises of capitalism. Internal panic was mainly caused by the withering away of the longest boom in its history. Accelerating international competition pushed the rates of profit into decline, which simultaneously blocked sources of new investment and slowed down economic growth, which meant in principle that even the social democratic version of capitalism seemed now too radical and expensive economic and political programme (ibid).

In *The Enigma of Capital* Harvey (2011, 112-113) argues that the internationalisation and increasing globalisation of trade were responses to the demands for continuous and expansive capital accumulation. Harvey states (2014, 235) that the privatisation of public assets, the creation of new markets and further enclosures of the commons have all expanded the playing field in which capital can freely operate. Before the 1970s the main source for investment was in production of surplus value through manufacturing, mining, agriculture and infrastructure (Harvey, 2014, 238-239). In contrast, Calhoun (2013, 137) claims that where financial instruments accounted for a quarter of invested assets in the 1970s, by 2008 the figure was 75%, as financial assets globally amounted to four times the value of all equities and ten times the total global GDP.

Regarding the heavy financialisation of the past decades, Calhoun (ibid) argues that USA and other core capitalist countries brought the Bretton Woods monetary system to an end while seeking to manage their economic difficulties in the 1970s. Bretton Woods was replaced by floating, infinitely tradable fiat currencies. This occurred, according to Harvey (2014, 240), at the time when profitability prospects in productive activities were at their lowest in almost three decades and *'when capital began to experience the impact of an inflexion point in the trajectory of exponential growth.'* One way to sustain economic growth and secure prospects for expansive capital accumulation in this situation was to pursue the so-called neoliberal politics[12] by opening up countries and various spheres of economic activity to market forces (Foster, 2009, 133; see also Jones, 2013). Thus, public utilities such as water, electricity, telecommunications, transportation, public housing, education and healthcare have been gradually opened up to 'market economics' (Harvey, 2011, 29). If one would look for a common denominator behind the breakthrough of neoliberal politics (see Jones, 2013), it would be the hegemony of capital. This is because accumulation and the prospects for capital expansion were seriously weakened in the 1970s – capitalism was in crisis, and due to this, there was a need to solve the 'capital absorption problem' (see Harvey, 2011, 28, 45).

During the 1980s and 1990s, state policies were adjusted in favour of capitalist globalisation, and globalisation coupled with neoliberal policies opened up new opportunities for transnational accumulation (Robinson, 2014, 54). However, as Robinson (ibid) argues, it was not the basic ideas of neoliberal ideology that convinced political administrators around the world and converted it into the dominant economic model, but the fact that the political programme that neoliberalism proposed was perfectly in line with the demands of capital at that particular historic moment.

---

12 According to Calhoun (2013, 150) the term neoliberalism is used to refer to a set of policies that seek to reduce government spending and interventions in economic activity and to reduce government regulation of the capitalist market structure. Robinson (2014, 56) argues that neoliberal policies typically include liberalisation of trade and finance, deregulating the movements of capital (but not an end of state intervention in assisting accumulation of capital), the privatisation of the so-called public spheres, and austerity packages involving lay-offs in public sector and cuts in social services.

But even in terms of economic viability the age of neoliberalism has brought diminishing returns (see e.g. Pollin, 2003; Brenner, 2006). Meanwhile, less and less of the surplus capital is being absorbed in production due to falling profit margins, and as a result, more and more capital has been directed to speculation on asset values (Harvey, 2011, 29). In much same way as Harvey (2011, 28, 45), Robinson (2014, 132) explains that the most recent financial crisis, which begun in 2007-2008, was one of overaccumulation, or from another perspective, due to the lack of outlets for profitable absorption of surpluses. Although, capitalist globalisation and neoliberal policies have been successful in opening up substantial opportunities for transnational capital accumulation, by the end of the 1990s, the limits of expansion of capital started to show, as global markets became increasingly saturated when the opportunities for profitable absorption of surpluses diminished (Robinson, 2014, 134). However, overaccumulation and lack of investment opportunities to foster further accumulation seem to be merely the flip side of the coin when explaining the falling profit and growth rates in the neoliberal era. The other side is, as Moore (2015, 97) explains, underproduction due to problems in the appropriation of work/energy. As Moore (2015, 87) writes, capitalism continually *'exhausts its sources of nourishment'*. When opportunities for appropriation of new work inputs and raw materials decline relative to the mass of accumulated capital, a certain course of events follows. According to Moore (ibid, 101), the cost of production rises, and the profitability of renewed capital accumulation now depends upon finding new frontiers of appropriation. Thus, new production complexes extend their arms to novel territories, and therefore every era of capitalism begins with a 'new imperialism' and with a new wave of industrialisation, as we have witnessed in China and India (ibid).

Neoliberal policies have, in particular, targeted the welfare duties of nation states (Harvey, 2005; Wood, 2005). Nevertheless, there seems to be little evidence that we would be witnessing a rundown of the state or even the disappearance of the welfare state in one form or another (Wood, 2005). While it is true that the left and the workers movements in general have been forced to withdraw, so-called social democratic governments have still been able to hold on to the basic social safety nets for citizens in most of the Western world (ibid, 168). Thus, instead of 'self-regulating market economy', a more accurate way to describe the neoliberal reality would be to rely on Magdoff and Foster (2011, 99) and claim that we are increasingly witnessing a reality where private interests regulate the state and not vice versa.

Consequently, 'neoliberalism' seems to be both an ideology and a means to an end – instrument. On the one hand, neoliberalism is an ideological arrangement and a political campaign, in the sense that its theorists and proponents claim that the private sector is more 'effective' than the public sector, and thus the public sector 'should be opened up' more to private accumulation, or that 'free trade', financial deregulation, and increased competition benefits everyone – rising tide lifts all boats – and so on. On the other hand, neoliberal politics is used as an instrument to alleviate the internal problems of capitalism (diminishing rates of profit since the 1970s) by extending the process of capital accumulation to, for example, public healthcare and education, or by proletarising and urbanising China and India, or by privatising global commons, or, and perhaps most importantly, by globalising and lifting barriers to the movements of capital (financialisation and integration of global financial markets). Similarly, Robinson (2014, 55) argues that the neoliberal project has a twin dimension, which is pursued by global elites backed up by a well-organised and well-funded transnational corporative lobby (see also Herrmann, 2013). One dimension of the neoliberal project is an agenda to push for worldwide market liberalisation and a shared regulatory framework for the global economy. The other dimension is internal restructuring and the global integration of national economies (Robinson, 2014, 55).

In parallel with neoliberalism, Robinson (2014, 81-82) argues that a transnational capitalist class become the dominant fraction of the capitalist classes worldwide. The class power of the transnational capitalist class, as a dominant class fraction of the dominant class or 'historic bloc', is anchored in global capitalist relations of production, particularly in its domination over the world's natural and cultural resources (ibid, 73). Kauppinen (2013) argues as well that the economic crisis of the 1970s and the following restructuring of capitalism, together with technological and organisational innovations, facilitated the formation of the so-called transnational capitalist class. Moreover, various transnational mechanisms and practices have played a key role in the integration process, including the rapid rise of transnational corporations since the 1970s (ibid). Simultaneously, a historically unprecedented concentration of wealth and power has occurred at the hands of few thousand global corporations, financial institutions, and investment funds. This concentration and centralisation means, in principle, also the accumulation of power by not only national but also increasingly transnational capitalist groups (Robinson, 2014, 21-22).

Robinson (2004, 36, footnote 1) argues that the transnational capitalist class consists of those individuals who own or control transnational economic capital. Thus, the transnational capitalist class is the propertied class. Sklair (2002, 9) offers, in contrast to Robinson's definition, a more elaborate portrayal of the transnational capitalist class. Sklair (ibid) argues that the members of the transnational capitalist class *'see their own interests [...] as best served by an identification with the interests of the capitalist global system*'. In a more specific manner, Sklair (2001, 12) explains that the mutual interests of the transnational capitalist class are *'the protection of private property and the rights of private individuals to accumulate it with as little interference as possible'*. Therefore, the members of the transnational capitalist class are those (individuals and/or organisations) who not only own but also make efforts to safeguard their interests and rights to accumulate capital. The transnational integration of national economies and their capitalist groups have created common interests concerning capital accumulation in the expanding global economy (Robinson, 2014, 44). Nevertheless, this does not mean there would not exist political tensions and conflicts of interest in international forums. However, as Harris (2009, 146) notes, global competition is *'rather the integration of economic interests creating competitive blocs of transnational corporations seeking to achieve advantage in a variety of fields and territorial regions.'*

As Kauppinen (2013) remarks, a consequence of these mechanisms and practices has been the uneven transnationalisation of production networks and the emergence of transnational social networks between economic actors. Whereas the former has provided a basis for the overall development of transnational capitalist class, the latter has provided the social spaces in which it became possible for the members to interact, and to develop common strategies and class-consciousness (ibid). From all this has resulted, and is equally particularly characteristic to the top layer of the global economy, the complex web of transnational capital (Robinson, 2014, 29). Seemingly, at the heart of this web is the pumping engine of the global financial structure. Harvey (2011, 16) notes that the phenomenon of 'going global' was indeed facilitated by a new financial architecture that was created to facilitate the international flow of capital to wherever it could be put into work most profitably (ibid). Hence, Robinson (2014,

135) has noted that the transnational financial capital is at the core of the global capitalist economic order and to be considered the hegemonic fraction of capital globally.

Meanwhile, as the movements of capital have globalised and have become hegemonic, global policy planning organisations have become vital elements for the capitalist historic bloc in bringing together transnational corporations, global-governance institutions and elite policy-planning organisations (Gill, 1995). International organisations such as the IMF, World Bank and WTO have worked together with national states to reformulate global production processes, labour relations, and financial institutions to be embedded into a structure of global accumulation (Robinson, 2014, 68). IMF, WTO, OECD and other international organisations can be seen as a web of decentred 'institutional ensemble' or network of institutions that are loosely unified in the function of capitalist globalisation (ibid). In another words, the primary purpose of these bodies is to secure the conditions of the reproduction of capital accumulation in and across territories of the global economy. The transnational capitalist class and its agents make use of these international bodies, and at the same time, these bodies organise the transnational capitalist class (Robinson, 2014, 78).

It is relative easy, I think, to recognise, which bodies benefit the most from the existence of capitalist globalisation and its reproduction. Transnational corporations - especially their leaders and owners – and international organisations (such as IMF, World Bank, WTO, OECD, EU) and leaders of nations states are obvious drivers and beneficiaries of the current world order. In addition to them, financial operators, various industrial organisations, parliamentary politicians, high-ranking public officials, various experts and consultants (including many university professors, faculty and administrative personnel), mainstream media and popular culture excecutives, sports and pop stars and also high earning and consuming middle-classes, clearly benefit from the established order and have seemingly little ambitions to change their ways. In contrast to this relatively small minority, located predominately in the global North, significant part humans live reasonably stable lives having their basic needs met, while a significant portion of humans are exploited and/or oppressed by capitalist production processes, or live in absolute poverty at the outskirts of vast cities or in rural areas (see Ulvila and Wilén, 2016). Also there still exist approximately 300 million people who remain at least somewhat untouched by modernity and live more or less self-sufficiently (see Böhm et al., 2015). This kind representation is, however, only limited and partial, as it is the non-humans who most heavily experience the harms of industrial capitalism and the 'age of humans' on the planet Earth.

The absolute contradiction: ecological unsustainability of capitalism

> It is impossible to exaggerate the environmental problem facing humanity in the 21st century. (Foster, 2009, 55)

Ecological economist Herman Daly is known for introducing the 'impossibility theorem', that is, the paradox between unlimited economic growth and a finite ecosystem (see e.g. Daly, 1991). John Bellamy Foster (2009, 15) has introduced an important extension or variation to Daly's impossibility theorem:

> The position that there is 'no absolute contradiction between capitalism and sustainability' is true only in the very limited sense that there is no insurmountable barrier, in each and every instance, between the capitalist market and shifts toward sustainability in particular areas. Things are altogether different, however, when capitalism as a planetary system is viewed against the backdrop of the earth as a planetary system. Capitalism as a world economy, divided into classes and driven by competition, embodies a logic that

accepts no boundaries on its expansion and its exploitation of its environment. The earth as a planet, in contrast, is by definition limited. This is an absolute contradiction from which there is no earthly escape.

Ultimately, there is no goal in capitalism, but to generate more profits and accumulate more capital *ad infinitum* (Magdoff and Foster, 2011, 42). It is quite obvious that this kind of maxim generates both growth and an imperative to grow the economy, again limitlessly and indefinitely, which will inevitably be in conflict with the planet and its limited natural resources (see Jackson, 2009). The authors of *The Limits to Growth* had already made this realisation over forty years ago. Meadows et al. wrote (1972, 46) that:

> Much of each year's output is consumable goods, such as textiles, automobiles, and houses that leave the industrial system. But some fraction of the production is more capital – looms, steel mills, lathes – which is an investment to increase the capital stock. [...] More capital creates more output, some variable fraction of the output is investment, and more investment means more capital. The new, larger capital stock generates more output, and so on.

The environmental impacts of expansive capitalist and industrial production are gruesome. After decades of exponential growth in production and consumption, it has been noted that every major ecosystem on earth is in decline (Foster, 2009, 46). Jackson (2009, 13) states that it is commonly known that about 60% of the world's ecosystem 'services' have been degraded or over-used since the mid-20th century. The pressure created by humankind on the Earth's ecosystems is not equally distributed; some parts of the earth and its species are already suffering from the consequences of over-production and consumption while some are blossoming, but eventually the damage done to ecosystems will negatively affect most living beings (Díaz et al., 2006), including the entire human population (Brown, 2011). The most recent and seminal predictions concerning the worst-case scenario, that is, if the business as usual continues, is the sixth mass extinction (Wake and Vredenburg, 2008; Barnosky et al., 2011), the collapse of civilisation or even to extinction of humanity (Morgan, 2009; Brown, 2011).

Diamond (2005) has studied the causes for collapse of local civilisations in the past and found eight linking ecological factors from population growth to soil erosion as the root causes for collapse. What is different in our times compared to Diamond's analysis of past civilisations is that we are now not only witnessing the same ecological problems locally, but also on a planetary level (Rockström et al., 2009; Steffen et al., 2015). Although it is clear that the human-caused ecological crisis is not reducible to a single denominator but rather consists of a complex bundle of problems (Foster et al., 2010, 15-16), it is nevertheless becoming commonly accepted that most ecological problems can be traced down to the growth in economic activities leading to expansive exploitation of natural resources (Foster, 2009; IPCC, 2014; Moore, 2015, Ward et al., 2016).

Concerning the severity of the ecological crisis, world's leading natural scientists, have produced the 'planetary boundaries' model (Rockström et al. 2009; Steffen et al. 2015), which attempts to trace down the limits to human activities on planet Earth. Staying within the so-called safe zone of each of these boundaries is considered critical in order to be able to sustain the relatively benign climatic and environmental conditions that have existed during the Holocene epoch, that is, the last 12000 years or so. The planetary boundaries figure below (Steffen et al., 2015) illustrates the current estimation of the 'safe operating space for humanity'. The green zone in the picture portrays the safe operating space, the yellow signifies the zone of uncertainty or increasing risk, and the red is high-risk zone. The planetary boundary lies at the intersection of the green and yellow zones. The grey wedges in the figure represent boundaries which cannot yet be quantified.

What we can observe from the figure is that biochemical flows and genetic diversity are at the high-risk zone, and land-system change and climate change are at the increasing risk zone (ibid). Steffen et al. (2015, 1-2) conclude that:

> The human enterprise has grown so dramatically since the mid-20th century that the relatively stable, 11,700-year long Holocene epoch, the only state of the planet that we know for certain can support contemporary human societies, is now being destabilized. In fact, a new geological epoch, the Anthropocene, has been proposed. [...] A continuing trajectory away from the Holocene could lead, with an uncomfortably high probability, to a very different state of the Earth System, one that is likely to be much less hospitable to the development of human societies.

The ecological crisis, as an outcome of the human-induced biospheric overshoot (see Meadows et al., 1972; 2002; Foster et al., 2010), is often reduced to a single phenomenon, such as climate change (IPCC, 2014). However, as Steffen et al. (2015) suggest, to address the whole gamut of it, and to find means to a sustainable return within the planetary boundaries would mean that all aspects of the ecological crisis, are to be considered. While the ecological crisis is very serious and complex phenomenon, the mitigation of it should not be. Arguably, there is only one way to correct the overshoot, and that is to produce and consume less in material terms. However, as Foster et al. (2010, 17) note, the essential problem concerning the ecological crisis *'is the unavoidable fact that an expanding economic system is placing additional burdens on a fixed earth system to the point of planetary overload.'*

Tragically, the expansive environmental destruction of industrial capitalism, is most often believed to be remedied by human ingenuity (e.g., Hamilton, 2013; Bannon, 2014; Hamilton et al., 2015). Hand in hand with this hubristic ethos goes the old Cartesian dualism, based on which humans and nature are seen as separate entities (Bateson, 2002). In contrast, a more accurate way to describe the connection is to insist that natural and human history are, and have always been, inseparable (Marx and Engels, 1998, 34). This is, of course, because humans are part of nature (Marx, 2011, 105). Everything on this planet is interconnected; there are no separate entities (Foster, 2000, 226). However, it may also make sense to differentiate analytically different realms of material reality (e.g. nature and society), as Malm (2018) has convincingly argued, to make sense for instance why climate is changing and biodiversity is collapsing, without losing focus that these realms are components of the same substance with different properties (substance monist but property dualist standpoint as Malm would argue).

Concerning capitalism, the fundamental problem is that capital (or rather its agents) operates in contradiction to its ontology, that is, in capitalism nature is treated as something external, and not only as a limitless external entity, but as an object to overcome and as a resource (or a free gift) to be exploited to foster endless accumulation (Moore, 2015, 95). Moreover, the reason why, for example, many of the citizens in affluent Western industrial countries refuse to recognise the full human dependence and embeddedness in nature, seems to be linked to their overall lifestyle, which gives the accumulation of wealth (or economic growth) the first priority in societal goal setting (Foster, 2001). As Meadows et al. observed in *The Limits to Growth: the 30-Year Update* (2002, 223-224):

If society's implicit goals are to exploit nature, enrich the elites, and ignore the long term, then that society will develop technologies and markets that destroy the environment, widen the gap between rich and poor, and optimize for short-term gains. In short, that society develops technologies and markets that hasten a collapse instead of preventing it.

Figure 1. Planetary boundaries (Steffen et al., 2015)

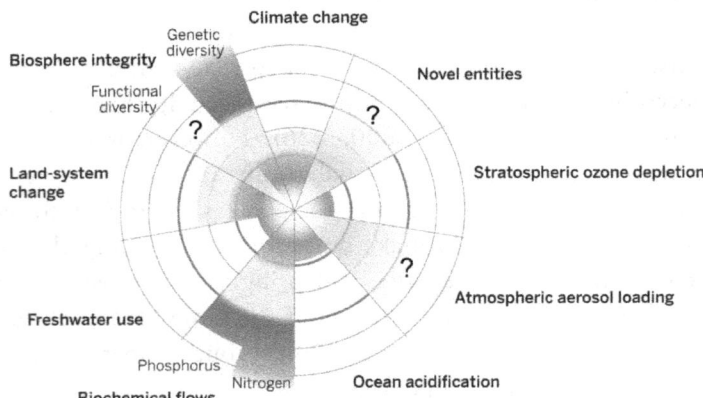

The imperatives of accumulation and growth seemingly define capital's indifferent relation towards life and future generations. While capitalist production goes on, the reproduction of capitalism requires more and more natural resources and labour (human or machine) to sustain growth, capital circulation and accumulation. The problematic relation of nature and capitalism was well recognised by Marx. In *Grundrisse* (1993, 410) Marx argues that:

> For the first time nature becomes purely an object for humankind, purely matter of utility; ceases to be recognized as a power for itself; and the theoretical discovery of its autonomous laws appears merely as a ruse so as to subjugate it under human needs, whether as an object of consumption or as a means of production.

As Foster (2009, 178) explains, Marx's conceptualisation regarding the concept *metabolism (stoffwechsel)* gave Marx analytical means to portray the dynamic interchange, between human beings and nature, through human labour. An essential aspect of the metabolism concept is Marx's notion that it constitutes the basis in which life is sustained and reproduction is possible (Foster, 2009, 180). Humans depend on ecosystems to be able to provide for themselves, and while providing for themselves their actions affect those very ecosystems that humans are part of and in which they interact. Thus, there is a necessary 'metabolic interaction' between humans and the earth (ibid). However, as Marx noted, the large-scale capitalist agriculture created a rift in metabolism between human beings and the soil endangering the reproduction, which also means that the basic conditions of sustainability are violated (ibid).

Foster (2000, 157) claims that metabolism was the key concept (especially for the later) Marx to his ecological accounts and analysis of capitalism. *'The German word "Stoffwechsel" directly sets out in its elements the notion of 'material exchange' that underlies the notion of structured processes of biological growth and decay captured in the term "metabolism"',* Foster (ibid, 157) writes. He continues that Marx himself made the concept of metabolism central to his analysis by rooting his understanding of the labour process upon it (ibid). Marx defines the human labour process in Capital, vol. 1 (1973, 183-184) as *'the necessary condition for effecting exchange of matter between man and Nature; it is the everlasting Nature-imposed condition of human existence',* meaning that the rift in this exchange caused by capitalist socio-economic structure would mean nothing less than undermining the *'everlasting nature-imposed condition of human existence.'*

Indeed, Marx recognised in *Capital* vol. 1 (1973, 506-507) that the rift in metabolism represented a sustainability problem both socially and ecologically. Marx's overall analysis of the capitalist mode of production, but also his perception of capitalist agriculture and the realisation of the necessity of recycling the nutrients of the soil (Foster, 2009, 181), led him to conclude that capitalist society was incapable of rational action regarding long-term planning and future generations as it violated and exploited both the soil and the worker. In *Capital*, vol. 3 (1981, 754) Marx wrote:

> The ways that the cultivation of particular crops depends on fluctuations in market prices and the constant change in cultivation with these prices – the entire spirit of capitalist production, which is oriented towards the most immediate monetary profits – stands in contradiction to agriculture, which has to concern itself with the whole gamut of permanent conditions of life required by the chain of successive generations.

As he maintained, humanity should conserve, but also, if needed, restore the earth so that it could be passed on in an equal or 'improved' state to the succeeding human generations (Foster, 2009, 147-148). In a famous passage in *Capital,* vol. 3 Marx (1981, 911) remarks that:

> From the standpoint of a higher socio-economic formation, the private property of individuals in the earth will appear just as absurd as the private property of one man in other men. Even an entire society, a nation, or all simultaneously existing societies taken together are not the owners of the earth. They are simply its possessors, its beneficiaries, and have to bequeath it in an improved state to succeeding generations as *boni patres familias (good heads of the household)*.

Marx referred to sustainability as a material requirement for any future society, implying the need to protect the earth for 'successive generations' (Foster et al., 20010, 160). However, Marx perceived that this could not be achieved by following the logic of capital, and argued for alternative communal and emancipatory ways of being instead of the commodification of life and the dominant role played by accumulation without an end (Foster, 2009, 202).

In contrast to the ideas of Marx, the conventional response to the incompatibility claims between capitalism and prospering planetary ecosystems is to appeal to 'sustainable' or 'green growth'. In this case, the idea of 'decoupling' is of essence. A typical ecological modernisation argument goes somewhat as follows: as the production processes are reconfigured, and goods and services redesigned, economic output becomes less dependent on material throughput (Jackson, 2009, 68). As Jackson (ibid) writes, it is vital in this case to distinguish between 'relative' and 'absolute' decoupling:

> Put very simply, relative decoupling is about doing more with less: more economic activity with less environmental damage; more goods and services with fewer resource inputs and fewer emissions. Decoupling is about doing things more efficiently.

Yet, relative decoupling does not mean that a decline in the material throughput in absolute terms occurs. Indeed, the proponents of green capitalism seem to ignore that there is little empirical evidence of absolute decoupling so far, especially at the global level (Daly, 1996; Victor, 2008; Jackson, 2009). In fact, there is strong empirical evidence, in addition to the theoretical arguments presented in this book, regarding correlation and causality of economic growth and ecological destruction (IPCC, 2014). This statement is also backed up by recent empirical evidence-based studies by Wiedmann et al. (2015) and Ward et al. (2016). Wiedmann et al. (2015) argue that, although some metrics of resource productivity used by governments suggest that relative decoupling (or even absolute decoupling in some cases) has taken place, the findings of the study, based on the material footprint (MF) calculations of nations, strongly contradict these claims. Meanwhile, Wiedmann et al. (ibid) state that achievements in decoupling, especially in advanced economies, are smaller than reported or even non-existent. Wiedmann et al. (ibid, 6271) conclude:

> By calculating raw material equivalents of international trade, we demonstrate that countries' use of nondomestic resources is, on average, about threefold larger than the physical quantity of traded goods. As wealth grows, countries tend to reduce their domestic portion of materials extraction through international trade, whereas the overall mass of material consumption generally increases. With every 10% increase in gross domestic product, the average national MF increases by 6%.

According to the study, even the claimed relative decoupling has seemingly been based on false accounting. By measuring only goods that move around from one nation to another, rather than measuring the total amount of raw materials needed to produce those goods, the previous calculations have greatly underestimated the total use of resources, especially in affluent nations (ibid). While an OECD report (2011) claims that G8 countries have halved their resource intensity between 1980 and 2008, Wiedmann et al. (2015, 6273) argue based on their metrics that *'the MF has kept pace with increases in GDP and no improvements in resource productivity at all are observed when measured with GDP/MF'*. In similar fashion, Ward et al. (2016) claim, again based on strong empirical evidence, that the growth in GDP quite simply cannot be decoupled from growth in material and energy use and, more generally, from environmental impact.

Even if we disregard false accounting and the inadequate indicators used in societal goal setting, one is nonetheless left to wonder, why is it that, despite the wide-ranging efforts to tackle environmental problems, our global predicament is not getting better but actually only getting worse? One decisive reason for this is, again, the logic of capital accumulation and circulation, along with other imperatives of capitalism. As Foster (2009, 15) explains:

> Yet, while it is true that energy and resource-use efficiency have continually risen along with the advance of production, the overall result has not been to reduce the consumption of energy and materials. This is because efficiency gains under a capitalist economy result in further accumulation and economic expansion, with the increase in scale typically overwhelming gains in efficiency (a phenomenon known as the 'Jevons Paradox'). Moreover, what appear to be environmental gains are often the result of simply shifting the problems elsewhere – from rich to poor regions and countries.

What is often neglected concerning energy efficiency is the notion that, in capitalism, savings in one place are consistently used to promote new capital formation and the proliferation of commodities elsewhere, demanding ever-greater resources (Foster et al., 2010, 180). William Stanley Jevons originally argued in *The Coal Question* (first published in 1865) that increased efficiency in using coal only generated increased demand for it, and not decreased demand as one might expect. This was simply because improvements in efficiency led to further consumption and economic expansion elsewhere in the economy (Foster, 2009, 123). Jevons (1865, 112) observed: *'every such improvement of the engine, when effected, does but accelerate anew the consumption of coal. Every branch of manufacture receives a fresh impulse – hand labour is still further replaced by mechanical labour.'* The situation today is largely similar to Jevons' day, and this is fundamentally because Jevons paradox continues to apply with the persisting logic of capital accumulation (Foster, 2009, 128). However, Jevons himself did not see the link between his observations and capital (ibid, 125).

Another argument presented in favour of 'sustainable capitalism', most frequently links to technological progression. It is regularly claimed that, through technological advancements, we are to reach a stage of development when technology is clean and emission free, thus creating conditions for sustainable growth (see e.g. Heikkurinen, 2016). However, this is, in many ways, a problematic statement (ibid). Similarly, Hornborg (2014, 12) argues that increased technological efficiency may be largely illusory. As he (ibid) remarks, economists, ecological modernisationists and politicians alike generally not only reject the pessimism of Jevons or Malthus, but also general concerns over economic growth versus limits of the planet, peak oil, overall environmental degradation and loss of biodiversity, and give faith to human ingenuity linked to technological advancements such as solar powered civilisation. Nonetheless, considering the serious doubts that have been expressed towards the large-scale applicability of solar power as a potential cure for future energy crises and substitute for fossil fuels, it is certainly relevant to ask whether this technological scenario should be viewed as unrealistic[13] (ibid), to say the least. As Hornborg (2014, 12) explains, there exists,

> glaring inefficiencies and unsustainable practices that paradoxically also seem to increase over time, such as waste of resources, environmental degradation, and economic inequalities. These inefficiencies are often referred to as externalities, which might be mitigated by modifying prices.

---

13 Solar power accounts for only 1% of global energy use, while its low EROEI (energy return on energy investment) and high material inputs cast serious doubts about its feasibility (see Andersen, 2013; Prieto and Hall, 2013).

At the same time, it has been suggested that the logic of capital accumulation, in fact, systematically seeks to keep such externalities external, and not to pay bills according to actual environmental impact (Moore, 2015, 299). Moreover, technological optimism is founded on a conception of technology reflecting the historical experiences from an era of unprecedented capital accumulation, that is, the Industrial Revolution based on fossil fuels (Hornborg, 2014, 16). This conception pictures technology as being primarily an engineering challenge, rather from being a societal strategy embedded in both economics and ecology (ibid). The latter perspective suggests that where and when technology is concerned neither the instruments nor technics, or perhaps more importantly, the context where technology is applied, is neutral (see Mumford, 1967; 1970; Hornborg, 2014). That is to say, modern technology is and has always been a matter of uneven distribution in the global society (Hornborg, 2014, 17). Thus, 'technological progress' is, in some sense, only another manifestation of capital accumulation and it being based on unequal exchange (ibid).

Moore (2015, 100) argues that capitalist *technics* (understood as specific crystallisation of tools, nature, and power) seek, in principle, to mobilise and to appropriate the 'forces of nature' so as to make the 'forces of labour' productive, that is, to produce surplus value. Calhoun (2013, 154) states that the new (industrial) organisation of social life has, in fact, multiplied demands for energy that have been primarily met by carbon but also by nuclear and other forms of energy. Moreover, the technologies by themselves have increased the demand for energy and a range of minerals (ibid), which are ultimately non-renewable in nature. Similarly, Harvey (2014, 236) argues that the needs of capital accumulation has systematically shortened the turnover time and life cycle of consumer goods by producing commodities that have to be replaced more often than before. In fact, it seems that the primary purpose of 'modernising' technology is to keep the growth economy rolling rather than to solve ecological problems (Foster, 2009, 20). This is not to say that there would not be honest and genuine attempts to solve ecological problems by developing technological solutions, but rather to claim that, when new technologies enter the capitalist markets, they are immediately undermined by the logic of competition and accumulation (see Gould et al., 2008), and more generally, that 'technology' as an instrument and practice is a problematic way to decrease material throughput (Heikkurinen, 2016).

Technological solutions are not created out of thin air, but fundamentally rely on labour and natural resources. Consequentially, and also given the unlimited and endless accumulation aspiration of capitalism, the new technologies that are supposed to overcome the contradictions between capitalism and ecological sustainability inevitably run up against the challenge of transcending the very laws of physics (see the law of entropy, e.g. Georgescu-Roegen, 1999). In the words of Georgescu-Roegen's (1999, 19):

> Had economics recognized the entropic nature of the economic process, it might have been able to warn its co-workers for the betterment of mankind – the technological sciences – that 'bigger and better' washing machines, automobiles, and superjets must lead to 'bigger' and 'better' pollution.

Overall, it is easy to become lost in the general declarations and ideologies regarding 'green growth'. While it is true that some efficiency gains have been reached locally, it is profoundly problematic to argue that the dilemma of growth can be remedied by producing more (Wiedmann et al., 2015; see also Hornborg, 2013) and by continuing capital accumulation in an expansive manner (Foster, 2009).

In addition to the myth of decoupling, modernisation of technology, there exists further bottlenecks for capital accumulation. Foster et al. (2010, 208) point out that the second law of thermodynamics (see Georgescu-Roegen, 1999) guarantees that there will be an increase in 'entropic degradation' as industrial production advances. Accordingly, the second law of thermodynamics indicates that order transforms into disorder, or highly organised matter is transformed into chaos (e.g. oil is transformed into CO_2 emissions when it is burned), and thus humanity cannot rely on resources that would always be in a form that would allow their easy utilisation (Georgescu-Roegen, 1975). Moore (2015, 97) argues that capitalist production constantly seeks to utilise matter and energy with low entropy, and turn it into products and waste. The characteristics of capitalism guarantee that entropic degradation (from low to high) tends toward the maximum economically feasible levels globally (Foster et al., 2010, 208). This is because capitalism continuously exhausts its 'sources of nourishment', or put simply, there are limits to how much additional labour capitalism can squeeze out from humans, forests, oilfields, and the rest of the available means of production (Moore, 2015, 87).

Capitalist socio-economic structure has been perfectly dependent on the continuous and expansive appropriation of energy and labour (ibid, 95), which is clearly manifested in the historical development of capitalism (Sarkar, 2012; Malm, 2016). However, fossil fuels are, by definition, exhaustible and their stock is continually diminishing (Foster, 2009; Sarkar, 2012; Järvensivu, 2016). At the same time, their substitution has proven difficult (see e.g. Andersen, 2013; Prieto and Hall, 2013; Hornborg, 2014) if not impossible, especially if we were to sustain the current levels of production (see Trainer, 2013; Zencey, 2013). Consequently, another serious bottleneck exists, that is, the existence and availability of cheap and abundant source of energy that would replace fossil fuels in sustaining economic growth and capital accumulation in the future.

In this respect, peak oil (the actual moment when oil production does not grow anymore) represents a crucial landmark in the timespan of modern civilisation, because it inevitably indicates the end of cheap oil (see e.g. Heinberg, 2005, 127-128; Klare, 2008, 41) which again also poses a problem for the transformation from fossil fuels to renewable energy (see also Zencey, 2013). As Foster (2009, 93) explains: *'The peak oil crisis is more sharply defined than the more general crisis in energy, since not only is petroleum the most protean fuel, but it is also the preeminent liquid fuel in transportation, for which there is no easy substitute in the quantities needed.'* Peak oil, therefore, presents an imminent threat to industrial capitalism, with the possibility of a drastic economic dislocation and slowdown (ibid).

To understand why this is so, we have understand what oil is and why its substitution has proven to be so difficult. Ultimately, there are two ways to grow production: to add or to increase labour, or to work more efficiently, i.e. more productively. The history of capitalism is a history of both of these 'streams' (Vadén, 2009; Salminen and Vadén, 2015). On the one hand, productivity gains have been achieved through the division of labour, specialisation, technology, and automatisation. On the other hand, a vast amount of labour has been added; more human labour, more labour done by machines, and more labour extracted from various (but mainly fossil) energy sources (Salminen and Vadén, 2015). In this regard, it is surprising how little Marxists have focused on the work and surplus extracted from 'non-human' sources, because when the total labour force or the amount of labour is measured, oil can be thought as 'non-human labour' (Vadén, 2009).

In this regard, *energy return on energy investment* (EROEI) is an important factor to be considered concerning bottlenecks of capital accumulation. EROEI calculates how much energy is gained with particular energy investment (net energy). According to some, the most productive oil fields in history have had a ratio up to 100:1, that is, a hundred barrels of oil were gained with one barrel of energy investment (Vadén, 2009). Naturally, the most productive taps have been exploited first, and therefore much of the remaining oil is located deep underwater or is in the form of shale or bitumen. In short, this means that more energy is used or invested to extract additional energy, which means a declining EROEI ratio, which on the other hand, is problematic for an economic structure or a civilisation that has come to rely on a high EROEI ratio (ibid). The problem is made worse because the fossil energy substitutes, such as nuclear, solar, and wind energy's EROEI ratios are substantially lower than fossil fuel's historical figures, and thus some scholars speak of an energy trap indicating the hardships linked to the transformation from fossil energy to renewables (Zencey, 2013).

Furthermore, another bottleneck regarding capital accumulation and the reproduction of capitalism is, as Moore (2015, 97-98) states, the decline of overall ecological surplus. This means that the mass of accumulated capital tends to rise faster than the appropriation of economic value from labour-force and natural resources. Likewise, the ecological surplus declines over time because the reproduction time of capital tends to exceed the reproduction time of the rest of nature (ibid). This is because the circulation of capital can, at least in theory, accelerate endlessly, and of course, there are good reasons why capitalists want to accelerate the speed of capital circulation (possible competitive advantage), but at the same time, there are limits how much grain can be harvested form a field, or how fast a pine tree grows (ibid).

A final bottleneck of capital accumulation is linked to overall industrial production and cumulating waste (Moore, 2015, 98). Industrial production entails that the share of unpaid work and energy tends to fall because the accumulation of capital becomes more wasteful over time (one example of this could be considered to be industrial agriculture). This is because, in the long run, capitalism (or other kind of productivist and industrial structure based on accumulation and growth) produces environments that are increasingly hostile to further accumulation (ibid).

To sum up, while substantial local, national and transnational efforts are made to advance conditions for uninterrupted and continuous capital accumulation, it certainly seems that historical and material preconditions are inevitably pushing us towards a looming crises, depression and the end of capitalism as we know it. The question is, therefore, will this happen, for instance, soon enough to avert catastrophic climate change? Or will capitalism or industrial civilisation collapse before rainforests have been burnt or cut down and turned into cattle farms or palm oil plantations? In any case, it is safe to say that the ongoing industrial growth project seeking to control, exploit humans and the non-human world is heading towards another systemic or even terminal crisis, or is perhaps already in the middle of one, and we can only guess what the consequences will be.

4

REPRODUCTION OF CAPITALISM

Marx's treatise of the concept of reproduction can be considered to include four different approaches: simple, extended, complex and transformation (Morrow and Torres, 1995, 121-122). Marx originally introduced the concept in the beginning of Chapter 23 called *Simple Reproduction* in *Capital* vol. 1. He (1973, 566) begins the chapter by stating that:

> Whatever the form of the process of production in a society, it must be a continuous process, must continue to go periodically through the same phases. A society can no more cease to produce than it can cease to consume. When viewed, therefore, as a connected whole, and as flowing on with incessant renewal, every social process of production is, at the same time, a process of reproduction.

Marx also remarks in *Capital* vol. 1 (1973, 574) that *'the reproduction of the working class carries with it the accumulation of skill, that is handed down from one generation to another.'* In the case of *simple reproduction* (see Capital vol. 1, 1973, 566-578; Capital vol. 2, 1973a, Chapter: *Simple Reproduction*) Marx explains how the continuity of production *in situ* is ensured by distinguishing the product of labour and subjective labour power. Regarding *extended reproduction* (see Capital vol. 2, 1973a, Chapter: *Accumulation and Reproduction on an Extended Scale*) Marx examines the reproduction of capitalism (including prospects for economic growth) on a more systemic/societal level, and refers to extended reproduction in the case where production increases but relations of production, that is, class relations, remain intact. As Morrow and Torres (1995, 122) argue, two other distinctions can be derived from Marx's treatise on reproduction: *complex reproduction,* and *transformation.* Morrow and Torres (ibid) remark: *'In the case of complex reproduction the overall stability of society is preserved but at the price of, or despite fundamental modifications of, relations of production, which do not thereby alter the identity of the system as such.'* Transformation, on the contrary, indicates a process that leads to an entirely different type of socio-economic organisation of a given society.

Morrow and Torres also propose that the emergence of the welfare state could be posed as an example of complex reproduction. They (1995, footnote 2, 451-452) define the welfare state *'as a form of capitalist state that has emerged in the industrial advanced social formations'*. The welfare state has three foundational features, which are represented arguably in their most exemplary form, in Nordic welfare states (ibid). First, the state promotes a policy of absolute equity among different classes, but without compromising or hindering the capitalist (private) ownership or the capitalist (relations of) production. Second, the welfare state is also defined by a formulation, implementation, and evaluation of bureaucratic public policy conducted by state administrators, funded in corporative mechanisms of control and cooperation (ibid). Third, the welfare state is characterised by a somewhat conscious notion that this type of state represents a 'tertium squad' between the classic capitalist state and the totalitarian communist state (ibid).

I do not reject Marx's remarks concerning simple and extended reproduction, but instead of dealing with them I concentrate on investigating the logic of capital accumulation as a social relation and as an imperative for economic actors in the capitalist socio-economic structure. Thus, I am dealing with complex reproduction, a task, which is made more difficult by the fact that neither Marx nor his followers have explicitly, extensively, or consistently dealt with complex reproduction (except Althusser and Poulantzas as outlined later). This is peculiar, especially because, retrospectively it is rather clear that the relative stability of capitalism, despite the recurrent crises in 20th and 21st centuries, has been achieved in this manner (Morrow and Torres, 1995, 122).

Althusser and Balibar (2009, 289) remarked in *Reading Capital* that *'if we return to Capital and try to read in it as a theory of the transition from one mode of production to another, we find first of all a concept which seems to be the very concept of historical continuity: the concept of reproduction.'* In *Sur la reproduction* (*On Reproduction of Capitalism*, 2014, 47) Althusser returns to the concept and argues that every social organisation must, in order to be able to produce in the future, *reproduce* the conditions of its production. In practice, this means the reproduction of 1) the productive forces, and 2) the existing relations of production (ibid); 3) but also, and in addition to, the relative stability of the prevailing socio-economic structure, and 4) suitable responses to internal and external crises linked to production and various societal upheavals and threats.

Following Althusser's reasoning, it is presented that the reproduction of the capitalist socio-economic structure is guaranteed by the interplay of the capitalist mode of production and so-called socio-ideological structures. The topography of this arrangement is drafted in the next page.

There are, however, some prerequisites (see e.g. 'circuit of capital' in Wallerstein, 2003, 15) before it is possible for the capitalist socio-economic structure to reproduce itself. I have already dealt with primitive accumulation and, to some extent, the creation of capitalist

Figure 2. Reproduction of capitalism in the 21st century

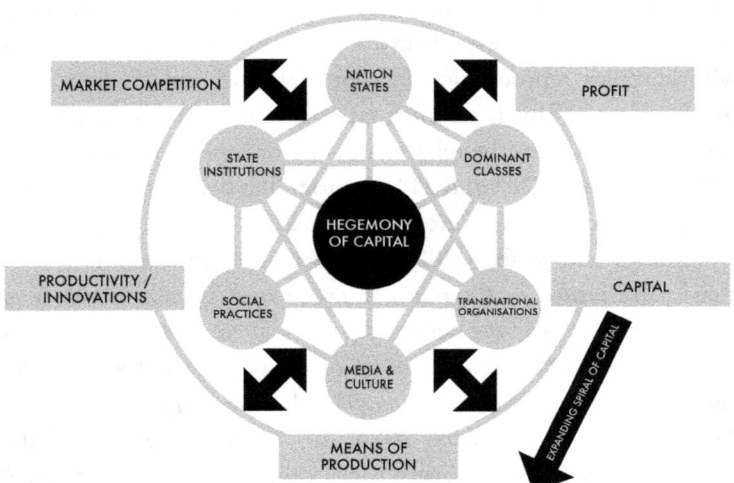

market structure in earlier chapters. In addition to capitalist relations of production, there exists other institutional structures that provide social stability and the necessary legal framework for property relations, for instance, but also physical force, to secure the reproduction of capitalism if needed. In fact, without the presence of the coercive or repressive state structures (police, military, law, taxation) it is very difficult to see how a system based on capital accumulation would have developed (see e.g. Perelman, 2000; Althusser, 2014; Graeber, 2014) or stayed in place (I will be discuss this in further detail later in this chapter). Moreover, these two spheres are not separate or static but rather intertwined and remain in flux, as presented in the topography above[14].

---

14 Any model or a theory should be treated, as they are, namely, a gross simplification of complex reality. Consequently, I propose that this theoretical model is primarily used to analyse the 21st century capitalist socio-economic structures in a liberal parliamentary and Western industrial settings.

The capitalist mode of production

The definition and operation of the capitalist mode of production was presented at length in Chapter 3. However, to briefly recap the main aspects of it, we might recall that a mode of production is characterised by *a particular unity* between the *relations* and *forces* of production (Althusser, 2014, 19-21, 25). In the unity of the capitalist mode of production there is, on the one hand, advanced commodity production for external bodies (to 'market') in order to produce a surplus (profit). On the other hand, there exists a class division between capitalists and wage-labourers, and institutions and social constructions (often guaranteed by the law) such as private property.

The imperatives of the capitalist mode of production, stemming from the unity of relations of production, forces of production and other characteristics of capitalism, push capitalism to continuously expand its scope, and to impose its imperatives to novel territories and spheres of both human and non-human life to ensure further capital accumulation and circulation in the future. The imperatives of capitalism essentially steer economic actor(s) within the capitalist socio-economic structure, who are compelled to maximise profits, to search for new markets, to enhance productivity, and to cut costs (Wood, 2002, 36-37) in order to succeed in the market competition and able to continue their pursuit of capital accumulation. Therefore, capital's need for endless accumulation and circulation of capital creates a compulsion to invest a part of the surplus created in the production back into production in order to expand the scope to be able to accumulate capital, pay debts, and succeed in the market competition in the future. The 'expanding spiral of capital' (see figure 2 above) illustrates the dynamic and logic of the capitalist mode of production, but also the increasing pressure it creates towards the natural environment. Indeed, the elements for growth in production, portrayed in figure 2, lead to an increasing use and exploitation of a wide range of natural resources (including human and non-human labour, such as the fossil fuels) to ensure the continuous expansion and accumulation of capital, that is, the reproduction of capitalist mode of production.

Socio-ideological structures

The internal 'laws' of capitalist mode of production are alone insufficient to explain the reproduction of capitalism. While the imperatives of capitalism may rise from the economic (Althusser, 2014, 19-21) and produce capitalism's signifying characteristics as a mode of production, the socio-ideological structures are as important for sake of the reproduction of capitalism, although they are not, necessarily, directly linked to material production.

May the capitalist mode of production be primary, yet there is not one without the other. It is together that these two elements form the capitalist socio-economic structure, that is, the way capitalist production and capital and wealth accumulation-driven society are organised materially, economically and politically. This structure remains in change, intertwined and both internally and externally in interaction with its surrounding natural, socio-cultural and historical circumstances. However, based on the history of the capitalist mode of production, it is also evident that there are also some necessary and permanent elements in the structure that characterise capitalism and without which it would not be recognised as capitalism. These include, for instance, production for profit and to a 'market' to gain profits, as means to accumulate capital.

I define the capitalist socio-ideological structures (see figure 3 below) as material arrangements, institutions and social practices and norms that are committed either directly or indirectly to the reproduction of capitalism. In addition, I perceive these structures as being ideological precisely because of their either direct or indirect commitment to the reproduction of capitalism. To provide background for this definition, in the following pages, concepts such as hegemony and hegemonic state apparatuses, and Ideological State Apparatus are applied. These concepts are utilised in order to make sense of how capitalism is reproduced in the 21st century.

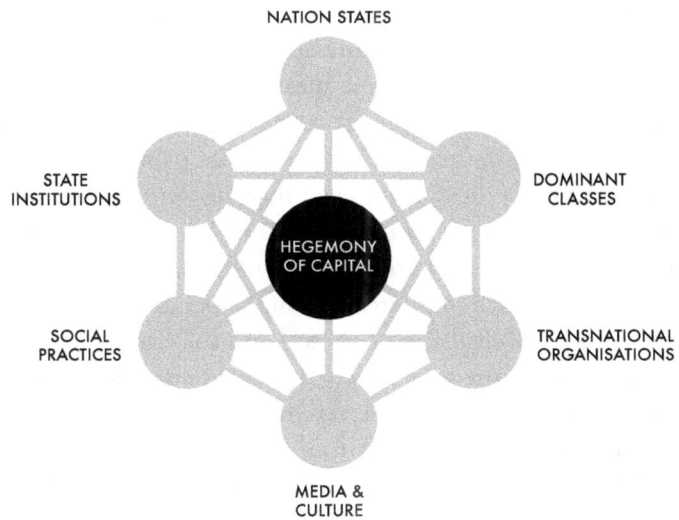

Figure 3. Socio-ideological structures of capitalism

The market liberalist utopia has been based on an idea of free trade between free individuals, who are free from state intervention. Historically, this has never been the case with capitalism (Wallerstein, 2013, 10-11). As Harvey (2014, 72) claims, *'stateless capitalism is unthinkable'*. It seems that, historically, the modern nation state has provided the necessary legal and social circumstances for both economic actors and capitalist markets. This is because the state organises the workforce and consumer markets, and creates trust and stability that capitalism needs to function (see Calhoun, 2013; Herrmann, 2013). The rise of the state is in conjunction with the appearance of significant surpluses and the division of society into classes, which is at the same time, a central political and historical milestone in the development of class societies. There is, thus, a historically constituted connection between state forms and the development of production processes with respect to the rise of capitalism and its current transnational phase (Robinson, 2014, 66).

Marxist theories of the state explicitly argue that neither the capitalist socio-economic structure nor the capital-labour relation can be reproduced by economic means alone (Robinson, 2014, 66). In other words, the capitalist mode of production needs the state (or a state-like structure) to secure its own reproduction (ibid). Poulantzas (2000, 17) argued that *'the political field of the State (as well as the sphere of ideology) has always, in different forms, been present in the constitution and reproduction of the relations of production'*, which indicates, among other things, that the 'market' is not self-regulating (subject) and the contradictions of the capitalist structure generate crises that the state must attempt to resolve to ensure the future reproduction and accumulation of capital (Robinson, 2014, 66-67). This is also to say that the capitalist socio-economic structure has been and continues to be a globally constituted social relation, in which the state is not external to capital and capitalism, but constitutive of capitalist relations of production (Robinson, 2014, 67). This is also because capitalist socio-economic structure is, to its very core, an anarchic system (see Boltanski and Chiapello, 2005, 5), in which the revolutionising nature of production continuously threatens to tear apart the persisting social fabric and social order (see also Polanyi, 1968). In fact, it seems that capitalist socio-economic structure probably needs stability and predictability more than any other previous social formation. This is because it is likely, that in a volatile social and political condition, the circulation and accumulation of capital are likely to be endangered. Hence, the nation state has, provided the required stability and predictability by providing legal and institutional framework – secured in the last instance by physical violence – to protect and sustain the capitalist relations of production (Wood, 2003).

The state indeed is the ultimate guarantor of capitalist socio-economic structure, and not least because it, indeed, holds the monopoly for violence (Poulantzas, 2000, 80), but also because of the property relations the state secures, protects, and maintains. For instance, as Harvey (2014, 250) argues, *'nature is portioned and divided up as private property rights guaranteed by the state.'* To reproduce, the capitalist socio-economic structure requires sovereign territorial entities to provide a reliable institutional and administrative 'environment' to underpin its proper functioning (Harvey, 2011, 199). It also requires the existence of individuals that are able to engage in all kinds of speculative and innovative activities that provide capitalism with its dynamism and keep the accumulation of capital going (ibid).

The 'interests' of the state as an institution and capitalists are interlinked for various and obvious reasons (Saad-Filho, 2003, 10). First, the state is committed to capitalism by custom and law, but also because state institutions are, and have been, historically modified and shaped by the capitalist market exchange, wage-labour and profit-orientation. Second, there are several interest groups serving the interests of capital that are trying to influence the state apparatus to their advantage. Third, the reproduction of the state is heavily dependent on the workings of capital; above all, because of the tax revenue is dependent upon the performance of corporations and the level of employment. Fourth, because of the overall overwhelming impacts the economic and political power and the influence capitalism has had on national and international culture, practices and language (ibid).

Capitalist socio-economic structure depends on social and economic solidarity of a range of state institutions from schools and hospitals to the police and military. These institutions often provide opportunities for capital accumulation even when they are organised based on a public or non-profit manner (Calhoun, 2013, 147-148). More importantly, these institutions provide services that capitalist corporations would otherwise have internalised into their operation (ibid). This kinf of expenditure, which is vital to the reduction of costs of multiple groups of owner-producers, such as energy, transport, infrastructure, education, have most often been developed and supported by public funds (Wallerstein, 2003, 55). To be sure, my intention is not so much to argue that the modern nation state is nothing but the right hand of capital, but moreover to suggest that nation states are increasingly steered by the powers, needs and logics of transnational capital (see Robinson, 2014, 42). This 'infiltrative' logic of capital is, of course, perfectly in line with the way capitalism functions, as Wallerstein has noted (2003, 14). Consequently, in the beginning of the 21st century, Marx and Engels's classic polemic from *The Communist Manifesto* (2002, 221) seems to hold true – perhaps more than ever – as they claimed that *'the modern State is but a committee for managing the common affairs of the whole bourgeoisie.'*

Although it seem now true that both 'liberals' and 'socialists' agree that politics and taking care of the needs of capital are one and the same (Ranciére, 1999, 113), historically the state has not been a mere instrument for capital accumulation (Thomas, 2010, 141-142). For example, Gramsci observed that, from the French Revolution until 1848, there was a period of expansion in which the 'new state' of the victorious bourgeoisie commenced a programme of social and political 'education' and elevation (ibid).

The first half of the 19th century marks a period in which the bourgeoisie, especially in France, presented itself as a revolutionary class guided by its universal claims of progress and new form of state (Thomas, 2010, 141-142). This is also something that Marx and Engels observed in their high praise of the revolutionary bourgeois class in *The Communist Manifesto*. The bourgeoisie had not yet developed its precise and explicit state apparatus that we witness today, but it had established an immutable principle of modern life, that is, thus far the state could not be a sovereign locus of power above 'civil society', but rather involve itself in all levels of society in a previously unprecedented manner (Thomas, 2010, 142-143). The state was no longer purely an instrument of coercion, explicitly representing the views and ideologies of the aristocracy, but it had become a network of social relations for the production of consent for the subaltern masses to be integrated in the expansive wealth accumulation project of the bourgeoisie (ibid).

The rise of capitalism and the bourgeoisie as the dominant class has been accompanied with the rise of a distinctively capitalist state power, that is, the 'fiscal military state' (Harvey, 2011; 2014). As Wallerstein (2003, 32) explains, the accumulation of capital in core areas created both the fiscal foundation and the political incentive to create relatively strong state-machineries. The first and most elementary component of modern state power was territorial jurisdiction; states created boundaries, which were determined by juridical procedures (Wallerstein, 2oo3, 48-49). The second fundamental element has been the right to determine the constitution of the relations of production: '*as a matter of law the states recognized no constraints on their legislative scope other than those that were self-imposed*' (ibid, 51). The third element has been state's exclusive right to tax. To be sure, taxation is by no means a creation of the capitalist structure. Previous socio-economic structures utilised taxation as a source of revenue for the state as well, yet as Wallerstein (ibid, 53) argues:

> historical capitalism transformed taxation in two ways. Taxation became the main (indeed overwhelming) regular source of state revenue, as opposed to state revenue deriving from irregular requisition by force from persons inside or outside the formal jurisdiction of the state (including requisition from other states). Secondly, taxation has been a steadily expanding phenomenon over the historical development of the capitalist world-economy as a percentage of total value created or accumulated. This has meant that the states have been important in terms of the resources they controlled, because the resources not only permitted them to further the accumulation of capital but were also themselves distributed and thereby entered directly or indirectly into the further accumulation of capital.

In addition to law and right to tax, modern state power is founded on the monopoly of violence. Nicos Poulantzas writes in *State, Power, Socialism* (2000, 80) that the European capitalist states were originally founded through pacification of territories torn by feudal wars, and once the modern state apparatus and its political power was institutionalised, the state had to rely less on direct physical violence in the 'normal' context of domination. This does not mean, however, that the power of the modern state would no longer be grounded in physical violence. Political power has been, according to Poulantzas (2000, 80), in particular concentrated and materialised by the state, which has meant that the state has been the central site of exercising power. Poulantzas (2000, 81) states that:

> state-monopolized physical violence permanently underlies the techniques of power and mechanism of consent: it is inscribed in the web of disciplinary and ideological devices; and even when not directly exercised, it shapes the materiality

of the social body upon which domination is brought to bear.

Marxist economic history reveals that the creation of national capitalist markets has been the result of conscious and frequently violent actions of a state that has forced a society to adopt capitalist relations of production because of reasons, which are not, in fact, related to the economy (see e.g. Perelman, 2000; Moore, 2015; see also Polanyi, 1968; Graeber, 2014). Equally, even after the capitalist relations of production had been imprinted, their reproduction was guaranteed by different forms of intervention of the state machinery. This has been precisely because it is fundamentally the state machinery that not only controls and governs the relations of production (Wallerstein, 2003, 48, 51), but also secures the reproduction of the dominant mode of production (Althusser, 2014). Poulantzas (2000, 81), in turn, claims that:

> The establishment of techniques of capitalist power, the constitutions of disciplinary devices (the great 'enclosure'), the emergence of ideological-cultural institutions from parliament through universal suffrage to the school – all these presuppose state monopolization of violence concealed by the displacement of legitimacy towards legality and by the rule of law.

Poulantzas (ibid) concludes that the very existence and reproduction of capitalism and modern state institutions presuppose a state monopoly of violence (a realisation originally elaborated by Max Weber), and argues that even the practice of bringing legislation into effect is unthinkable without the modern national army. More generally, state law plays an important (positive and negative) role in organising repression and creating consent, because the legal and judicial system above all institutionalises and materialises the dominant ideology as the legitimate 'code of conduct' (Poulantzas, 2000, 14, 27; see also Althusser, 2014). However, as Poulantzas (2000, 82-83) remarks, the law is never exclusively negative and repressive, but also always involves positive aspects, such as the conservation of forests and wetlands.

Nevertheless, the sovereign power of the state has been eroded to some extent during the last few decades, principally because of the hegemony of transnational capital (see Robinson, 2014). However, the state is nothing but powerless. Rather, state power has become more 'contingent' upon the interests of the global financial apparatus, often at the expense of ordinary citizens (Harvey, 2014, 159) and public services.

A shift from international economic integration to global productive integration has occurred during the past decades, which means that global capitalism is not reducible to a web of national economies, national capitalists, and national circuits of accumulation connected by the international market (ibid). The state, for its part, is caught up in a process of transformation contingent with the overall neoliberal restructuring of global capitalism (Robinson, 2014, 27-28). This transformation has not meant the end of the nation state, but rather altered and modified its role and purpose (Robinson, 2004) within this structure. Although the transnational capitalist class has decentralised its activities in numerous countries and regions, they still turn to local nation states in the regions in which they operate. Robinson (2014, 7-8) explains:

> Just as in previous epochs, they (transnational capitalists) require that these local (national) states provide the conditions for accumulation within their respective territories, including disciplining labour. Reciprocally, local managers of the national capitalist state are compelled, just as they were in the past, by structural power of the capitalist system. The legitimacy of these states and the reproduction of the status of the state elites as privileged strata depend on their ability to attract and retain now-globalized accumulation to the territories over which they exercise political authority.

> Competition among national states to attract transnationally mobile capital becomes functional to global capital and to its ability to exercise a structural power over the direct power of states [...]. In this way, the continued existence of the nation-state and the interstate system appear to be a central condition for the class power of transnational capital and for the reproduction of global capitalism.

The nation state is still an integral element from the perspective of the reproduction of capitalism. This is, above all, because of the reproduction of workforce and the local institutional framework and regional conditions upon which the process of capital accumulation is dependent. As Struna (2009, 246) acknowledges, the worker is still considered national. Workers in general do not enjoy the same transnational mobility as capital does, because national borders still remain mechanisms for controlling movements of labour (Robinson, 2014, 51). At the same time, competition has taken on new forms, as increasingly global competition steers companies to establish global as opposed to national or regional markets (ibid, 27-28). In this process, transnational corporations turn to numerous bodies to secure their interests, including nation states and various international institutions.

While it is true that the nation state is still important for the reproduction of global capitalism (Wood, 2005), it also seems clear that transnational state apparatuses are needed to secure the conditions for global accumulation (Robinson, 2014). There are key functions through which the nation state contributes to the reproduction of capitalism including the formulation of local economic policies aimed at achieving macroeconomic equilibrium, providing a legal framework (property laws, etc.) and infrastructure, and social control (army, police, law) and ideological reproduction (education, church, popular culture, media, parliamentary politics) (ibid, 120). But at the same time, there are other conditions that transnational capitalists require for the proper functioning of the global capitalist structure, which go beyond nation states or a web of nation states (ibid). For example, nation states are hardly capable of organising supranational unification of macroeconomic policies, or to be capable of creating a unified field for transnational capital accumulation, or capable of imposing transnational trade agreements, and so on (ibid). As Robinson (ibid, 74) convincingly points out:

> The class power of the transnational capitalist class is constituted on the extensive and intensive enlargement in recent decades of capitalism, on the more fully and completely capitalist nature of the world capitalist system, and on the unprecedented control and domination that transnational capital exercises over the global means of production and over global labour. But this class power is exercised through the transnational state. Global corporations could not reproduce their control if it were not for national state apparatuses that provide property rights, arbitration, and social control, and that open up national territories for transnational corporations. The transnational capitalist class could not exercise its class power if the IMF did not impose structural adjustments on countries, if the World Bank did not make its lending conditional on the reform of labour laws to make workers flexible, if the WTO did not impose worldwide trade liberalization, and so on.

The institutions of the transnational state in comparison to nation states should be seen, as Robinson (2014, 67-68, 78, 82) suggests, as a network that provides structural channels for the transnational capitalist class and its agents through which they exercise their power. Because of the hegemony of transnational capital, the transnational elites have been able to take hold of the transnational state institutions over the nation states and popular classes. Meanwhile, the fiscal functioning and legitimacy of a particular nation state is dependent on the global capitalist economy and global financial markets (ibid, 8-9).

From the perspective of the reproduction theory, the state's transformed role in the global capitalist structure has not changed its core function when it comes to the reproduction of capitalism, that is, providing a suitable legal framework and infrastructure, suitable political and ideological setting, and disciplined and skilful labour. What has instead changed, is the global power balance. Nation states are increasingly integrated in a global structure, controlled by the movements and logic of transnational capital. In this structure, the legitimacy and competitive position of a single nation state depends on its ability to attract and maintain conditions for transnational capital accumulation, as Robinson (2014, 78) and Harvey (2014, 159) remark. At the same time, competition to attract transnational capital has become functional to global capital and to its ability to exercise structural power over nation states. Consequently, we are increasingly witnessing the hegemony of transnational capital and transnational capitalist classes.

Reproduction of capitalism and education: theoretical grounds

To establish a connection between reproduction of capitalism and contemporary higher education, the remaining pages of this chapter are devoted to theoretical argument building. Combining the theoretical work of Antonio Gramsci, Louis Althusser, and Nicos Poulantzas reveals how institutional education plays an essential role in reproducing the dominant relations and mode of production, and ideology.

A suitable way to reflect upon the relation between Gramsci and Althusser[15], but also to examine the preconditions of the

---

15 In this book, I am focusing on the issues where these two classics (Gramsci and Althusser) can be brought together in order to understand the reproduction of capitalism. Yet, this does not mean that we should neglect the philosophical legacy of

theory of reproduction is to study Karl Marx's infamous base/superstructure metaphor – Marx's presentation of the transformation and composition of a socio-economic structure. Both Gramsci and Althusser praise and criticise the metaphor, but also develop Marx's thesis, especially regarding the composition of the superstructure. Marx's famous discussion of the metaphor can be found from the preface of *A Contribution to the Critique of Political Economy*. Marx (1970, 20-21) writes that:

> In the social production of their existence, men inevitably enter into definite relations, which are independent of their will, namely relations of production appropriate to a given stage in the development of their material forces of production. The totality of these relations of production constitutes the economic structure of society, the real foundation, on which arises a legal and political superstructure and to which correspond definite forms of social consciousness. The mode of production of material life conditions the general process of social, political and intellectual life. It is not the consciousness of men that determines their existence, but their social existence that determines their consciousness. At a certain stage of development, the material productive forces of society come into conflict with the existing relations of production or – this merely expresses the same thing in legal terms – with the property relations within the framework of which they have operated hitherto. From forms of development of the productive forces these relations turn into their fetters. Then begins an era of social revolution. The changes in the economic foundation lead sooner or later to the

Gramsci and Althusser, nor the significance of their disputes, or their conflicting ideas. A reader who is interested in the disagreements of Althusser regarding Gramsci's work may want to take a look at, in addition to Althusser's and Balibar's *Reading 'Capital'* (2009), Peter Thomas's *The Gramscian Moment* (2010) and his article *Althusser's Last Encounter: Gramsci*, in *Encountering Althusser* (in Diefenbach et al., 2013) or, for example, Jan Rehmann's *Theories of Ideology* (2014).

transformation of the whole immense superstructure. In studying such transformations it is always necessary to distinguish between the material transformation of the economic conditions of production, which can be determined with the precision of natural science, and the legal, political, religious, artistic or philosophic -- in short, ideological forms in which men become conscious of this conflict and fight it out.

Marx's metaphor[16] has been extensively criticised – especially the latter part dealing with historical change – by both Marxists and critics of Marxism (Eagleton, 2012, 155) as it has been noted to be static (ibid), and abstract and incomplete (Althusser, 2014). But this does not mean that Marx's elaboration would be of no use (Eagleton, 2012, 155).

What Marx means by the 'economic foundation' or the 'base' in this case are the forces and relations of production. By the 'superstructure', he implies institutional structures such as state, law, and politics, as well as religion (Eagleton, 2012, 154). Marx insists that one of the main purposes of these institutions is to support the dominant mode of production. Some of these institutions such as politics and religion accomplish this task by producing ideas that legitimate the overall structure. This can also be defined as ideology (ibid). Marx and Engels famously argue in *The German Ideology* (1998, 67) that:

> The ideas of the ruling class are in every epoch the ruling ideas: i.e., the class, which is the ruling material force of

---

16 One may ask: what is the relationship between Marx's metaphor and the theoretical elaboration presented in this book? To answer, Marx's theory is a frame to explain historical change, but also a useful platform to analyse the reproduction of the capitalist socio-economic structure. This said, I want to emphasise that the updated theory of reproduction of capitalism does not include an analysis of historical change (transformation). In other words, I perceive Marx's metaphor as a 'broader' historical explanation and description of the socio-economic dynamics than that which I am pursuing.

society, is at the same time its ruling intellectual force. The class which has the means of material production at its disposal, consequently also controls the means of mental production, so that the ideas of those who lack the means of mental production are on the whole subject to it.

Despite the critiques, Marx does not want to argue that society would be divided into two different realms, but rather that the relation between base and superstructure is dialectical (Eagleton, 2012, 155). May it be that the base, at last instance, determines the superstructure (Althusser, 2014, 54), the superstructure is also of the essence, in terms of the reproduction of a mode of production (Eagleton, 2012, 155). Without the legal system or military, it seems that capitalism, for instance, would have been considerably more volatile than we have witnessed throughout its history. Therefore, the superstructure is not secondary to the base insomuch that it would be somehow less real – although the base is primary in the sense that before anything else can happen, humans have to fulfil their basic needs, and thus before a civilisation can see the light of day, there has to be enough surplus to support the creation and reproduction of a civilisation (Eagleton, 2012, 155). Universities, churches and hospitals are materially as real as banks and coalmines, and some institutions are part of both the base and the superstructure, for instance the state, which can simultaneously operate as a capitalist business and provide social security (Eagleton, 2012, 156; see also Harvey, 2014). Similarly, there are countless things that do not fit or belong to the model, because the model ultimately merely seeks to explain historical social structures and their transformations, not the purpose of human existence or acidification of oceans for instance (Eagleton, 2012, 156-157).

From the perspective of reproduction theory, it makes more sense to note that, instead of simply categorising things to base or superstructure, if one examines law, politics, religion, or for example education and the culture of a capitalist class society, one is likely to observe that most of the institutions, either directly or indirectly, support the current capitalist establishment (Eagleton, 2012, 159). Hence, it indeed seems that the main purpose of the superstructure is, in fact, to sustain the base, and this is above all because the base, in its capitalist form, is bound to create anxieties, because it is based on conflict of interests and exploitation (ibid, 161-162). Therefore, as Marx and Engels argue in *The German Ideology* (1998) the existence of the state is contradictory, because the state does not actually represent the people, but is concentrated in protecting the mode of production dominated by the ideas of the dominant class.

Regarding Althusser's and Gramsci's take on the base/superstructure metaphor, both, in fact, agree on its basic character, but noticeably depart on their perceptions concerning the superstructure. However, peculiarly, both write about the 'superstructures' (see Gramsci, 1971, 371-372; Althusser, 2014, 53-56), but in a different manner. Althusser sees the superstructure being saturated by the ideas of the ruling class, as ideology is, for Althusser, a trans-historical process, 'ideology in general', which ultimately gives the superstructure a more static and rigid character compared to Gramsci (Thomas, 2010). As Thomas (ibid, 100-101) remarks, Gramsci sees ideology translating to hegemonic struggle *'and the forging of composite social bodies via the contestation of collective meanings and values.'* Gramsci developed his theory of the superstructures to encompass both 'civil' and 'political' society, which is nevertheless dominated by the historic bloc (or dominants classes).

Herein lies a crucial difference. Althusser's general theory of reproduction is partially reliant on Marx's base/superstructure model. Althusser (2014, 149) argues that *'a mode of production subsists only insofar as the reproduction of the conditions of production is ensured.'* It follows that *'the entire superstructure is grouped around, and centred on, the state, considered in its two aspects as a class force of repression and a class force of ideologization.'* In other words, Althusser (ibid, 1-2) argues the reproduction of the relations' production is warranted by the state apparatuses; Repressive State Apparatuses (e.g. military, police) and Ideological State Apparatuses (education, church, law, etc.). In the early phase of his studies, Gramsci specifies and extends his discussion of the base/superstructure metaphor, as he speaks about the 'material structure of the superstructure', what is soon to be developed in relation to the concept of 'hegemonic apparatus' (Thomas, 2010, 97). Gramsci reviews 'the superstructures' not directly or mechanically derived from the base but as constituting a dialectical unity or 'historical bloc' with the dominant relations of production, that is, the means by which the relations of production are organised, guaranteed, and made to endure (ibid). In addition, according to Thomas (ibid, 172) Gramsci distinguishes between the 'civil society' and the 'political society', which are conceived as two major superstructural 'levels'. Accordingly, civil society is not opposed to the state, although it presupposes the state, but rather a plateau of difference *'between the family and the state'* (Thomas, 2010, 179). Hence, Gramsci's civil society has a dialectical, non-exclusionary and functional relationship to political society or state (Gramsci, 1971, 12). Therefore, the essential difference between Gramsci and Althusser concerning their views on the base/superstructure metaphor and overall on ideology and domination, is that Gramsci's perception of the superstructure(s) seems to be more dialectical and less rigid than Althusser's.

Gramsci: Hegemony and hegemonic apparatuses

Antonio Gramsci's theoretical investigations concerning hegemony are drafted in his *Prison Notebooks[17]*, written during the last eleven years of his life that he spent in prison in the 1920s and 1930s. Gramsci deploys the term hegemony in order to analyse the history of the bourgeois social formations, and class domination in Western Europe in particular, within the bourgeois capitalist class state during the so-called passive revolution (Thomas, 2010, 222). As Lears (1985, 568) argues, Gramsci's treatment of the concept hegemony can help us to understand, for instance, how '*ideas reinforce or undermine existing social structures*' yet also how to recognise and comprehend the contradiction between '*the power wielded by dominant groups and the relative cultural autonomy of subordinate groups whom they victimize*'. Although Gramsci's writings do not contain a precise definition of hegemony, a frequently quoted passage from the *Prison Notebooks* (Gramsci, 1971, 12) states that hegemony is:

> the spontaneous consent given by the great masses of the population to the general direction imposed on social life by the dominant fundamental group; this consent is 'historically' caused by the prestige (and consequent confidence) which the dominant group enjoys because of its position and function in the world of production.

A crucial point to understand is that hegemony is accomplished, not (only) by means of legal coercion or authoritarian leadership, but by means of manufacturing consent (Hall, 2006). Consent is not only manufactured by means of political discourse or representational democracy, for example, but also through

---

[17] I predominately make use of Peter Thomas's reading of Gramsci's theories that Thomas explains and interprets in his seminal book *The Gramscian Moment* (2010). I have three reasons for this choice: first, Gramsci's writings in his *Prison Notebooks* are often cryptic and ambiguous for various reasons. Second, because of this reason his writings are often interpreted in a conflicting manner. Third, and more importantly, I perceive that Peter Thomas's interpretation of Gramsci is the most compatible and sensible in terms of the main argument. This is so, above all, because of Thomas's investigations regarding Gramsci's conception of the state, which presents the state as a social relation, rather than an instrument or a thing-for-itself.

different societal practices and institutional structures, such as wage-labour and the institutional education that Gramsci calls hegemonic apparatuses. Moreover, based on Gramsci's conceptualisation and deployment of the term hegemony, it is possible to grasp how ideas, practices and institutions are signified by the dominance of the historical bloc, and how that dominance overshadows the social fabric and 'common sense' of a particular society.

Gramsci (1971, 57) explicitly remarks that *'a class is dominant in two ways, that is, it is 'leading' (dirigente) and 'dominant'. It leads the allied classes, and dominates over the adversarial classes.'* Therefore, leadership-hegemony and domination are to be comprehended as strategically differentiated forms of a unitary political power (Thomas, 2010). Furthermore, as Lears (1985, 569-570) argues, the maintenance of hegemony does not necessarily require the active commitment of the subordinate classes to the legitimacy of the elite rule, that is, consent is never engineered with complete success, but *'the outlook of the subordinate groups is always divided and ambiguous'*. Lears (ibid, 569) states that:

> Less powerful people may be thoroughly disaffected. At times they may openly revolt through strikes, factory takeovers, mass movements, and perhaps the creation of a counterhegemony. But normally most people find it difficult, if not impossible, to translate the outlook implicit in their experience into a conception of the world that will directly challenge the hegemonic culture.

Gramsci (1971, 263) states that *'the general notion of the State includes elements which need to be referred back to the notion of civil society (in the sense that one might say that the State = political society + civil society), in other words hegemony armoured with coercion.'* Interestingly, in this 'equation', hegemony is the consensual political practice on the terrain of civil society, but again inherently linked to the state. Gramsci leaves no doubt that the exercise of hegemony also impacts upon the political society or state, above all because political society itself is integrally linked to civil society and its social forces. Therefore, hegemony is always political (Thomas, 2010, 194).

Gramsci himself uses the concept of hegemony to analyse the specifics of the Western social formation, which is followed by broad analysis of the complex cultural forms and practices that emerged in the hegemonic relations of the *Risorgimento*, ranging from newspapers, popular literature, education, language policies, and other characteristics of the embryonic Italian civil society (Thomas, 2010, 223-224). In order to grasp these societal developments theoretically, Gramsci developed the concept of a 'hegemonic apparatus', and while so doing, he further concretised and developed this notion as a part of his theory of class power (ibid). The hegemonic apparatus is the concrete form in which hegemony is exercised, as Buci-Glucksmann (1980, 48) argues:

> The hegemonic apparatus qualifies the concept of hegemony and gives it greater precision, hegemony being understood as the political and cultural hegemony of the dominant classes. As a complex set of institutions, ideologies, practices, and agents (including 'intellectuals'), the hegemonic apparatus only finds its unity when the expansion of a class is under analysis.

The concept 'hegemonic apparatus' is used by Gramsci to explain the ways of domination and the influence of the historic bloc, or more precisely, how power and ideas are used and materialised through the complex network of social relationships in civil society (Thomas, 2010, 223-224). As Thomas asserts, this materialisation must be repeated constantly if a class's project is to secure its dominant position by assuming institutional power in a society. Rehmann remarks (2014, 136), based on Gramsci, that in most developed capitalist countries, the socio-economic structure is reproduced and maintained in two complementary ways: by the political society with its predominantly repressive apparatuses (army, police, judiciary-system and prison-system), which is usually highly centralised and hierarchical, primarily relying upon coercion. Political society is complemented by a civil society that consists of institutions such as schools and universities, churches, and various associations, which are, to some extent, controlled by the government but formally independent (ibid). It is within and through these institutions, which Gramsci labelled as hegemonic apparatuses, where consent of the general public is manufactured, constructed, but also contested.

Althusser: Ideological State Apparatuses

It is well known that Louis Althusser drew part of his inspiration from Gramsci when he drafted his theory concerning ideology and Ideological State Apparatuses (Morrow and Torres, 1995, 146; Thomas, 2010, 225; Bidet, 2014, xxv; Rehmann, 2014, 148, see also Sotiris, 2014). Jacques Bidet states in the introduction of Althusser's study *On the Reproduction of Capitalism* (2014, xxv) that Althusser was stimulated by Gramsci's work in this particular area, yet Althusser turned Gramsci's conception about ideology and indoctrination around by *'presenting the ensemble of institutions as elements of the state machinery thanks to which the bourgeoisie secures its domination.'*

In Althusser's favour, one can certainly argue that his emphasis on the 'socialization from above' by the dominant state ideology communicated and indoctrinated in the 'Ideological State Apparatuses', gives a realistic portrayal of the relations of power and influence within capitalist societies (Rehmann, 2014, 154; Sotiris, 2014, 136). At the same time, several critics have expressed their concerns over Althusser's arguments on power, agency and ideology. According to some readings, Althusser's thesis concerning structure and agency may lead to a situation where individual agency and the contradictorily composed forms of everyday consciousness no longer fit into his theoretical framework (Giroux, 1980; 1983, Morrow and Torres, 1995, 151; Thomas, 2010, 224-225; Rehmann, 2014, 10).

However, and in more dialectical accounts and readings of Althusser, Lahtinen (2015) has proposed that Althusser was not nearly the rigid 'Structural Marxist' he has frequently been claimed to be, but in fact Althusser attempted to find theoretical possibilities for individual agency disregarding the 'ideologisation' of capitalist state and capitalist rationality (see also Resch's definition of Structural Marxism, 1992, 22-24). Althusser argues that societal change is a complex and mutual interaction between societal structures and agents in which they produce each other (Lahtinen, 2015), while, and as Resch (1992, 27) argues, for Althusser and other Structural Marxists, the social structures and social relations, which produce social subjects, are held as primary. Indeed, Structural Marxists seek to explain first the structures and processes by which social subjects are created, and then the relationships between social subjectivity, power and practice (ibid). Moreover, Structural Marxism analyses the contradictions, tensions as well as forces of empowerment of social subjectivity. Therefore, as Resch (ibid) remarks Structural Marxist do not consider that social agents would be mindless robots, but instead *'they are creative, decision-making players within a rule-bound yet open-ended and interactive system of dispositions, discourses, and interests.'*

In the case of economic and social reproduction, Althusser's point of departure is to argue (2014, 233) that the reproduction of conditions of production not only requires the reproduction of productive forces, namely, the means of production, but also existing relations of production. The latter entails not just simply labour power or skills, but also the *'reproduction of its subjection to the ruling ideology or the 'practice' of that ideology'* (ibid). To explain this process, Althusser complements the base-superstructure metaphor with his theory of the state and ideology. While he wants to keep Marx's thesis in regard to economic determination in 'the last instance', Althusser, in contrast, stresses the importance of the superstructure and abandons instrumental thesis regarding linear, mechanical determination (ibid, 237). Althusser's two theses on this matter state: first that there is a 'relative autonomy' of the superstructure with respect to the base, and second that there is a 'reciprocal action' of the superstructure and the base (ibid, 237-238).

In his influential essay *Ideology and Ideological State Apparatuses* (1968/2014), Althusser argues that the reproduction of the workforce has to be studied separately from the reproduction of means of production (e.g. factories, machinery, raw materials). Althusser (ibid) claims that the sole material or physical reproduction of the workforce is not enough, but in addition to this, the workforce has to be competent, because of the complex nature of the capitalist socio-economic structure. In *On the Reproduction of Capitalism* (2014, 50) Althusser argues that the development and the complexity of the means of production demands that the workforce has to be skilled and continues to be reproduced so as to correspond to the modern societal division of labour, and to fill in its different 'posts' and 'jobs'. Consequently, Althusser (ibid) asks how this kind of professional and skilled reproduction is ensured within capitalism, and provides the following answer:

> the reproduction of the qualifications of labour-power *no longer tends* (it is a question of a tendential law) to be ensured *'on the job'* (instruction during production itself) but, increasingly, *outside* production, by the capitalist school system and other instances and institutions.

Althusser (ibid, 51) states that what is learned in school is different kinds of 'know-how', that is, *techniques and quite a few other things besides, including elements (rudimentary or, on the contrary, advanced) of 'scientific culture' or 'literary culture' that are of direct use in different jobs in production.* In addition to know-how, 'rules' of good behaviour are taught in school, that is, customs and practices to be observed, depending from the future position one is 'destined' to hold (ibid). These are rules of professional ethics and professional moral codes of conduct, i.e. *'rules of respect for the social and technical division of labour, and, in the final analysis, the rules of the order established by class domination'* (ibid).

Althusser (2014, 51-52) further argues that the school teaches know-how in a form which ensures one's dependency on the dominant ideology. He claims that, within the industrial and mature capitalist societal structures, the dominant Ideological State Apparatus is now, as the result of political and ideological class struggle, the educational Ideological State Apparatus. This is so, above all, and as Althusser (2014, 37-38) argues, because the reproduction of the workforce takes place outside the enterprise in the modern industrial capitalism. In this regard, it is worthwhile to quote Althusser (ibid, 37-38, footnote 24, italics in original) at more length:

> What happens in an enterprise (since we are taking an enterprise as our example) is never more than an effect of what happens in the capitalist system as a whole, and thus an effect that can in certain cases be literally *undecipherable* at the level of the enterprise alone. Precisely that holds for the social 'distribution' or 'penning in' of people that we are here denouncing. Any 'engineer' will tell you: 'Fine but so what? I need someone to run a milling machine, so I run an ad. A milling machine operator answers it. I hire him. Is it my fault that he's *just* a milling machine operator?' Literally taken in its own limits, this is not 'wrong'. But

> precisely, 'competencies', that is, qualifications or the lack of them, *owe their existence not to the enterprise* as such, but to a system *external* to the enterprise, the school system that 'educates', more or less, different individuals [...] in ways that vary with the milieu from which they come. These mechanisms reinforce the practical, economic and ideological prohibitions [...] which *distribute in advance*, or a class basis, the individuals recruited by the enterprise. In this respect, the entrepreneur's (sic) reasoning it not 'wrong'. It simply proves that he is not 'in control of'' events. But these events that 'are beyond his control' nicely correspond *in advance*, by an amazing coincidence, to a dispositive for 'distributing-penning in' people that is always already ready and waiting in his enterprise, for the purpose, precisely, of exploiting workers. The reason is that the school system that supplies ready-made, at the national level, a predisposition for the 'distribution-penning in' of people that becomes concrete reality in the enterprise is the capitalist school system corresponding to the capitalist class's systems of exploitation, *not some other school system.*

It is explicitly clear for Althusser that ideology has a material existence (2014, 184). Moreover, he argues that public institutions are the 'organs' of 'class struggle', in which one class subjugates the other and ensures that this domination will be reproduced (Bidet, 2014, xxv). This is not, however, a functionalist thesis, an accusation which has more than often been provided by his critics, because, accordingly, the state apparatuses are merely instruments of class struggle, which goes beyond ideology and indoctrination (ibid, see also Althusser, 2014, 219-220). In addition, to develop the theory of capitalist state, Althusser (2014, 75) argues that it is important to note the distinction between state power and state apparatus, but also between Repressive State Apparatus and Ideological State Apparatus. He (ibid, 77) defines Ideological State Apparatuses (ISAs) in the following way:

An Ideological State Apparatus is a system of defined institutions, organizations, and the corresponding practices. Realized in the institutions, organizations, and practices of this system is all or part (generally speaking, a typical combination of certain elements) of the State Ideology. The ideology realized in an ISA ensures its systemic unity on the basis of an 'anchoring' in material functions specific to each ISA; these functions are not reducible to that ideology, but serve it as a 'support'.

Whereas the Repressive State Apparatus is, by definition, repressive, one that makes use of direct or indirect physical violence if necessary, and holds the official monopoly for its use, the ISAs cannot be called repressive in the same manner, because they do not involve themselves in the use of physical violence (Althusser, 2014, 78), although they operate behind the 'protective shield' of the Repressive State Apparatus (ibid, 201). ISAs are not only distinguished from Repressive State Apparatuses by violence or lack of it, but on ideology (ibid, 78). In *Ideology and Ideological State Apparatuses* Althusser (ibid, 243) lists following institutions as ISAs: religious (the system of the different churches), educational (the system of the different public and private 'schools'), family (obviously has also other functions, as Althusser notes), legal (belongs to both Repressive and Ideological State Apparatus), political (the political system, including different parties), trade unions, communications (press, radio, television, etc.), and the cultural ISA (literature, the arts, sports, etc.).

As Althusser points out, Marxists are well aware that the state itself, notwithstanding the constitutional law, is always the state of the dominant class. In the case of capitalist socio-economic structure, the state is the state of the bourgeoisie, in which the bourgeoisie hold state power and exercise it through the Repressive and Ideological State Apparatuses. Yet, Althusser (ibid, 82) maintains that *'institutions do not 'produce' the ideologies corresponding to them. Rather, certain elements of an ideology (the State Ideology) 'are realised in' or 'exist in' the corresponding institutions and their practices.'* ISAs are the materialisation of the ideological configurations dominating them, although the ISAs are objectively distinct, relatively autonomous, and do not form an organised whole with shared and conscious leadership (ibid). Althusser (2014, 140) concludes that the reproduction of the relations of production *'is ensured by the exercise of state power in the state apparatuses'*, that is, the Repressive (military, police, juridical and prison system) and Ideological State Apparatuses (educational, religious, political, cultural, etc.).

Althusser elevates the scholastic ISA as the dominant one, as he provides the following answer to a question: why is the educational apparatus the dominant ISA in the capitalist social formation?

> [...] one Ideological State Apparatus certainly has the dominant role, although hardly anyone lends an ear to its music: it is so silent! This is the School. It takes children from every class at infant-school age, and then for years, the years in which the child is most 'vulnerable', squeezed between the family state apparatus and the educational state apparatus, it drums in to them, whether it uses new or old methods, a certain amount of 'know-how' wrapped in the ruling ideology (French, arithmetic, natural history, the sciences, literature) or simply the ruling ideology in its pure state (ethics, civic instruction, philosophy). Somewhere around the age of sixteen, a huge mass of children are ejected 'into production': these are the workers or small peasants. Another portion of scholastically adapted youth carries on: and, for better or worse, it goes somewhat further, until it falls by the wayside and fills the posts of small and middle technicians, white-collar workers, small and middle civil servants, petty bourgeois of all kinds. A last portion reaches its summit, either to fall into intellectual semi-employment, or to provide, as well as the 'intellectuals of the collective labourer', the agents of

exploitation (capitalists, managers), the agents of repression (soldiers, policemen, politicians, administrators, etc.), and the professional ideologists (priests of all sorts, most of whom are convinced 'laymen'). (Althusser, 2014, 250-251)

Meanwhile, Althusser reminds us that many of the 'virtues', such as modesty, resignation and submissiveness, are also acquired in families, in the church, in the army, through culture, and in sporting events (ibid, 146). Yet, no other ISA, as Althusser (ibid, 146) argues, has *'a captive audience of all the children of the capitalist social formation at its beck and call [...] for as many years as the schools do, eight hours a day, six days out of seven.'* It is, without a doubt, the education apparatus in which the future holders of different social positions get their know-how in terms of formal knowledge but also regarding conformity, dominant ideology and societal practices. For Althusser, the education system is not simply a provider of knowledge, but rather various forms of rules and behaviour that reflect the current social division of labour (Sotiris, 2013, 109). Althusser (2014, 236) remarks in *Ideology and Ideological State Apparatuses* that:

the reproduction of labour power requires not only a reproduction of its skills, but also, at the same time, a reproduction of its submission to the rules of the established order, i.e. a reproduction of submission to the ruling ideology for the workers, and a reproduction of the ability to manipulate the ruling ideology correctly for the agents of exploitation and repression, so that they, too, will provide for the domination of the ruling class 'in words'.

This is why Althusser thinks the educational apparatus, in a developed capitalist society, is the dominant Ideological State Apparatus (Sotiris, 2013). The weight of this claim seems undeniable, especially in the time of neoliberal higher education restructuring, as we will come to realise later. However, although Althusser's thesis remains to be convincing, his remarks uphold certain degrees of structural determinism, as well as problematic notions regarding the (capitalist) state, which is where we turn next.

Poulantzas: Relational state and economic reproduction

The works of Nicos Poulantzas are of great importance when bringing Gramsci and Althusser together because, and as Sotiris (2014) argues, Poulantzas had both the Althusserian ambivalence towards Gramsci, but also at the same time, he was a strongly influenced by Gramsci in his work. Although Althusser's theory on reproduction is, in many ways, valuable, especially in explaining the relation between capitalist state and education, Poulantzas (1975, 2000) argues that it gives too narrow a portrayal of the state. Althusser is often accused of disregarding, in particular, the class struggle and the contested circumstances from where the dominant ideas originate or are manufactured in the form of class hegemony. Personally I'm not sure of this claim. For example, Lahtinen (2015) has recently shown how Althusser has indeed incorporated the class struggle into his theories of societal change. For instance, in *On the Reproduction of Capitalism* Althusser (2014, 138) writes that:

> The unity of the State Apparatus and the Ideological State Apparatuses is ensured by the class politics of those who hold state power, acting directly in the class struggle by means of the Repressive State Apparatuses and indirectly by means of the realization of the State Ideology in the Ideological State Apparatuses.

In addition, Althusser explicitly takes class struggle into consideration, for example in his later comment *Note on the ISAs* (see Althusser, 2014, 218-231), and generally comments upon class struggle in the chapter *The Political and Associative ISAs* in *On the Reproduction of Capitalism*.

In contrast, much more prominent and apt streak of criticism regarding Althusser's remarks – including also the previous quote – is linked to the more general composition of his thesis. In *Political Power and Social Classes* (1978), Poulantzas criticises Althusser's dualistic categorisation – Repressive and Ideological State Apparatuses – as too schematic. Poulantzas' (ibid, 33) main argument is that Althusser's theory assigns functions in an essentialist way, and overlooks the fact that a number of apparatuses *'can slide from one sphere to the other and assume new functions either as additions to, or in exchange form, old ones'*.

It is apparent that Althusser's distinction and framing omits the state's specific role in the constitution of the relations of production, which may also indicate that his theory is not able to explain – in contrast to Gramsci's I would add – how power of the dominant classes is constructed, or how the state is heavily involved in the economic reproduction, and at the same time, produces 'among other things', a 'material substratum' of consensus that binds the subaltern classes to domination, as Poulantzas (2000, 30-31) argues. Poulantzas (ibid) uses the expression 'among other things' in this instance, because the state acts, according to him, within an unstable equilibrium (Gramsci) of compromises between the dominant classes and the subaltern classes. Therefore, the state *'continually adopts material measures which are of positive significance for the popular masses, even though these measures represent so many concessions imposed by the struggle of the subordinate classes'* (Poulantzas, 2000, 30-31). Similarly, Poulantzas (1975, 95) has stated in *Classes in Contemporary Capitalism* that *'the state is not an instrumental entity existing for itself, it is not a thing, but the condensation of a balance of forces'*. Hence, it seems that through Althusser's theory, the essential material and institutional aspects of reproduction cannot be explained if the complex relation between state and general public is reduced to the repressive-ideological dichotomy.

For Poulantzas, the state has, in addition to its coercive and ideological functions, an organisational role, but the state is likewise indispensable in guaranteeing the necessary conditions of capitalist production, which also, and necessarily, leads to an increased role for the state over the course of history (Sotiris, 2014). The state guarantees the capitalist production in several ways, and not only by educating the needed workforce and by holding the monopoly of violence. For example, state guarantees the legal framework for capital accumulation, that is, property relations and class relations, as well as offers a wide variety of other supporting services such as public schooling, healthcare and infrastructure, while it, at the same time, stimulates the economy with financial investments and gives monetary subsidies for industries and companies.

Moreover, another misconception arises from the repression-ideology dichotomy especially concerning state ideology, as Poulantzas (2000, 31-32) notes. This is because the state does not produce a unified discourse, but rather several discourses that are set for and against various classes and apparatuses (ibid). Poulantzas (ibid, 31-32), argues that state's role is essentially organisational in relation to the dominant classes, including that of *'formulating and openly expressing the tactics required to reproduce its power.'* As Poulantzas (2000, 14) remarks:

> The State really does exhibit a peculiar material framework that can by no means be reduced to mere political domination. The state apparatus – that special and hence formidable something – is not exhausted in state power. Rather political domination is itself inscribed in the institutional materiality of the State. Although the State in not created *ex nihilo* by the ruling classes, nor it is simply taken over by them: state power (that of the bourgeoisie, in the case of the capitalist State) is written into this materiality. Thus, while all the State's actions are not reducible to political domination, their composition is nevertheless marked by it.

Therefore, the basis of the material framework of power and state has to be sought elsewhere, i.e., from the relations of production and social division of labour (Poulantzas, 2000, 14), a remark, which can also be considered to be missing from Gramsci's work. This is because, and according to Poulantzas, the conception of state activity regarding the reproduction of capitalism, based on the dichotomy repression-ideology, quite simply diminishes the specificity of the *economic state apparatus* (ibid, 33), and thus, prevents one from locating the power relations of the dominant classes. As Poulantzas (2000, 28) argues, leaning herein to Althusser, ideology involves a series of material practices:

> embracing the customs and life-style of the agents and setting like cement in the totality of social (including political and economic) practices. Ideological relations are themselves essential to the constitution of the relations of possession and economic property, and to the social division of labour at the heart of the relations of production.'

Poulantzas argues also, now following Gramsci's line of argument, that ideology is always class ideology, and in particular, the ruling ideology constitutes an indispensable power of the ruling class, which is then, again following Althusser, elaborated, instilled and reproduced in the Ideological State Apparatuses (ibid, 28-29). When it comes to the dominant classes – to the bourgeoisie in our case – the state's primary role, in addition to representation, is to organise (Poulantzas, 2000, 127). The state represents and organises political interests of a power bloc, which is constituted from several different class fractions. This means that the state is organised in a conflictual unity of the alliance in power and the 'unstable equilibrium', as Gramsci called it, of compromise among its constituents, that is the hegemonic class fractions (ibid). Poulantzas (ibid, 127) argues that:

> this fundamental role of organization does not involve just

one apparatus or branch of the State (political parties), but concerns, in varying degrees and manners, the totality of its apparatuses – including pre-eminently repressive ones such as the military or police. The State is able to play this role in organizing and unifying the bourgeoisie and the power bloc insofar as it enjoys *relative autonomy* of given fractions and components, and various particular interests. Such autonomy is indeed constitutive of the capitalist State: it refers to the State's materiality as an apparatus relatively separated from the relations of production, and to the specificity if classes and class struggle under capitalism that is implicit in that separation.

In a nutshell, Poulantzas' treatise of the capitalist state indicates that it is a relationship of forces, and a material condensation of such a relationship among classes and different class fractions (2000, 128-129). The contradictions among the dominant classes is indeed the reason which makes the state's existence necessary as the organiser of the unity of the power bloc (ibid, 133). Thus, the state apparatuses concentrate and reproduce hegemony by organising the power bloc into 'game of provisional compromises'. As Poulantzas (2000, 35) argues, power is not – in Marxist literature – by any means reducible to the state. He (ibid) states that:

> In the case of classes, power comes down to objective positions rooted in the division of labour: it designates the capacity of each class to realize its specific interests in a relation of opposition to that capacity in other classes. It is therefore impossible for power to escape economic relations. Rooted in the production of surplus-value and in their relation to the politico-ideological powers, these power relations are furthermore concretized in specific institutions-apparatuses: the companies, factories or production units that are the site of the extraction of surplus-value and of the exercise of these powers.

To my understanding, what Poulantzas means is that it is impossible to escape the 'agency' and the influence of the relations of production in the capitalist socio-economic structure. Hence, not only the specifics of the capitalist relations of production, but also the structural imperatives of capitalism have to be taken into consideration when analysing power and domination, as well as their contribution to reproduction. Thus, the capitalist 'economic compulsions', have to be taken into account as well in education.

Poulantzas (2000, 29-30) argues that Althusser's development of Gramsci's theory assumes that the state's *'efficacy somehow lies in what is forbids, rules out, and prevents; or in its capacity to deceive, lie, obscure, hide, and leave people to believe what is false.'* Poulantzas argues that Althusser's theory simultaneously suggests that the economic is, for instance, capable of self-reproduction and self-regulation, and the state's role is merely to set the negative rules of the economic 'game'. Consequently, Poulantzas maintains that, with such a conception, one simply cannot understand or analyse the state's role in the constitution of the relations of production, or the state's interventions in relation to the reproduction of capital (ibid). More importantly, Poulantzas (2000, 167-168) maintains that the economic role linked to the accumulation and reproduction of capital is manifested in the very modification of the respective spaces of state and economy. He (ibid) argues that the changes in the relations of production, in the division of labour, in the reproduction of workforce, and in the extraction of surplus value (in fields such as education, urban planning, transport, and healthcare) are directly integrated, in an expanded and modified form, into the process of reproduction and valorisation of capital. Moreover, as these changes have occurred, the state has, at the same time, assumed a fresh meaning. Poulantzas (ibid, 167-168) explains that:

> It is this transformation of the economic space-process which shifts the targets of state activity and brings the State increasingly to bear on the heart of the reproduction

of capital. In a parallel movement, the space of the State expands and changes to the extent that whole areas of the valorization of capital and reproduction of labour power (the areas of public and nationalized capital, amongst others) are directly inserted in the State.

In other words, Poulantzas argues that, whether they are repressive or ideological or some other kind, the functions of the state cannot be considered in isolation from its economic role. According to Poulantzas (2000, 167-168) it is apparent that state's economic functions occupy the dominant place within the state apparatus, which means that the state operations have been, and are, reorganised to support its economic role in providing conditions for capital accumulation (ibid). It follows that, just as we cannot consider the economic role and actions separately from the state's other operations, we cannot consider the economic state apparatus as being separated from other state apparatuses, which do indeed carry out economic functions and undergo restructuring in relation to the formation and functioning of the current state's role and its economic apparatus, and this is, arguably, because the economic state apparatus dominates other functions of the state (ibid, 172).

Furthermore, and of critical importance are a whole set of state activities *vis-à-vis* scientific research and technological innovation, restructuring industry, education and occupational training, as well as healthcare, transportation, social welfare, urban development, and collective consumption. All these fields are integrated around the state's role in the 'expanded reproduction of labour-power' (Poulantzas, 2000, 176). Such reproduction is no longer simply the *'condition' of exploitation; it is located at the very heart of surplus-value production'* (ibid, 176). Finally, Poulantzas (ibid, 177) notes that:

> The reproduction of labour-power takes place within the limits imposed by the relations of production: what is

at issue is never merely technical training, but expanded reproduction referring to the social division of labour.

Thus, Poulantzas clearly rejects a simplistic conception of the capitalist state that primarily has to do with coercion and ideological justification. On the contrary, he emphasises the importance of the state as an organiser of class hegemony, but also its role in social and economic reproduction. Moreover, for Poulantzas, the state is essential in guaranteeing the conditions of capitalist production, (Sotiris, 2014). Poulantzas' relational conception of the state, in general, offers a dialectical way of understanding how institutions are determined by class struggle. This is because, for Poulantzas, the state is not a *thing-for-itself*, nor does it have an instrumental essence, but is rather a relation, or more precisely a condensation of class relations (Sotiris, 2013).

Based on these theoretical remarks, it seems clear that the economic role of the state cannot be downplayed from the theory of reproduction of capitalism. Similarly, the state's role in the reproduction cannot be reduced to mere repression-ideology, again because of the organisational role of the state. Consequently, through these realisations, it is possible to grasp the complex unity of the capitalist socio-economic structure, and its reproduction in which economic compulsions of the capitalist structure and relations of production are intertwined with state apparatuses, power relations and class interests. Also this way the connection between reproduction of capitalism and institutional education is revealed and explained. However, a theory should not be overly abstract, and thus, in the following two chapters, the connection between contemporary higher education and reproduction of capitalism is taken to a more concrete level.

5

CAPITALISM, HIGHER EDUCATION AND ECOLOGICAL CRISIS

> No other ideological state apparatus [...] has a *captive* audience of *all the children of the capitalist social formation* at its beck and call (and – this is the least it can do – at no cost to them) *for as many years as* the schools do, eight hours a day, six days out of seven. *The relations of production* of a capitalist social formation [...] are primarily reproduced in this process of acquiring what comes down, in the end, to a handful of limited types of know-how, accompanied by massive inculcation of the ideology of the dominant class. (Althusser, 2014, 146)

The emergence of so-called knowledge capitalism has emphasised the importance of higher education because universities are, in the current epoch, identified as one of the key sources of economically valuable information and knowledge (Kauppinen, 2013). This is, above all, because the rapid increase in complexity is one of the fundamental features of modern capitalist socio-economic structure (Harvey, 2014, 121). While artisanal skills continue to be of diminishing importance, the agents of capital have become more and more interested in a workforce that is literate, flexible, disciplined and obedient enough to fulfil a wide variety of tasks that are needed to reproduce the relations of production (ibid, 182-183). In a similar fashion, Burton-Jones (1999, vii) has argued that the economic demand for increasingly skilled workforce leads to the development of a global learning industry and, along with this, to significant changes to the relationships involving learners, educators and companies. More explicitly, Rikowski (2000, 23) has argued that the *'social form (of schooling and training) develops over time in the history of capitalism – in definition and in intensity, and increasingly as productive systems of labour power.'* And as the intensity and influence of capital increases over the rest of the society, Rikowski (ibid) accurately states that the *'the intentionality and social drive to reduce education and training to the social production of labour power in capitalism [...] grow stronger with time.'*

Due to these and various other factors, universities have been pushed into the centre of the global political economy (see Pusser et al. 2012). Thus, it is no wonder that higher education institutions are experiencing pressure for fundamental change (see Torres and Rhoads, 2006). Sievers (2008, 238) argues that, during the last decades, the landscape and organisational climate of higher education has changed dramatically. Whereas the legitimacy of universities in the 1970s was not exclusively derived from the demands of society, this is no longer the case with the present reform of higher education seen in most European countries (ibid). In addition, Olssen and Peters (2005) maintain that the era of neoliberalism has produced a fundamental shift in the way universities and other higher education institutions define their institutional existence[18]. Olssen and Peters (ibid))

---

[18] The relationship between neoliberalism and higher education has been widely and extensively dealt with in several academic publications in the 21st century (to list just a few: Apple, 2000; Nixon, 2004; Ross and Gibson, 2007; Kumar, 2012; Pusser et al., 2012; Sotiris, 2012; 2013;).

claim that higher education has a greater importance for the capitalist economy, as higher education is seen by governments as a key way to succeed in economic competition in the modern knowledge economy (see Jessop, 2008), and consequently, higher educational institutions have been encouraged to develop closer connections with industry (Olssen and Peters, 2005).

Sotiris (2012, 112) argues that, since the 1980s, the restructuring of higher education has been primarily connected with adjustments and opening up of universities towards markets and the interests of private businesses. This transformation has entailed a closer connection with the economy, making the overall higher education apparatus more responsive to the needs of industry, but also bringing novel accountability demands for higher education institutions regarding their capacity to be productive and competitive in the 'knowledge market'. Likewise, transformations in the relations between higher education, economy and state, have brought changes in the funding of higher education but also increased universities' pressure to seek external funding (ibid). In addition, there have been changes in university administration, as formal and informal management methods from the corporate world have been introduced (ibid, 113), with indications of more authoritarian and business-like forms of public management (Deem et al., 2007).

In stricter terms, Kumar (2012, 5) argues that in neoliberal capitalism education is perceived principally from two dimensions: first, education is a commodity contributing to the expansion of capital, and second, education is reduced to skills development to support the first aim. Sotiris contends (2013, 132) that there have been new forms of productive processes, new areas for the accumulation and valorisation of capital, which require the application of scientific knowledge, and new technologies, all pointing to a workforce with increased skills. Sotiris (ibid, 136) claims that:

> Entrepreneurial Higher Education is both a class strategy aiming at ensuring conditions for the reproduction of the conditions of capitalist accumulation (steady flow of qualified personnel, applicable scientific knowledge, product development) and a hegemonic project aiming at undermining the aspirations of the subaltern classes (as attempt towards inscribing precariousness in the form and hierarchy of degrees, reproducing neoliberal ideology, fragmenting collective aspirations and practices). It not only extends knowledge and skills but also promotes the identities, habits and illusions of a particular kind of worker within neoliberal capitalism. Entrepreneurial Higher Education involves not only the transformation of university governance into more managerialism modes and structures but also a particular culture of knowledge, a particular view of knowledge acquisition and utilisation.

One of the main objectives and consequences of the ongoing restructuring of higher education has been to introduce relations of competition to academic life as a way to increase productivity, accountability and control (Olssen and Peters, 2005, 326). This has, dubiously, denoted marketisation and commodification of higher education as being under the scope of neoliberalism. Beginning in the 1980s, human capital and competitiveness discourses started to gain strength in the public sphere, in part because they were in line with the rising neoliberal market-oriented narratives. Along with them came audit exercises, league tables, and various rankings and benchmarking operations to assess the success of universities in different fields of national and international competition (Slaughter and Cantwell, 2012, 589-590). Barnett (2000) argues that marketisation has become a new universal theme in the commodification of teaching and research and other ways in which universities are supposed to meet various performance criteria. Similarly, Graeber (2015, 134) claims that the increasing interpenetration of state, university and private corporations has resulted in each of them adopting language, sensibilities, and organisational forms that originate from the corporate world, which has, in part, speeded up the process of coming up with new marketable products, but has meanwhile had a devastating effect in terms of fostering original research. Thus, the last thirty years in academia have seen a rise in the amount of time spent in working with administrative paperwork, which Graeber (ibid) argues is the result of the introduction of corporate management techniques that are justified as ways to increase efficiency by introducing competition at every level of academia.

It certainly seems that performance indicators and new management techniques have been an important part of the streamlining operation of higher education, but are also closely bound to international policy trends, as for instance, the EU's competitiveness statements and policies indicate (see e.g. European Commission, 2000; 2006). Since the 1980s, groups of European political and business elites have been increasingly lobbying and operating within European institutions in order to create a discourse on European global competitiveness (Bieler and Morton 2001). For instance, in early 2008, the EU held the first meeting of a newly formed Higher Education-Business Forum, which brought together university administrators, European Commissioners, representatives from chambers of commerce, and business executives. The purpose of this forum is to network and coordinate the activities of academia and industry, so that European educational institutions would better serve the economy (Slaughter and Cantwell, 2012).

Sievers (2008) states that economic value and practices are the guiding paradigm in the ongoing university reform, which is characterised by the view that knowledge, above thinking and understanding, is the primary purpose of education. In terms of the reform, neoliberal restructuring of the global economy is, arguably, a precondition for the changing relations between universities and markets (Slaughter and Cantwell, 2012, 585), which has also indicated substantial organisational changes in the field of higher education, such as reduction and closure of departments, establishment of interdisciplinary units, and resource allocation.

Academic capitalism is a useful concept and a theory to analyse and further understanding of how and why higher education has become more managed and penetrated by capitalist logic in the era of neoliberalism. Overall, academic capitalism, as a concept and theory, refers to a wide variety of market and market-like activities and institutions that are made use of by faculties and other higher education institutions to ensure external funding, for instance, due to reduced public funding (see Slaughter and Leslie, 1997; Slaughter and Rhoades, 2004). In *Academic Capitalism* (1997), Sheila Slaughter and Larry Leslie define academic capitalism as market-based or market-like activities of higher education faculties and academic personnel to acquire funding from external sources. Slaughter and Leslie (ibid) argue that academic capitalism is the most suitable way to describe how the profit motive has spread to higher education. Moreover, they argue that, along with this development, university employees have become state-supported entrepreneurs (ibid). In another key publication in the field, Slaughter and Rhoades (2004) argue that the object of the theory of academic capitalism is to understand and portray the integration process of higher education to the new capitalist knowledge economy. Moreover, the focus in the research, according to Slaughter and Rhoades (ibid), is in the blurring boundaries between state and higher education institutions, as well as in networks that transcend the boundaries of public and private sectors. Furthermore, as Kauppinen (2012, 545) explains:

> The focus of academic capitalism (as a theory) is not restricted to commercialization of research but also takes into consideration other aspects of universities (e.g. instruction and administration) and changing relations between universities and their social environment. Thus, academic capitalism is many-sided framework for developing understanding also of such a diverse phenomenon as the influence of neoliberalism, new managerialism, and calls for accountability, assessment and rankings.

Both the neoliberal state and the globalising knowledge economy are seen as important features of the broader structural context that compels universities to move towards the markets (Kauppinen and Kaidesoja, 2013). In this respect, Slaughter and Leslie (1997) remark that although countries choose various paths and means to strengthen and support academic capitalism, globalisation is such a strong force that a convergence of higher education policies between countries occurs at least to some extent. This policy convergence manifests itself, for instance, in science and technology policy that supports techno-scientific innovations and ties to private sector rather than basic research or policy suggestions coming from scientific communities, and consequently, techno-scientific fields of research become the growth and focus areas of higher education (ibid). By techno-scientific research, Slaughter and Leslie (ibid) denote scientific fields that are directly tied to production, such as information technology, telecommunications, electronics, advanced materials, artificial intelligent and biotechnology. In the techno-science scheme, basic and applied research, inventions and innovations and technology and science mix together, and while the division between knowledge and commodity is blurred and knowledge becomes a market good (ibid).

In the academic capitalist regime, higher education has a dual role from an economic standpoint. One is the generation of revenue for academic organisations, and the other is to produce knowledge that facilitates the global economic competitiveness of corporations (Rhoades, 2005). This also means that academics, in their part, are increasingly forced to extend their human capital stocks to competitive environments (Slaughter and Leslie, 1997). Universities, faculties and individual academics are on the one hand compelled to move closer to the market because of increased competition. On the other hand, the state, through mechanisms such as privatisation, commercialisation and deregulation of the public sphere, has created opportunities for different groups to move closer to the market (ibid).

Slaughter and Cantwell (2012, 587) argue that the theory of academic capitalism *'teases out the ways in which new institutional and organizational structures that link state agencies, corporations and universities developed to take advantage of the openings provided by the neoliberal state to move toward the market.'* State agencies, NGOs, corporations and universities are all involved in this process. It is also important to note that universities are not simply affected by some external force, but parts of the university apparatus, indeed, embrace market activity, while other parts resist or neglect these measures (ibid). Likewise, in the academic capitalism regime, new circuits of knowledge are developed to facilitate entrepreneurial research projects linking state agencies, corporations and universities. These projects are supported and funded by novel funding streams and interstitial organisations. At the same time, universities build managerial capacity that enables them to function as economic actors in the market (ibid).

Although, some might claim that there is nothing new in this type of development, and that universities have surely collaborated with industries for a long time, Kauppinen (2013) claims that academic capitalism is an actual trend, not a historical tendency, because academic capitalism is not immanent to the higher education system. While it is true that universities have been accountable to their funding bodies throughout their history, and interacted with the rest of the society, during the last decades we have seen the rise of such networks and practices that have '*introduced direct market behaviours, the profit motive and the capitalist ethos increasingly into universities*' (Kauppinen and Kaidesoja, 2013, 5). On this matter, Slaughter and Rhoades (2004) have also attempted to portray in their book how universities have actively promoted activities that have spread the ethos of academic capitalism.

According to Slaughter and Rhoades (2004), a signifying feature of academic capitalism is that the content of 'public' is transformed, and that the spread of academic capitalism is based on the transformation and unification of higher education. This change, Slaughter and Rhoades (ibid) argue, does not necessarily indicate a decrease in the public support of higher education, but its reconfiguration. Kauppinen (2013) claims that in the academic capitalism regime, knowledge is commodified, and while this is being done, the system of information distribution within universities is transformed by encouraging secrecy. To be sure, universities are complex institutions with various disciplines and practices. Some disciplines are, due to their nature and applicability, more able to interact with economic actors, while others (such as humanities and social sciences to a large extent) are not, which means that there are differences among disciplines to what level they are engaging and able to engage in market activities that characterise academic capitalism (Kauppinen and Kaidesoja, 2013).

In any case, it can be well argued that many of the contemporary changes in higher education are based on the deepening functional linkages between knowledge-based capitalism and higher education. Yet, Kauppinen (2013) argues that the theory of academic capitalism, for instance, lacks a sufficient transnational element in its analysis, which relates to a more general point regarding higher education studies, that is, contemporary higher education studies seldom deal with broader social theoretical debates, not to mention ecological ones, to inform their research. Kauppinen and Cantwell (2014) note that globalisation has been the central element regarding the theory of academic capitalism from the beginning. Moreover, Kauppinen and Cantwell (ibid) argue that in the global economy knowledge production and its application have become key factors. This also entails a greater role for universities in the global economy as producers of knowledge, but at the same time, knowledge is contracted to a measurable and transferrable commodity. Kauppinen and Cantwell (ibid) argue as well that the globalisation of academic capitalism may indicate that academic capitalism becomes transnational.

More explicitly, Kauppinen (2012) argues in his article *Towards transnational academic capitalism* that we are currently witnessing transnationalisation of academic capitalism, which ultimately challenges the common assumption that universities are primarily promoters of national economic competitiveness. While national competitiveness certainly seems to have a significant role in the level of national higher education policy (see Chapter 6 for the Finnish case), strong external forces are pushing for transnationalisation of higher education. Therefore, it is safe to say that academic capitalism is not only blurring the boundaries between higher education, states and markets, but also blurring these boundaries transnationally (ibid). This observation is also backed up by studies regarding global capitalism (see e.g. Robinson, 2004; 2014). As presented earlier, scholars in this field argue that a shift from a world economy to a global economy has occurred, based on transnationalisation of production processes and development of global financial structure. Transnationalisation of global capitalism has resulted to a situation where transnational capitalists have mutual interests (although this does not mean that there is no competition or conflict of interests among transnational capitalists), and thus, they are forming networks and other collaborative forms to cement their position as the dominant fraction of capital (Robinson, 2014, 24). Nonetheless, as Kauppinen (2012) notes, it is not only the production processes, but also research and development and innovation networks that have become more transnational during the past decades (see also Kauppinen and Cantwell, 2014a). Kauppinen (2012, 553) explains that:

> networks, and circuits of knowledge that characterize academic capitalism tend to operate increasingly transnationally partially because nation-states and supranational entities have developed favourable conditions for various knowledge-intensive transnational economic practices (e.g. transnationalization of R&D) as part of their knowledge-based economy strategies and visions.

This, in turn, has opened up possibilities for academics and universities to diversify their funding. Finally, a wider implication regarding transnational academic capitalism is the link between it and transnational circuits of capital. Through its transnational character, higher education is also contributing to the emergence of the newest chapter of global capitalism, that is, global knowledge capitalism, which is characterised by transnational production processes and research and development networks together with global financial structure (ibid).

Neoliberal higher education as hegemonic and ideological state apparatus

The developments in the neoliberal era have led to the point where contemporary higher education functions as a *hegemonic apparatus* (Sotiris, 2013). Accordingly, higher education supports the reproduction of class structures and communicates the dominant class strategies, fosters capitalist accumulation, and undermines the resistance of the subaltern classes (ibid, 133). This is because the shift towards neoliberal higher education or entrepreneurial higher education *'is not limited to questions about degree structures, access and hierarchies, but also to the ideological and political balance of forces both within and outside academia'* (ibid, 134). Sotiris (2013, 134) argues that contemporary higher education is integral in corresponding to the crucial challenge in present-day capitalist society, that is, to the need to have a labour-force, which is at the same time more qualified, but at the same time has less collective rights and aspirations, and is thus more likely to conform and submit to a more oppressive, insecure, and exploitative environment.

In order to escape overly rigid and functionalist theorising in this sense, it is important to consider and emphasise the dual character of the capitalist state and its organisational forms, i.e., while the state represents itself as an official representative of the whole nation, it is at the same time place and object of class conflict (see Thomas, 2010, 93-95, 167-195). The capitalist state is, at the same time, directed toward the constitution and reproduction of capitalism, while it protects the accumulation process from various threats, as it acts as a factor of social cohesion, and meanwhile supports at least somewhat democratic processes and provides social security (Morrow and Torres, 1995). Notwithstanding these various, and conflicting ambitions, the primary concern for capitalist state's is in the long-term planning and synthesising of the goals of economic and social reproduction of capitalism, despite its internal and external conflicts and disputes of individual or corporative groups (ibid, 351). The contradictory role of the capitalist state in terms of social conflict is evident also in the field of education. Carnoy and Levin (1985, 50) state that:

> schools are part of social conflict. Education is at once the result of contradictions and the source of new contradictions. It is an arena of conflict over the

production of knowledge, ideology, and employment, a place where social movements try to meet their needs and business attempts to reproduce its hegemony.

While it is important to consider the process of state mediation of contradictions in education, such as equality and democracy in contrast to capital accumulation, it is even more important to consider the 'correspondence' between education and capital accumulation (see also Bowles and Gintis, 1976), and how in this respect the object of capital accumulation not only affects education but also undermines and limits democratic and egalitarian reforms. The demands and pressures for restructuring higher education originate from various fields and directions, as we are dealing with a phenomenon that is highly complex in character. In this sense education is, by no means, not *only* a factory (see Sotiris, 2012). Notwithstanding, it is argued by Sotiris (2012) that contemporary higher education is to be considered as a hegemonic apparatus of the state, that is, a condensation of practices and rituals that have to do with social reproduction, but especially, and more importantly in our time, increasingly to do with commodifying and supporting capitalist production processes (ibid, 118) and more generally the reproduction of capitalism.

To bring about the idea of economic reproduction and its accompanying ideology to education is, at the same time, an opportunity to discard the high structuralist tendency to think of the social whole in terms of respective 'specialisation' (Sotiris, 2012, 117-119). Meanwhile, to perceive the contemporary higher education as a manifestation of the hegemony of capital, as well as the dominance of transnational capitalist class hegemony, calls for dialectical conception of power and ideology, but also regarding the relation between state and higher education. Similarly, to avoid overly structuralist, teleological, and functionalist lines of argumentation, it is important to contrast these observations with resistance and class struggle regarding higher education that is ongoing, both internally and externally. This is because the 'turn' towards neoliberal higher education should not be seen one-dimensionally as the result of universities becoming private businesses due to the hegemony of capital, but as certain condensation and reorientation of class strategies vis-à-vis in a period of capitalist restructuring (ibid). Thus, the recent and ongoing higher education restructuring does not denote some simple process of managerialism and privatisation but is part of a more complex transformation in line with bourgeois class interests, manifested in the ideology and hegemony of neoliberal capitalism (see also Duménil and Lévy 2004). In this respect, Gramsci's understanding of hegemony, indeed, offers a way of conceptualising higher education in the current historical setting. This is because, as Sotiris (2013, 127-128) argues, the complex relation between civil society (see Thomas, 2010) and state offers a more dialectical conception of the relations between power, society and state, crystallised in Gramsci's conception of the state.

Furthermore, Gramsci's conceptions regarding hegemony offer a way to integrate different purposes and practices that we generally define to be part of 'education'. This is particularly true regarding the class struggle, which is composed of hegemonic and counter-hegemonic projects, marked by a constant struggle between dominant and subordinate classes. In addition, it becomes apparent that Poulantzas' conception of the state supports Gramsci's thesis and understanding of hegemony and power, that is, Poulantzas (2000) perceives state and/or education, and the class hegemony these institutions reflect, as being a condensation of certain social relations. Meanwhile, and evidently, higher education institutions (in their neoliberal outlook) are indeed what Althusser postulated to be Ideological State Apparatuses, that is, locations where social force is transformed into power with a condition that we perceive power as class strategy (Sotiris, 2013, 128-129). Altogether, this relational conception of higher education, which can be at the same time considered a synthesis of Gramsci's and Althusser's remarks, can help us understand, as Sotiris (ibid, 129) argues, *'the hegemonic function of state apparatuses. It is not the result of some inherent structural determination, nor of conscious design, but of the articulation of singular practices and strategies.'* Thus, the neoliberal higher education as *hegemonic and ideological state apparatus* is not necessarily a conscious or coordinated project but rather a reflection of certain class relations, structural imperatives linked to the reproduction of capitalism, and hegemony in a certain historic moment. This is also to say that although capitalist relations of production, ideology, and conditions for capital accumulation are reproduced through contemporary higher education, there is also ongoing struggle and resistance embedded in the higher education apparatus regarding its purpose and orientation.

Higher education and ecological crisis

To conclude the arguments put forward so far, the common denominator for the entire capitalist socio-economic structure is the hegemony of capital. The endless capital accumulation imperative is the glue that both creates common interests and influences the actions of different economic operators including individuals, corporations, universities, states, banks, and international organisations. Concerning contemporary higher education and its neoliberal restructuring, capitalism, as an increasingly complex organisation, is in constant need of skilled labour and different kinds of innovations to advance its expansion and to guarantee its reproduction. In addition to this, and because of the ongoing integration between capitalist markets and higher education, there are compelling reasons to argue that higher education institutions either directly or indirectly serve the purposes of capital, especially because of higher education's increased role as an element in the so-called knowledge economy. Likewise, the demands for intensifying global competition and pressure for further capital accumulation, in particular from the state's perspective, affect the purpose and orientation of the higher education apparatus and push higher education into a more instrumental direction, influenced, managed, and controlled by different public and private interests.

This being so, the role of higher education from the perspective of the reproduction of capitalism can be considered threefold:

1) to 'educate' the workforce to become part of the processes of capital accumulation (Althusser, 2014; see also Bowles and Gintis, 1976).

In addition to this, two other contributions to the reproduction of capitalism are to be considered. These are:

2) knowledge and innovation production to foster economic growth (Slaughter and Leslie, 1997; Slaughter and Rhoades, 2004), and;

3) a further involvement in fostering profit-making opportunities through commodification and commercialisation of education (e.g. Bok, 2003).

Human-caused ecological crisis, although complex as a phenomenon, is largely due to expansive economic activities leading to over-exploitation and over-consumption of natural resources (Foster, 2009; Jackson, 2009; Barnosky et al., 2012; IPCC, 2014; Moore, 2015; Steffen et al., 2015; Ward et al., 2016). Therefore, it stands to reason that instead of continuous expansion in consumption, production, and capital accumulation (or more exactly expansion in the material throughput of economies) there is rather an urgent call for reversed 'degrowth economics' especially concerning the over-consuming and over-producing economies (see e.g. Victor, 2008; Jackson, 2009; Latouche, 2010).

However, by contributing to the reproduction of capitalism, or in other words to the processes of expansive economic activity, higher education, in its current outlook, is, in fact, making the ecological crisis worse, and it is of critical importance to understand by what exact means.

As argued, contemporary higher education has three primary ways through which it contributes to the reproduction of the capitalist socio-economic structure. First, higher education contributes by 'educating' the workforce to become a part of the processes of capital accumulation (Althusser, 2014; see also Bowles and Gintis, 1976). In addition to persuasive theoretical arguments, arguably one of the most straightforward practical examples of this particular contribution is the CEMS program in management education. According to the CEMS program website[19]:

> CEMS is a global alliance of academic and corporate institutions dedicated to educating and preparing future generations of international business leaders.
>
> The CEMS academic and corporate members work collectively to develop knowledge and provide education that is essential in the multilingual, multicultural and interconnected business world.
>
> The joint CEMS Master's in International Management is the main vehicle for achieving this goal.

The CEMS program was founded in 1988. In 2017, CEMS consisted of 30 higher education institutions on five continents. The program had 73 corporate partners, all of which were transnational corporations, including ABB, Bayer, BNP Paribas, Facebook, Google, Hyundai, KONE, Maersk, McKinsey & Company, Microsoft, Procter & Gamble,

---

19   http://www.cems.org/about/mission, page visited 24.2.2017

PriceWaterhouseCoopers, Statoil, and UBS. In addition to these corporate partners, the program also had seven social partners (NGOs), including Fairtrade and Global Alliance for Banking on Values. According to CEMS's graduate survey, in September 2016, 78% of CEMS's graduates worked for transnational corporations, of which 30% in consulting, 15% in technology, 13% in consumer goods, 12% in finance, and 4% in health/pharma[20].

As an overview of the program, according to the CEMS website[21], CEMS Masters in International Management *unites high-calibre professors from leading universities and business schools, multinational companies and non-profit organisations jointly designing and delivering theoretical knowledge and practical know-how.* Furthermore, it is stated that CEMS corporate partners *'contribute strongly in the creation, implementation and delivery of the local curricula.'* On a more institutional level, it is remarked that *'a distinguishing factor of the programme is that it brings together all stakeholders (schools, companies, students and alumni).'* Finally, it is concluded that *'in addition to being the most international management programme on the market, it is the starting point for lifelong professional and personal networks.'*

In this case, the connection between capitalism, higher education, and ecological crisis is explicit and direct. The CEMS program, for its part, offers to the transnational corporations a setting to offer a suitable education for future business leaders with a certain skill set, qualifications, and knowledge. The students, on their behalf, become part of the capitalist processes of accumulation, as they become employees of transnational corporations, which, by definition, maximise profits, market share, and target economic growth in their operations. Thus, higher education, in this case,

---

20 http://www.cems.org/about-cems/overview/key-facts-figures, page visited 24.2.2017

21 http://www.cems.org/mim, page visited 24.2.2017

reproduces and supports the structure that contributes to over-consumption and over-exploitation of natural resources in an expanding scale, and consequently, rather than mitigating, ends up exacerbating the ecological crisis.

Second, higher education contributes to the reproduction of capitalism by producing knowledge and innovations to foster economic growth. Ward (2012, 91) states that, by the 1970s, technology-based businesses began to emerge around university zones in the United States (for instance in Berkeley, Stanford, and the Massachusetts Institute of Technology). At the same time, the National Science Foundation in the US started to support the funding of these operations by developing what was to be called 'technology transfer' or knowledge transfer between universities and businesses (McSherry, 2001, 149). The trend to establish technology transfer offices (see e.g. Slaughter and Leslie, 1997; Mowery et al., 2004; Slaughter and Rhoades, 2004; Kauppinen and Kaidesoja, 2013), as go-between organisations that facilitate cooperation between universities and corporations, can be understood as a direct marker of academic capitalism (Slaughter and Leslie, 1997; Slaughter and Rhoades, 2004; Kauppinen and Kaidesoja, 2013; Kauppinen, 2014a). This is because, as Slaughter and Leslie (1997, 19) argue, *'technology transfer is perhaps the most direct form of academic engagement with the market'*.

In the US context, it has been argued that changes in federal law (in particular the Bayh-Dole Act) have resulted in increased patenting and licensing operations by universities during the 1980s and 1990s (Mowery et al., 2004; Ward, 2012), and more generally to a shift towards academic capitalism (Slaughter and Rhoades 2004, 28–30, 76–77). Whereas corporations have utilised universities in search of new products and services, universities have sought novel external funding channels after the decline in state financing (see e.g. Slaughter and Leslie, 1997, 6-7, 15), and means to measure up in competition against other universities for students and faculty (Bok, 2003). More generally, as Kauppinen (2014a, 1737) argues, academic capitalism represents the 'second enclosure movement' (Boyle, 2003), in which *knowledge is treated as a private good and subjected to commodification*' (Kauppinen, 2014a, 1737; see also Ward, 2012, Chapter 3). Thus, the normative position in the academic capitalism regime is that knowledge should be converted into profitable innovations (Kauppinen, 2014a, 1737). Accordingly, knowledge is seen as valuable only when it leads to commodities or services that generate profit (Slaughter and Rhoades, 2004, 29). Hence, there has been a trend to establish technology transfer offices (Slaughter and Rhoades, 2004; Ward, 2012).

A large-scale practical example of technology transfer and technology transfer office is the Massachusetts Technology Transfer Center (MTTC). According to its website[22], the mission of MTTC is to facilitate and accelerate technology transfer between research institutions and Massachusetts companies, to promote collaboration between research institutions and the Massachusetts technology industry, assist in the growth of Massachusetts companies, and to support regional and state-wide economic development priorities. In the website, it is concluded that:

> Fundamental research is the primary building block for technology-based and knowledge-based industries. To develop and support these industries, creative ideas must make the transition from research labs to companies, where they can be developed into products.

Also, it is noted that federal research and development expenditures in Massachusetts' academic and non-profit research institutions exceed 4.5 billion dollars annually. In this respect, more

---

22 www.mttc.org/about-mattcenter/overview/, page visited 28.2.2017

than 30 technology transfer offices in Massachusetts universities, research hospitals, and non-profit research institutes support the commercialisation of research. In the website, it is also remarked that MTTC enhances the commercialisation of research by:

> implementing programs aimed at increasing the quantity and quality of new technologies transferred, educating researchers on entrepreneurship and the technology commercialization process, and bringing together researchers, company executives and professional financiers to learn about new technological advances.

Concerning the ecological crisis in particular, technology transfer should be considered a prominent example of the questionable ecological impact of contemporary higher education. Again, the main ecological problems are related to overproduction and -consumption, as well as the processes that target and contribute to expansive economic activity. The overall aim of technology transfer is, as Kauppinen (2014a, 1736) argues, to commercialise research and to introduce the profit motive into academia through intellectual property rights and, consequently, to contribute to processes of capital accumulation and economic growth. For instance, in the case of MTTC, the aims and agenda concerning research outputs are clearly economic growth-driven. Another point to consider is the scale of MTCC's operations, which indeed are substantial. Subsequently, it can be argued that because of the increasing commercialisation of research outputs and due to their contribution to the processes of capital accumulation, higher education, at least indirectly, adds to environmental degradation instead of alleviating it.

Third, higher education contributes to the reproduction of capitalism by the commodification and commercialisation of education to foster profit-making opportunities and economic growth. One of the most clear-cut examples in this case is the so-called 'education exports' (for a more general account on the commercialisation of higher education see e.g. Bok, 2003). Bennell and Pearce (2003, 215) note that the internationalisation of the landscape in higher education has been identified as a major trend since the late 1980s. Among other measures, universities in the Northern hemisphere have sought to attract a greater number of students and to develop collaborative ties with foreign institutions to enable foreign students to study for their qualifications (ibid). As Bennell and Pearce (2003, 215) remark, these measures, which comprise the bulk of education exports, have sought to *generate much-needed income as well as foreign exchange for the universities*'. As a whole, Bennell and Pearce (ibid, 215-216) state that the value of education exports has grown exponentially during the past decades. Meanwhile, higher education institutions and state governments have recognised the potential of international education markets for an array of education and training services (ibid).

Universities in the UK and Australia, in particular, have been successful in recruiting students and developing overseas-validated courses and partnerships as sources of income (Bennell and Pearce, 2003, 217). In the UK, education exports are a relatively big business that is also well organised. One of the examples of this is Exporting Education UK (ExEdUK), which is a group of 20 UK organisations in international education promoting UK's educational services in the global economy. On ExEdUK's website[23] it is argued that:

> Education exports are worth over £18 billion to the UK economy and have the potential for year on year growth. The international students of today are the business and cultural leaders, politicians and citizens of the growth economies of the future. The cultural and personal links

---

23 http://exeduk.com/why-are-we-campaigning/, page visited 3.3.2017

they forge as students at British institutions will shape their future decisions in all sorts of ways.

The founding members of ExEdUK believe that this is of enormous importance to the UK's own economic future and there is a need for the all parts of the sector to work more closely together to promote the contribution of education exports to politicians, policy makers and the media to ensure we create the most positive climate we can to ensure education exports continue to grow in the short and long term.

The UK government is also involved in the promotion of education exports. For instance, a UK government press release issued on July 29, 2013, noted that *'an ambitious strategy to expand UK's education export industry'* has been published. In the press release it is declared, among other things, that

the International Education Strategy will ensure British schools, universities, colleges and education businesses continue to stay ahead in the global education market – worth almost £3 trillion annually.

It aims to secure an extra £3 billion worth of contracts for the UK's education providers overseas, and attract almost 90,000 extra overseas university students by 2018.

The British Council, a UK government-funded organisation promoting international cultural and educational opportunities, concludes in its website[24] that:

More and more countries are recognising the benefits available from the internationalisation of education, and its implications for their economies' competitiveness and productivity. They are also increasingly realising the difference that supportive national policies can make in

---

24 https://www.britishcouncil.org/organisation/policy-insight-research/insight/education-goes-global, page visited 3.3.2017

fostering innovation and growth.

This is important for the UK. International education brings £17.5 billion into the country every year. The education sector is the second largest global market, growing at 7% per year.

As we see in these exhibits, education is portrayed in a very instrumental fashion; being an integral element of the processes that seek further capital accumulation and economic growth. While it is certainly true that higher education is no oil or mining industry when it comes to its direct ecological footprint, for instance in the case of education exports, its indirect consequences on the environment and ecological crisis are arguably significant. While, it is true that education is somewhat immaterial (although many aspects of it are not, including campus buildings, sports arenas, information networks, computers, books, and also people with material needs), the overall aims and wider socio-economic repercussion count in this case. The explicit aim of education exports is to acquire revenue from commodifying education. This revenue is likely to be used to foster further opportunities for future capital accumulation and economic growth, which is, because of the absolute contradiction and Jevons paradox, going to cause a negative impact to already overburdened ecosystems of this planet. Therefore, it is argued that the contemporary higher education apparatus is increasingly functioning in an unsustainable fashion, from an ecological standpoint, indeed because of its contribution to the processes of capital accumulation and economic growth. In the next chapter, the connection between the reproduction of capitalism, contemporary higher education, and ecological crisis is reflected upon from a perspective of a single nation state, as the Finnish higher educational apparatus is scrutinised.

6

HIGHER EDUCATION AS A FACTORY OF COMPETITIVENESS AND INNOVATIONS
The Finnish Context

The mid-19th century seems to be suitable place in history to start this short narrative concerning Finnish educational history and education policy. This is because it was this time in Finnish national development (although the country was, at this time, still under Russian rule) when education and its school-like formats truly started to gain foothold in the Finnish socio-economic sphere. From this moment on, education was to become more significant and purpose-oriented, especially from a political standpoint (Heikkinen and Leino-Kaukiainen, 2011, 11-12). This was because, from the mid-19th century onwards, religious and demotic educational traditions and institutions were gradually transformed and merged with new educational structures (ibid).

Along the lines of this development, 'modernity' found its way to Finland. A class society based on Christian morality was incrementally replaced by a civil society, in which one's position was not to be determined by birth, but more and more one's economic and socio-political agency, in which education was to play an important part. As the Russian Empire's foreign-political position went through turmoil in the mid-19th century, cumulating pressures for change erupted in the Finnish great-principality (Heikkinen and Leino-Kaukiainen, 2011). One of these eruptions concerned the fact that the contemporary demands of government and economic life no longer responded to the teachings of ABC books and catechisms. Inherited from the 18th century enlightenment, the ideas based on the importance of information, rational action and utility casted the ground for the designated educational thinking for the next century. This was re-cultivated by popular movements (such as the Fennomans) trying to elevate the level of the standard of education for the entire Finnish population. One of the guiding principles was that, to succeed or flourish, a small nation would need more than just an educated upper class; every citizen should possess a range of basic skills (ibid).

To respond to this challenge, arguably, a more extensive educational system would be needed. The creation of this started from elementary schools that were extended to cities and countryside across the country beginning from the 1860s, gradually followed by more wide-ranging educational arrangements including occupational and higher education (Heikkinen and Leino-Kaukiainen, 2011, 12). This development also meant that education began to institutionalise and professionalise, which itself indicated that education became regulated and defined by decision makers, and organised institutionally (ibid).

Meanwhile, the barriers for trade and production were to be lifted from the mid-19th century onwards. One milestone was the year 1879, when freedom from occupation was declared in Finland. In general, widespread industrial breakthroughs occurred during the 1870s and 1880s along with the improved railroad connections. In spite of this, life for the majority was still anchored in small-scale farming and peasantry (compared to many other European countries urbanisation took place rather slowly in Finland; in the year 1900, 13% of the population lived in cities, and by 1920, 16%) (Leino-Kaukiainen and Heikkinen, 2011, 17).

In the beginning of the 20th century, Finnish industry and commerce had diversified and gained strength. At the same time, educational choices and possibilities had grown exponentially. Nonetheless, the economic and social differences between town and country kept on growing – the present educational system still primarily supported the education of the elites (officials, industrial managers and owners, landowners). Tensions grew more marked at the time of the First World War, when international trade dried up. Finland became independent in 1917, in the shadow of the October revolution in Russia, in volatile domestic and international circumstances. Ultimately, the harsh civil war of 1918 tore the country in half for decades. Bourgeois Finland was the undeniable winner of the war, which meant that bourgeois values defined Finland's political and cultural atmosphere up until the Second World War, as the country remained predominately rural (in the late 1930s over half of the citizens were still peasants, and only 24% lived in cities) (ibid, 21).

Political and demographic circumstances of the country turned dramatically around after the Winter and Continuation wars (1939-1944) against the Soviet Union. Right-wing movements were abandoned, and the left – supported by the Soviet Union – increased in power. In any case, in the spirit of post-Second World War reconstruction, both the right and the left seemed to agree that the current educational arrangement no longer served the needs of the industry, or the needs of an internationalising country, and thus another reform was needed (Heikkinen and Leino-Kaukiainen, 2011, 19-20).

Jalava (2011, 75-76) argues that it was not so much for the sake of the need to strengthen the social cohesion of different classes or mutual national identity, but rather to reformulate the ideas regarding the worker and ideal citizen as being disciplined, hardworking, responsible and moral according to the principles of new kind of nation building. In a societal situation, where industrial production processes pressured the former class society dominated by the church and patriarchal morals to change, there was a need for an educational arrangement that would socialise and discipline the workers accordingly (ibid). As production and work moved further away from the direct life-sphere of families, a new kind of societal institution was, arguably, required to socialise citizens to working life and citizenship, meaning that instead of educating and reproducing the agrarian class society, the novel education system would raise individuals that would integrate themselves to the level of bourgeois-capitalist class society as wage-labourers (ibid). Nevertheless, Jalava (2011, 75-76) claims that the link between education and industrialism was, in reality, not this direct. Rather what was pursued at the level of national and education policy was the old and familiar logic that even a small nation could become, with the help of mass education, a noteworthy actor in the international arena.

The idea of national competitiveness originally came to Finland from Sweden in the early 19th century. One of the central premises of the competitiveness ideology was that nations and cultures should aim for perfection and towards world citizenship, and the essential being of cultures manifested itself through mutual contest. Across the 19th century, this idea was attached to darker colours, when the idea of cultural contest turned to imperialist and militarist conflicts between nation states. Regardless, the notion grew stronger in Finland, indicating that the cultivation of human capital was the only way the nation would survive in the international competition, and thus, all the talents had to be discovered and utilised (Ikonen, 2011, 235).

Nevala and Rinne (2012) argue that behind the Finnish higher educational reform in the 1960s was a rapid change in economic and societal structures, the need to educate the baby boomers, and an idea of the welfare state. Thus, higher education came under the spotlight because it was perceived as an instrument to steer and manage societal development (ibid). In other words, the restructuring and expansion of higher education was an integral part in the building project of a modern education state to support urbanisation, modernisation and the overall welfare state. In this regard, the process and developments concerning the formulation of the welfare state were especially turbulent. Uljas (2012) writes in her dissertation that the most intense political battles surrounded the questions regarding the nature of the state, that is, whether to build a welfare state and a social security system, or return to the old night watchman-like state, and cancel even the modest redistributions of income that had been carried out in the post-war years. Generally speaking, social changes started late but took place rapidly in Finland. In this regard, Kettunen (2010, 9) has noted that Finnish society remained regionally and socially polarised for a long period of time, and the educational system, for its part, supported this division. It was only in the 1960s and 1970s that efforts began to build an education system based on the idea of social equality. In the post-war setting, an agrarian country was transformed in a remarkably short period of time to an urban society, in which the service industry was the largest employer (Kettunen and Simola, 2012, 13-14).

During the 1960s, trust in public governance was strengthened, as was political organising of different interest groups, and the belief in knowledge as 'capital', which would serve the benefit of the whole society. These developments, accompanied by an era of unprecedented economic growth, led to the creation of Finnish welfare society, which is, in many respects, considered a success story (Uljas, 2012). Yet, to support a society based on the idea of human capital and equality, an increasingly mass-based education system would be needed to integrate and serve this project (ibid). Hence, coming into the 1970s, the Finnish higher education system had been transformed completely. Economic growth, vernacularisation, mass education and politicisation were the central elements of the new higher education apparatus of the welfare state era. This also indicated that the scientific community was no longer as autonomous entity as it used to be, which manifested itself, for instance, in the foundation of several new higher education institutions and in education and public policy (see Ikonen, 2011).

While investigating the role and purpose of higher education, one has to ask what kind of duties do, for instance, universities have, to whom and in what way? Consequently, one has to ask whether universities create public or private well-being, or whether universities are local, national or global institutions (Kankaanpää, 2013, 26). From the state's point of view, the duties of universities can be divided at least into economic and other wider societal perspectives. These other perspectives include, for instance, the promotion of universal science and well-being of humanity, various private interests, as well as interests of industry, which can, of course, be overlapping and in a paradoxical relation to one another (ibid).

Higher education institutions have also been caught up with globalisation in many ways throughout their history. At the same time, universities have had an important role as national cultural institutions taking care of the education of the national elites (Välimaa, 2012). Moreover, universities have provided a cultural and academic basis for different disciplines (such as history, sociology, economics etc.) and supported the existence of a nation state as a social entity (see Beck, 1999). In this respect, universities have been both symbols of the sovereign state and also encompassed various social arrangements, such as citizenship, norms and values, and identity (see Beerkens, 2004). This is particularly true in Finland where universities and other higher education institutions have had an essential role in the creation of national identity (see Välimaa, 2001). Nonetheless, the most central role of universities has been for centuries, in addition to educating national elites, their position and entity as a mediator and facilitator of knowledge based on scientific research (Ikonen, 2011, 227).

Although in many respects, the history of universities has been and remains in a state of change regarding to what purposes and whose interests they serve, the nation state has, from early on, come to steer and influence its operations (Kankaanpää, 2013, 28). In fact, the development of the modern university is also deeply intertwined with the development and rise of nation states in the 19th century (ibid). This 'union' of the nation state and universities has guaranteed a steadier institutional foundation to universities, whereas the state has benefitted from universities in building a national culture and educating its citizens to serve the state (Kwiek, 2000; 2001). Neave (2000) argues that the modern state defined the purpose, 'place', and responsibilities of universities as the fundamentals of the modern state were outlined, and thus the nationalisation of universities occurred. Even Humboldian University was originally founded for national purposes in the 19th century. According to Jónasson (2005), it was perceived as an important instrument in nation building, in maintaining and in progressing Prussian culture, and later in securing German economic strength, whereas Napoleonic universities in France were founded to serve national interests even more tightly. The Humboldian university emphasised 'pure science' and 'education through science', characterised by a notion of 'freedom and loneliness', and thus it has sometimes been perceived as 'an ivory tower', an entity that is somewhat detached from the rest of society (Niiniluoto, 2015). Similarly, its Finnish equivalent, the Snellmanian University has, from the beginning, cherished freedom of research and scientific education, but at the same contained more explicit demands for those who have received education to serve their country (ibid).

Overall, the higher education structure in Finland has been in a state of transformation for the last hundred years. Until 1908, there was only one university in Finland, which had been transferred from Turku to Helsinki in 1828. It was renamed from the Imperial Alexander University to the University of Helsinki in 1919, and in the beginning of its academic history had philosophical, theological, judicial and medical faculties (Leino-Kaukiainen and Heikkinen, 2011). In 1908, the Polytechnic School was promoted as the University of Technology, meanwhile higher education became, for the first time, an integral part of Finnish industrial and commercial policy (Ikonen, 2011; see also Niiniluoto, 2015).

Since the Second World War, the development of higher education apparatus in Finland, along with other Western countries, has experienced an era of substantial expansion and massification (Välimaa, 2001; Nevala and Rinne, 2012). On the whole, the expansion and massification of the higher education apparatus has changed its societal position and significance, not only because of the number of students who study in these institutions (according to the Ministry of Education (2004) around 65% of particular age group is offered an opening in the Finnish higher education system), or the number of faculties, but also because of the increasing costs these institutions require to function, and the results they are expected to deliver. Thus, it can be argued that higher education has moved from the periphery to the core of society, and that Finland has become an education state in the post-war years (Nevala and Rinne, 2012).

To highlight this transition, in the beginning of 1950s there were three universities (the University of Helsinki, the University of Turku and Åbo Academy) and eight other higher education institutions in Finland (Ikonen, 2011). In contrast, at the beginning of the 2000s, the Finnish higher education apparatus consisted of ten multi-faculty universities, three universities of technology, three schools of economics and business administration, four art academies, and 29 polytechnics (Opetusministeriö, 2004:6). As of 2015, after several national university mergers, there were 14 universities[25], of which 12 are public corporations and two foundations, and 26 polytechnics[26], of which 24 are private or municipal institutions.

Many Finnish universities were private at first and then nationalised; 1985 marks the year when all the universities of Finland were public. However, soon after the tide turned, at least in principle, towards favouring autonomy and strategic steering of universities (Kankaanpää, 2013). Nevala and Rinne (2012) argue that Finnish higher education apparatus was caught up with major external structural pressures to change its composition and orientation in the 1980s and 1990s. In many respects, the relationship between higher education and state remained the same during the post-war years. The relationship was based on an unspoken contract that higher education institutions would offer education to those who would qualify, and the state, in turn, would secure necessary funding for universities. The quality and orientation of higher education was steered internally, which gave

---

[25] http://www.minedu.fi/OPM/Koulutus/yliopistokoulutus/yliopistot/ ?lang=en, page visited 12.11.2015

[26] http://www.minedu.fi/OPM/Koulutus/ammattikorkeakoulutus / ammattikorkeakoulut/?lang=en, page visited 12.11.2015

it strong autonomy despite being part of the state apparatus. In the 1980s, the relationship between state and higher education, however, began to change again. As Nevala and Rinne (ibid) write, autonomy turned out to be only conditional and negotiable after all. The 'conditional autonomy' of higher education institutions would only materialise if a particular higher education institution would succeed in fulfilling the norms set by the Parliament and Ministry of Education (ibid).

In addition to globalisation, the most significant feature of Finnish higher education after the Second World War has been massification (Välimaa, 2001). Välimaa (ibid) asserts that four trends are to be found linked to massification: democratisation of higher education, equalisation, levelling of regional differences and the tradition of elite universities, which has also implied the differentiation of higher education institutions in Finland. Perhaps more importantly, education has always been considered as a national project in Finland, although the word 'national' has been understood differently in the course of time (ibid). Along with massification, Finnish higher education policy became state-led during the 1960s, 1970s and 1980s. The state took a notable role in the formulation of education policy, as universities were nationalised, and the formulation of education policy was centred upon the Ministry of Education (see e.g. Nevala, 1999; Rinne, 2010; Kauko, 2011). The 1980s are considered to be another turning point in Finnish national education policy, because this decade is marked by a period when transformation began from state regulation and control towards managing by results (see e.g. Tomperi, 2009; Nevala and Rinne, 2012; Niiniluoto, 2015).

Originally, changes in the Finnish political and economic landscape were inflicted by an economic downturn in the mid-1970s (see e.g. Kuisma, 2013; Yliaska, 2014). However, especially since the beginning of the 1980s, alternative international trends such as New Public Management (see Yliaska, 2014), which challenged the social democratic spirit, penetrated Finnish national policy, and thus, reform would no longer mean the extension of public governance, but instead competition and freedom to choose.

In any case, the ongoing restructuring of higher education in Finland is linked to wider set of social and economic restructurings that were triggered by a wide variety of factors such as the oil crisis of the 1970s, the end of the Cold War, the deep financial recession of the 1990s, European integration, and the international economic policy trends. Yliaska (2014), for example, portrays in his dissertation how the ideas of New Public Management penetrated into public government and eventually gave away to centralisation, commodification and marketisation of the public sector, starting from the late 1970s. Many prominent Finnish social scientists have also identified this change from state planning to market-based competition economy, or namely the change from the welfare state to the competition state (see e.g. Eräsaari, 2002; Kantola, 2002; Alasuutari, 2006; Heiskala and Luhtakallio, 2006; Julkunen, 2006; Patomäki, 2007; Kettunen, 2008; Mäkinen and Kourula, 2014). This political change has, in particular, indicated how the way of speaking or the orientation of the state changed during the 1980s, 1990s and 2000s. During this period, competitiveness became a central indicator of performance in the state economic and social policy (including higher education), though this does not necessarily imply that the economy, government, politics or values of the public would have come to the core penetrated by a 'competitive logic' (Heiskala and Luhtakallio, 2006).

Developing capitalist globalisation has entailed a situation, in which national, regional and local activities attempt to produce competitive locations and settings for economic actors, who compare national and local conditions for investments from a transnational perspective (Kettunen and Simola, 2012, 13). In this framework, knowledge, know-how, innovation and lifetime learning have been raised as the state's explicit goals to respond to these new challenges (ibid). Rinne (2004) has written that the transformation towards market orientation in higher education was exceptionally rapid and profound in Finland in the 1990s. To Rinne (ibid), the most important reasons were the massification of higher education, harsh economic recession, EU membership (1995), and turn to the right in politics. As a result, the new guiding principles of higher education included *'entrepreneurialism, managerialism, competition, funding by results, continuous assessment, Centre of Excellence policy, contracting and fighting for external funding'* (Rinne, 2004, 129). Consequently, the overall restructuring, Rinne (ibid) argues, was a reflection of more globalised and international changes concerning the role and functions of higher education, state and transnational organisations.

According to Patomäki (2007), the liberation of the financial markets started the neoliberal era in Finland in the beginning and mid-1980s. To be sure, it is difficult to draw a timeline for the spread of neoliberalism, since the majority of countries that have embraced neoliberalism, have done so only partially or in a unique manner (see Harvey, 2005). The Finnish context differs a great deal from the USA, the UK or even Sweden. Nevertheless, is has been argued that the neoliberal structural changes such as privatisation of public services and the deregulation of financial markets have had significant effects on institutions and institutional practices in Finland during the past three decades (Patomäki, 2007). At the same time, there has been a change in discourse and way of thinking in the public sector as public sector policies have, in general, shifted from resource-driven towards market-driven policies (Alasuutari, 2006). The changes in the policy-making level and in the mindset have meant that education is increasingly perceived as an instrument of competition but also that competition is perceived as an instrument of education (Kettunen and Simola, 2012, 15-16).

Another telling example regarding state education policy transformation from quantity to quality is that, if the catchphrase for education policy in the 1970s was *democratisation*, in the 1990s it was *innovation*. Research and development appropriations grew steadily in Finland in the 1980s, over 10% annually, which was the highest increase among the OECD nations (Kettunen et al., 2013). An important milestone in the course of this development was the foundation of Tekes (The Finnish Funding Agency for Innovation) in 1983. In addition, the newly founded (1986) governmental scientific and technology council (later science and innovation council) contributed to this development, which brought the concept of the *national innovation system* along with its policy outline. From the national innovation system's perspective, the institutions linked to working life, education and technology were, in particular, to be perceived and integrated from the point of view of global economic competition. This novel way of looking at things gained strength, while the Finnish economy went through a recession in 1990s (ibid). Kallunki et al. (2015) note that the notion of national innovation system was attached to the Finnish higher education policy in the mid-1990s, and consequently universities were attached as part of the 'national innovation system'. In education, the Ministry of Education's Development Plan published in 1995 stated that universities are part of the national innovation system, which is an essential foundation for the development of employment and the economy (ibid). From this moment forward, innovations and innovation policy would play a central role in Finnish higher education policy, as would the case for the concept of national innovation system that integrated education, economic and employment policy (Kallunki et al., 2015).

One of the goals of state's innovation policy has been to make Finland one of the world's leading economies based on education and the quality of the educational system (Kettunen et al., 2013). Accordingly, this has implied that universities and other higher education institutions were elevated to a key position, as it was in their responsibility to both educate the needed workforce and to produce research in order to facilitate the creation of innovations. The innovation policy in the Finnish context has also suggested that educational resources have been reallocated in a more 'efficient' manner to those areas of research where Finland possessed opportunities for 'top-notch' research that would bring a competitive advantage (ibid). As Välimaa and Hoffman (2008, 274) point out:

> The distinctive feature of the Finnish welfare state version of the knowledge society is the strong expectation that the state should play a key role between society and the market. The State acts as regulator via legislation, making it a flexible organiser of the development activities needed to reach the goals of a knowledge society.

The nation state in this case plays an active and significant role in bringing together researchers and companies in order to focus resources on economically strategic operations. It is also politically notable that, in Finland, the national research and innovation council, chaired by the Prime Minister, defines national strategies concerning research and innovation, in which higher education has a substantial role. In addition, it is also precisely in this context, that the role of contemporary higher education policy becomes important regarding the role of higher education (Välimaa and Hoffman, 2008).

Niiniluoto (2015) observes that, in the beginning of the 1980s, the 'pureness' of science was still protected from the corporate world in Finland. However, soon science was to be perceived as a means of production, or as a catalyst for economic growth, which is the foundation of knowledge and the knowledge-intensive economy[27]. Likewise, Kauppinen and Kaidesoja (2013, 13-14) explain that in Finland *'universities' role in society was construed in a new way in science policy: they were no longer seen mostly as promoters of democracy, welfare state and systematic social planning, but rather as sources of new technologies.'*

Therefore, Kauppinen and Kaidesoja (2013) also suggest that, since the beginning of the new millennium, there has been a qualitative shift towards academic capitalism in Finland. They argue that this is because the institutional conditions for 'academic entrepreneurship' were strongly facilitated, for example through technology transfer offices and changes in legislation (see also Kauppinen, 2012). One of these changes in legislation was *The Act on the Right to Inventions Made at Higher Education Institutions*, which institutionalised the ownership of intellectual property by universities, which in principle, means that researchers are identified in relation to invention activities as any other employee who is working for an employer (Kauppinen and Kaidesoja, 2013). The new status of academic workers closely reflects, in this case, developments that have occurred in the US context (see Slaughter and Leslie, 1997). Another even more significant change in legislation was the *Universities Act* (2009) that terminated universities' status as state organisations and faculties' status as civil servants (see Välimaa, 2012). As Slaughter and Cantwell (2012, 595) remark, because of the *Universities Act* universities in Finland:

---

27 This change in education policy and in discourse is well documented by Kankaanpää in her dissertation (2013).

must choose whether they will be public corporations or private foundations, the various choices conferring somewhat different autonomy from the state. Universities will continue to receive funds from the state for their statutory public duties, but levels of funding will depend on the quality and impact of their activities as well as on national education and science policy objectives. Universities will be able to apply for public research funding, as well as decide how to use revenues from their business ventures, donations, gifts as well as return on their capital.

The *University Act* also emphasises the need for promoting an 'entrepreneurial culture' in academia by increasing organisational autonomy and flexibility (Aarrevaara et al., 2009). Kettunen et al. (2013) have argued that the distinctive feature and explicitly stated goal of the university reform was a call for tighter connection between universities and industry and commercial bodies in order to maintain Finnish national competitiveness. Rinne (2010) in contrast argues that, along with the University Act, a new era has begun in Finnish higher education policy. By this, Rinne means that the neoliberal doctrine has been adapted to the national policy. A reflection of this doctrine is, according to him, a transformation from emphasising competition and cutting-edge research to the specialisation and positioning of individual institutions, a change, he argues, that will bind universities tighter to the 'national innovation system'. Other noteworthy changes in Finnish academia (see e.g. Rinne, 2004; Patomäki, 2007) in the 2000s include the implementation of a performance-related pay system (2006), the system of time management (2006) and systems regarding quality control (2004). Hence, Kauppinen and Kaidesoja (2013) argue that the managerialisation of Finnish universities has transformed administration of universities into the direction of management of private corporations (see also Välimaa, 2012).

Overall, it seems evident that the restructuring of Finnish higher education is poorly understood if it is studied only from a single nation state perspective or more generally by using a nation state-centric framework. Scholars such as Rinne (2004), Välimaa and Hoffman (2008), and Kauppinen (2012) have argued that transformation in Finnish higher education are closely linked to the development of supranational higher education policy in continental Europe (e.g. Bologna Process) and the EU's competitiveness policy (e.g. Lisbon Agenda), but also the OECD's policy suggestions (see also Kauppinen and Kaidesoja, 2013). In particular, the importance of the Bologna Process (a procedure to ensure the comparability of standards and quality of higher education qualifications in Europe), as pointed out by Välimaa and Hoffman (2008), is that is simultaneously influences several levels of European higher education. As Välimaa and Hoffman (ibid, 276) explain:

> National higher education policy makers aim to implement the reform at the system level, higher education institutions are developing institutional policies to implement the Bologna Process and individual academics are occupied with the requirements of adapting curricula changes which can accommodate the idea of two cycles of degrees

Moreover, issues such as, the EU's aim to become the most competitive knowledge-based economy in the world have been translated in Finland into policies aiming to increase the country's competitiveness in the global knowledge economy. In addition to this, increased global competition has been used as one of the ways to legitimate Finnish higher education reforms (see Rinne, 2004; Välimaa, 2012). Thus, because of the ongoing higher education reform, it has been argued that Finnish higher education is becoming more and more EU- and OECD-like, rather than being national or Nordic (Rinne, 2004). However, and as Kauppinen

(2013) states, while it is important to analyse national university reforms in relation to international politics and political trends, it is still plausible to speak of national university structures, and furthermore to argue that nation states are still important in legitimising and resourcing these reforms. Whereas the national economy has become less relevant as a concept, the nation state still has important functions in respect to the economy, and thus, capitalist globalisation has, by no means, indicated a separation between state and capital. In this respect, the nation state is a site of an ongoing class struggle but also a site of struggle between transnational and national capitalist classes, which try to influence and to regulate it for their benefit (Kauppinen, 2013).

Higher education's contribution to the reproduction of capitalism and ecological crisis: introduction to empirical illustration

The choice to illustrate how higher education is expected to contribute to the reproduction of capitalism, from the Finnish state's perspective, is to provide more solid grounds to the main argument of this book, which is in short:

> One of the primary purposes of 21st century higher education is to reproduce capitalism, and being that higher education is organised in an ecologically unsustainable manner.

One has to be clear on what is really meant by the state's perspective in this case? Quite simply, the state's perspective means here that the aim is to illustrate how the documents, which originate from the state administration, express the overall orientation and purpose of higher education, and then conclude how this is linked to the reproduction of capitalism and ecological crisis. I am aware that the state is not a uniform entity – the state is not a thing, but a (contested) social relation, as presented based on Gramsci's and Poulantzas' remarks. While this is undoubtedly true, it is at the same time clear that the state does not remain impartial, but is defined by the dominating classes and their class ideology, which equals to specific state ideology on a specific time and place. Although the documents that originate from state administration do not have a uniform definition, portrayal or purpose of higher education, there can nonetheless be found to be a dominant way of expressing the purpose and orientation of higher education. This dominating expression can be considered to represent the state's overall portrayal or condensation of higher education. Furthermore, I have decided to use the state's perspective because I consider that the state is an integral element in both the reproduction of capitalism and also for the sake of overall higher education (in Finland). For instance, it is seemingly clear that, in Finland, the state is the most prominent body that steers higher education through legislation and policy (see also Rekilä, 2006), as well as the primary funding body of higher education (Niiniluoto, 2015).

One of the primary ways to communicate the state's expectations and aims concerning higher education is through higher education policy documents (Ranson, 1995). From the state's perspective, policy documents have a specific and formal purpose in codifying the values for future reforms (ibid). Thus, policy documents can be considered one of the main ways to steer education, in addition to various performance criteria, from the state's perspective. As Brand (2013, 431) argues, *'the concept of public policy needs to be developed in conjunction with other concepts, i.e. a sophisticated understanding of the state'*. This means, according to him, (ibid) that state policy should be seen primarily as a mechanism for structuring policy, rather than being a problem solving instrument. Therefore, state policy can be seen as a manifestation and condensation, although contested and based on unstable compromises (Brand, 2013), of the state's portrayal and ideal of a particular matter (such as higher education).

This portrayal of state and state policy is very much in line with the overall theoretical and philosophical foundations of this book. We might recall a certain quote by Marx in Chapter 2, where Marx and Engel's materialist conception of history (ontological and epistemo-logical stance) or in this case rather historical materialism (method of study upholding the ontological and epistemological stance of the materialist conception of history) was also briefly outlined. To repeat the quote from before, Marx (1979, 103) wrote in *The Eighteen Broodmare of Louis Bonaparte:*

> Men make their own history, but they do not make it just as they please; they do not make it under circumstances chosen by themselves, but under the circumstances directly encountered, given and transmitted from the past.

In short, humans 'inherit' natural, socio-cultural and material conditions from the past generations of human and non-human beings. In more elaborate terms, Marx and Engels (1998, 61-62) write in *The German Ideology* that:

> history does not end by being resolved into 'self-consciousness' as 'spirit of the spirit', but that in it at each stage there is found a material result: a sum of productive forces, an historically created relation of individuals to nature and to one another, which is handed down to each generation from its predecessor; a mass of productive forces, capital funds and conditions, which, on the one hand, is indeed modified by the new generation, but also on the other prescribes for it its conditions of life and gives it a definite development, a special character. It shows that circumstances make men just as much as men make circumstances.

From these rather broad statements, one can take note that the state and state policy is always a cumulation as well as an embodiment of particular historical circumstances and struggles, as Brand (2013) also argues. The political and material situation today may be something else tomorrow, but the situation is nevertheless conditioned by the historical legacy and prevailing natural and socio-cultural circumstances. Moreover, the type of state and state policy in a particular moment in history, according to Marx and Engels and many Marxists after them, is considered to be a manifestation and condensation of the dominant class's values and ideals, although it is, at the same time, clear that the situation has been and remains to be constested and conditioned by the ongoing political and class struggle (Marx and Engels, 1998; Poulantzas, 1978; 2000).

Accordingly, educational policy is to be considered as a culmination of historical choices made in the past that manifest and take a particular form as they become entwined with today's societal circumstances, as well as reflecting dominating ideas, social dynamics and relations that influence the contemporary and inherited socio-political reality. By perceiving educational policy documents from this perspective, we are also able to witness the materiality and historicity of these documents, but also, and more importantly, their nature as representations of dominant ideas, social relations and dynamics of a given time and place. Therefore, it is possible to argue that the state indeed perceives education in a particular fashion, although it is, also clear that this is only one of the state's many perceptions concerning education, albeit the dominant one. Moreover, it is possible to attach this dominant perception to a wider socio-political frame and contemplate how this perception is linked to the reproduction of capitalism, for instance.

The education policy documents used in the empirical illustration consist of a total of 51 documents[28] (approx. 3200 pages), and three websites from the beginning of 2000 to the end of 2015. They include:

- 4 government platforms (Vanhanen, 2003; 2007; Katainen, 2011; Sipilä, 2015)

---

28   All the documents are listed in the end of the references section.

- 2 Council of State's principle decisions (*periaatepäätös*)
- 36 reports and accounts published by the Ministry of Education (*Opetusministeriö*)
- 5 Research and innovation council reports and definitions of innovation policy
- 4 other documents (three passed laws, and one 'core initiative' from Prime Minister's Office)

The documents were primarily retrieved from the Ministry of Education and Culture's web page (except the passed laws, and the core initiative). In the Finnish Ministry of Education and Culture's web page, there is the opportunity to search for publications (*Julkaisuhaku*) by year. On a yearly basis (2000-2015) I collected documents of relevance in terms of education policy, that is, I gathered the documents that dealt with matters regarding education and education policy. This procedure gave me a total of 70 documents. The number of documents was then reduced to 47 (plus three laws and one core initiative) based on the relevancy of the documents in terms of education policy. I chose to use the 51 education policy documents because I contend that they reflect the overall views and ideas of Finnish education policy and portray the general expectations, demands and aims from the state's perspective concerning higher education. The content of those 51 documents is diverse, as is the style and tone of the text. Some of the documents are strict policy documents, and some are more informal reports. Some of the documents target small details, as some of the documents try to define general lines of future education and education policy, for instance. Yet, and somewhat surprisingly to me, the treatment of the purpose of higher education is quite unanimous. Disregarding the documents' purpose and style, it is clear that economic issues dominate the education policy documents (see table 3)[29].

Words such as *economy* and *economic* (*talous, taloudellinen*), as well as *economic growth* (*talouskasvu*), *competitiveness* (*kilpailukyky*), and *innovation* are frequently repeated in the majority of the 51 documents. In contrast, words like *all-round education* (sivistys, yleissivistys), *well-being* (hyvinvointi), *nature/environment* (luonto, ympäristö) are considerably less frequently used to portray the overall purpose of education. Overall, issues regarding innovation, economic 'development', growth, and competitiveness are dealt with rather consistently throughout the fifteen-year period, as can be noticed also from the table. The financial crisis that began in 2008 seemed to entail some changes in the content of the state's education policy. During the years 2009-2015, the emphasis on the cooperation between the private sector and educational institutions seems to increase, as well as the demand to strengthen the production of innovations, competitiveness, the internationalisation of education, the focus on employment and, in general, suitable economic development. At the same time, 'softer' aims regarding education, such as all-round education (yleissivistys), well-being and sustainable development seem to appear in the documents less frequently.

There are two documents that explicitly deal with sustainable development in education – *Education for Sustainable Development* (Opetusministeriö, 2002), and *Towards Sustainable Development in Higher Education – Reflections* (Opetusministeriö, 2007) – but in other documents the treatment of sustainable development as a purpose of education and educational policy remains marginalised. Meanwhile, when the term sustainable development is used, aside from the two mentioned reports, it is generally used to mean sustainable economic and social development, while sustainable

---

29 This kind of table is merely an approximate description of the content of the education policy documents, although the table in this case quite accurately testifies on the manner in which economic issues dominate the policy documents.

Table 3. Key word count

Year	2000	2001	2002	2003	2004	2005	2006	2007	2008	2009	2010	2011	2012	2013	2014	2015	Sum
No. of documents	1	1	2	3	2	2	3	6	7	5	3	3	2	1	5	5	51
Pages	59	51	145	152	99	43	174	644	335	247	93	277	172	34	183	502	3210
Economy, economic	52	6	53	153	21	5	67	890	114	61	103	305	153	1	135	489	2608
Economic growth	81	1	1	89	6	0	14	80	57	12	93	160	8	0	114	309	1025
Competitiveness	15	2	12	46	15	8	14	89	41	19	43	56	28	0	32	76	496
Innovation/-system	128	3	8	255	31	16	24	211	204	65	160	58	17	0	116	320	1616
Business	29	23	20	84	17	8	16	464	46	26	47	34	30	0	49	237	1130
Jobs	6	4	6	20	13	0	9	31	10	6	14	80	5	0	64	73	341
Wellbeing	6	1	3	21	12	1	29	35	10	10	44	48	16	0	48	106	390
All-round education	9	0	6	8	15	0	34	26	30	15	11	16	15	0	3	33	221
Nature, environment	5	2	83	15	6	1	3	248	3	0	4	32	0	0	4	19	425

ecological development is rarely mentioned.

In the next chapters, my aim is to present the quality of the documents in more detail, as it was only briefly portrayed here. To be sure, the primary aim is to illustrate how the purpose of higher education is expressed from the state's perspective, and to conclude how this portrayal is linked to the reproduction of capitalism. I begin by illustrating the link between higher education and the so-called Finnish national innovation system. I subsequently discuss the general purposes of higher education from the state's perspective, before going deeper into the more instrumental and utility-based perspectives concerning higher education. In the 'factory' -subchapters, I depict how the state perceives higher education as a factory-like institution – as I call it – that is expected to deliver certain predetermined outcomes. Finally, I bring the sub-themes together and discuss the state's view concerning the restructuring of the global economy and regional competitiveness, before I draw general conclusions on the Finnish higher educational context and ecological crisis.

National innovation system

A report by state's Science and Technology Council (Valtion tiede- ja teknologianeuvosto, 2000, 5) notes that since the year 1990 Science and Technology Council has perceived the advancement of science, technology and innovations from the perspective of *national innovation system*. The report argues (ibid, trans. mine)[30]:
'National innovation system is a field of interaction of knowledge and know-how, which is founded on cooperation of the all the creators and users of knowledge. The development of the innovation system has strongly relied upon the good cooperation of public and private sector.'
In the report (ibid) it is concluded that because of global trends

---

30 In these chapters, I often use direct quotes from the public policy documents, which I have personally translated from Finnish. When the translation is mine I have marked it accordingly (trans. mine).

the role of a functioning and efficient national innovation system and regional systems will be emphasised as a provider of economic growth and social well-being.

Another report from the state's Science and Technology Council (Valtion tiede- ja teknologianeuvosto, 2003, 35) suggests that Finnish strengths are mostly self-created. These include the education and research system, a knowledgeable workforce and strong basic societal structures. However, the globalisation of markets and of economic and technological development have challenged national structures to international competition.

Research.fi is a website produced by a group whose members include representatives from the Ministry of Education and Culture, the Academy of Finland, the Finnish Funding Agency for Technology and Innovation (Tekes), the Committee for Public Information in Finland, Statistics Finland, Ministry of Employment and the Economy and CSC – IT Centre for Science. According to the website[31]:

> Finland has a whole national innovation system, which comprises several independent actors involving research and innovation activities. Its central activities include education, research and product development as well as knowledge-intensive business activities.
>
> The actors can be divided into those who create, utilise and facilitate a new innovation. Creative actors are, for example, universities and higher learning institutions, research institutes and businesses. Utilisers include businesses, private citizens as well as an increasing number of public service providers and decision makers. The actors who facilitate new innovations set the administrative framework and resources. The most important facilitators include the Finnish

---

31   http://www.research.fi/en/finnish-strategy-and-policy-guidelines/innovation-system, page visited 7.12.2015

Government and Parliament, the ministries and research funders. The actors may have different roles, depending on the situation.

The task of research, education and innovation policy is to see that the system is balanced in its development, its internal cooperation works and the actors' roles are clear and that it answers to the changing needs of society. Knowledge and skills are essential requirements of the sustainable development and competitiveness of society, and as a result, cooperative relationships with other sectors, such as economic, industrial, labour market, environmental and regional policies as well as social and health care are essential.

- The framework and grounds for a functional innovation system are:
- a working labour market
- a comprehensive and efficient research and educational system
- legislation supportive of the utilisation of intellectual property rights
- legislation favourable of business activities
- trustworthy fundamental institutions in society

According to the Development Plan of Education (Opetusministeriö, 2004:6, 45, trans. mine) for the years 2003-2008, *'higher education institution forms an extensive regional foundation for national innovation system.'* The same report (ibid, 46), asserts that science and research create the foundation for operations of different societal sectors, as well as for economic, technological and social innovations. The national innovation system is based on the active interaction between different actors, and on the knowledge and know-how produced by higher education institutions and to its effective utilisation (ibid).

The following statement is found from the government platform of Prime Minister Vanhanen's second government (Valtioneuvoston kanslia, 2007, 49) as well as from the report Higher Education Institutions (*Korkeakoulut, 2007*, Opetusministeriö, 2008:30, 8). In these reports, it is stated that, in the government platform, a target has been set to develop Finland as the best innovation system in the world. In addition, in the *Yliopistot 2006* (Opetusministeriö, 2007:17, 49) report it is specified that, behind the ongoing higher education reform, is an ambition to consolidate the quality and impressiveness of Finnish research and teaching.

In general, within the period (2000-2015) the role of the national innovation system, including the role of its components, is perceived in a largely consistent manner. In 2014, the Research and Technology Council (before 2008 state's Science and Technology Council) argues in its report *Uudistuva Suomi: Tutkimus ja Innovaatiopolitiikan suunta 2015-2020* (Tutkimus ja innovaationeuvosto, 2014, 12) that a high-quality education system, good quality scientific research, and application and combination of technologies, as well as a desire for growth and to produce innovation that responds to needs, are needed. This entails encounters, multilateral choices, and cooperation from higher education institutions, research institutes, working life, industrial and commercial bodies, and the arts.

The role of the state, in the national innovation system is also perceived consistently. The state's Science and Technology Council (Valtion tiede- ja teknologianeuvosto, 2000, 6) notes that, from the perspective of a knowledge-intensive economy, the objective of the public sector is the maintenance and creation of stable macroeconomic and pro-innovation operational environment. The report (ibid) states also that the objective of the public sector is to maintain and develop such regulative and administrative structures that encourage innovative activities. This objective includes, among other things, education, research and development, and its public funding, as it does the development of financial markets to promote innovations and other means that support structural change. In addition, the report (Valtion tiede- ja teknologianeuvosto, 2000, 6, trans. mine) notes that:

> The availability of a well-educated workforce that possesses the needed know-how, the accumulation of intellectual capital, norms and standards, international rules, circumstances of competition, and a positive atmosphere for businesses, are areas in which companies need the operations of the public sector.

In general, the nurturing of intellectual capabilities and the growth of the overall knowledge base are the core functions of the public sector (Valtion tiede- ja teknologianuvosto, 2000, 20). This statement is reiterated in the State Council's Education Policy Report (Opetusministeriö, 2006:24, 19). The report notes that, in an open economy, the purpose of the public sector is to secure a sufficient knowledge base, and thus promote existing business activities, the development of entirely new entrepreneurship, and investments that are important for the sake of growth.

Education and research are not only combined with innovations to support favourable conditions for businesses but also to support sustainable well-being, competitiveness, creativity and education of citizens in the Research and Technology Council's report of 2008 (Valtion tiede- ja teknologianeuvosto, 2008, 17). Moreover, it is argued that the object of state government is to manage the structures and finance in such a way that these goals could be achieved. On similar lines, in 2014, the Research and Technology Council (Tutkimus- ja innovaationeuvosto, 2014, 12) notes that the public sector is primarily responsible for prerequisites of the operational environment (education that produces quality workforce, functionality of markets, statute environment, taxation). The same report (ibid) argues that Finland has to be an attractive location for research and innovation activities, and that the public sector takes care of the operational environment for research and innovation and guarantees conditions for new research, innovation openings, and growth. In addition, the public sector speeds up innovation, creates demand and supports the development of markets and companies (ibid, 2014, 22).

In brief, higher education is perceived from the perspective of the national innovation system as an 'outlet' of a knowledgeable and well educated workforce, meanwhile higher education is considered a facilitator and producer of innovations as an important component of the national innovation system. In contrast, state's responsibility from the perspective of national innovation system is among others to guarantee suitable operational environment, and a favourable atmosphere for business and innovation.

Higher education from the state's perspective

Based on the studied education policy documents, the purpose and role of higher education from the state's perspective is not unambiguous in Finland. However, it is also clear, based on the documents, that economic questions and aims dominate Finnish education policy in the 21st century (see also Kauko, 2011; Kankaanpää, 2013; Kallunki et al., 2015). Other missions, such as equality, active citizenship, well-being, sustainable development, and education as such, are present in education policy documents but they seem to appear merely as footnotes or aims that can be achieved by first fulfilling certain economic aims. These economic aims include a good employment level, competitiveness, economic growth, and productivity, through which higher education is portrayed, for instance, as an investment for the future, or as a source of competitive advantage from the state's perspective.

The government platform of Prime Minister Matti Vanhanen

(Valtioneuvoston kanslia, 2003, 23) argues that Finland, as an education society, is founded on know-how, knowledge and creativity, and education promotes cultural rights (*sivistyksellisiä oikeuksia*) and active citizenship. The Development Plan for Education (Opetusministeriö, 2004:6, 3) stresses the importance of educating the whole age group, as well as the utilisation of all talent reserves, and improving the possibilities for education concerning the adult workforce. The State Council's Decision in Principle (Valtioneuvosto, 7.4.2005, 1-2, trans. mine), in contrast, gives a more precise and holistic account of Finnish education policy:

> Finnish national objective is a sustainable and balanced social and economic development. Good employment, productivity and competitiveness are the key factors. In this development, determined intensification of the exploitation of research and technological development and their results play a crucial role. [...] The aim of the development of university institutions is, in all respects, a high-level university system, which is internationally first-class and operates in Finland's strong areas, and in which the internal ability for renewal and adaption continuously generates new research and research initiatives. Polytechnics will be developed as regional forces defined by their specific aims and by the practical needs of companies.

The Education and Research report (Opetusministeriö, 2006:8) is even more explicit regarding competitiveness but also international influences in Finnish education policy. It (ibid, 5, trans. mine) states that:

> In the Finnish education and science, the policy emphasis is on quality, efficiency, equality and the internationalism of science. The education and science policy promotes the competitiveness of the Finnish welfare society. Sustainable

economic development will continue to create the best opportunities to ensure the cultural, social and economic well-being of the nation. The basic lines of education and science policy are parallel to the European Union's Lisbon Strategy.

Notable here is how the word 'sustainable' is used to primarily refer to economic development. This kind of use of concept sustainable development was not atypical in the documents, as sustainable development was generally used to indicate economic and social development. However, there were two documents that contradict this observation. In both the *Education for Sustainable Development* (Opetusministeriö, 2002) and *Towards Sustainable Development in Higher Education – Reflections* (Opetusministeriö, 2007) reports, sustainable development is predominately used to refer to sustainable ecological development, although this does not mean that economic, social and cultural sustainability are also frequently mentioned. Although these two reports explicitly deal with matters regarding sustainable development, ultimately they seem to have had little impact on the Finnish education policy.

To return to the overall aims of state's education policy, aims concerning especially competitiveness, education as an investment, and economic growth are attached to education in the State Council's Education Policy Report (Opetusministeriö, 2006:24). The report notes that the equality of education possibilities forms the foundation of Finnish well-being and the country's competitiveness (ibid, 12), and that resources invested in education are an investment in the future (ibid, 13). Later, in the same report (ibid, 18-19, trans. mine), the importance of education and higher education is emphasised regarding economic growth and international competition:

> Education has a key role in how well Finland is able to maintain economic growth, competitiveness, innovation

and a high standard of living. In the future, the quality of education will be an increasingly important factor. A high level of know-how and education ensures the adaptability of the national economy in a rapidly changing world. In an era of increasingly fierce global competition, it is imperative that higher education and research are near the top international level, and that Finnish universities are at the forefront in the key areas regarding our national economy and societal development.

The government platform of Prime Minister Matti Vanhanen's second government (Valtioneuvoston kanslia, 2007, 28) states that the high education level of Finnish citizens, and the availability of good quality and free education are the foundation of the Finnish welfare society. The Development Plan for Education (Opetusministeriö, 2008:30, 39), based on the aims set out in the government platform, notes that the national strategy of Finland is the consolidation of the basis of know-how by reforming education, adding resources for research and development, and by enhancing their economic and societal applicability.

More specific aims and purposes regarding higher education are listed in Ministry of Education's report *Koulutus ja tiede Suomessa* (Opetusministeriö, 2008:24) in 2008. The report repeats the claim that investments in know-how and education are the best policies for the future, and that education has been a success factor for Finland, and its meaning in a global world is likely to increase (ibid, 4). Concerning higher education and higher education policy the report (ibid, 35, trans. mine) notes that:

> The Finnish higher education system consists of two complementary sectors: polytechnics and universities. Polytechnics train experts to serve working life, as well as engage in teaching and, in particular, regional development, by supporting research and development activities. Universities carry out scientific research and provide education based on

it, as well as doctoral education. The higher education policy aims to safeguard the educational needs of society as well as to produce enough highly skilled experts for the needs of industry and society at large.

In its definition of policy report, the state's Science and Technology Council (Valtion tiede- ja teknologianeuvosto, 2008, 7 trans. mine) present that the statement founded in the 2006 report is still valid concerning the Finnish national strategy. Again, it is noticeable how the concept 'sustainable' is used, as well as the way the 'environment' is seen as an 'instrument' to enhance the well-being of citizens:

> Finland's strategy is to ensure sustainable and balanced social and economic development. It continues to be valid to be able to combine the economic development of society and the environment for the enhancement of the well-being of citizens. A positive development is maintained alongside other factors through a good level of education of the population, as well as large-scale development and deployment of information and know-how.

In the 2008 (ibid, 7) report, the council supplements the previous report by stating that the execution of the national strategy, written above, is based on stable economic operational environment, high employment and productivity, as well as sound international competitiveness, and that the purpose of the Education, Research and Innovation policy (ERI policy) is to ensure the strategy and conditions for its execution. The council adds (ibid) that the education policy is an increasingly important part of this ensemble. Accordingly, Prime Minister Mari Kiviniemi states in the Research and Innovation Council's report (Tutkimus- ja innovaationeuvosto, 2010, 3) that investments in education and know-how are investments in the future and an integral part of the Finnish long-term strategy to ensure well-being and competitiveness. Prime Minister Kiviniemi also notes (ibid) that actions needed in education, research and innovation investments should yield good quality education, successful innovations and employment in growth enterprises. In addition, she (ibid) states that reforms could be considered successful if Finland is able to improve its position among the top countries regarding knowledge and know-how.

Prime Minister Katainen's government platform (Valtioneuvoston kanslia, 2011, 31) maintains that the purpose of the Finnish education and culture policy is to secure equal opportunities and rights to free and good quality education for all citizens, disregarding their origins, background or financial situation. The government platform (ibid) also states that the government's objective is to raise Finland as 'the most skilful nation' by the year 2020, and that the supply of education will be scaled to meet the educational needs and the needs of the job market in the long term. In addition, the government platform (ibid) states that the connections between education and working life will be strengthened, as well as the information of working life and entrepreneurial education, and information of the rights and responsibilities of citizens, employees, and entrepreneurs will be strengthened in all education levels.

In the *Korkeakoulut 2011* report, from the same year, (Opetus- ja kulttuuriministeriö, 2011:10, trans. mine), joint aims for universities and polytechnics[32] are listed. This time, sustainable ecological development is mentioned among other societal goals, yet, the latter piece of text explicitly stresses the foundational role of higher education institutions in the innovation system.

Universities and polytechnics contribute to the well-being of citizens and their education, as well as sustainable economic,

---

32 The same texts can be found in the Ministry of Education's report *Korkeakoulut 2009* (2009, 18).

cultural, ecological and social development. The operations of higher education institutions are of high quality, effective, ethical, and support the development of a multicultural society. (16)

Universities and polytechnics are the foundation of the innovation system. Higher education institutions function as active parts of society. Companies, working communities and authorities are interested in participating in the development of higher education and making use of their competence. (21)

In 2012 (Opetus- ja kulttuuriministeriö, 2012:1, 3), the Minister of Education, Jukka Gustafsson, presents, in the Development Plan of Education, that the main focus in developing the Finnish education system regards poverty, inequality and the alleviation of marginalisation, along with stabilising the public economy, sustainable economic growth, and strengthening employment and competitiveness. The most recent accounts concerning education policy are listed in the government platform of Prime Minister Sipilä (2015). According to this, the aims for Sipilä's term of office are (ibid, 17): modernisation of education environments, inclusive education, increased interaction between education and working life, increased quality and impressiveness of research and innovation activities, increased internationalisation of education, and dismantling the obstacles to education exports.

To conclude, it is clear that the state has numerous aims and various commitments regarding education and higher education. Meanwhile, it is also clear that education is perceived in an instrumental fashion from the state's perspective. That is to say that, from the state's perspective, higher education can be perceived as a factory-like institution that serves as a means to an end to achieve various but mostly economic goals such as national competitiveness, productivity, innovations, and stable economic and social development through economic growth, as is further concluded in the following sub-chapters.

Higher education as a factory-like institution vol. 1: skills, know-how, and employment

By the term 'factory-like institution', I mean an institution that is expected to produce certain instrumental and predetermined outcomes. According to the notion, which has partly arisen from the education policy documents and partly from the existing literature ('*Education* [...] *is not only a factory*', see Sotiris, 2012, 118), I argue here that education, and especially higher education, is perceived as a factory-like institution from the Finnish state's perspective that provides possibilities for employment, innovation, competitiveness and economic growth.

To this particular chapter, I have gathered excerpts to describe how the state's aims regarding skills, know-how and employment in higher education are pursued to enhance Finnish national competitiveness and to produce technological innovations. These educational outcomes are primarily to be achieved, from the state's perspective, by increasing the cooperation, interaction and connections between working life and education (see e.g. *Koulutus ja tutkimus Suomessa*, Opetusministeriö, 2004:6, 18; *Valtioneuvoston koulutuspoliittinen selonteko*, Opetusministeriö, 2006:24, 19; *Koulutus ja tutkimus Suomessa 2007-2012*, Opetusministeriö, 2008:9, 49-50; *Pääministeri Jyrki Kataisen hallituksen ohjelma*, Valtioneuvoston kanslia, 2011, 31; *Koulutus ja tutkimus vuosina 2011-2016: Kehittämissuunnitelma*, Opetus- ja kulttuuriministeriö, 2012:1, 12; *Pääministeri Juha Sipilän hallituksen ohjelma*, 2015, 17-18).

In the Education and Science in Finland report (Opetusministeriö, 2006:8, 31) it is argued that, as the economy is increasingly based on knowledge, the importance of universities and polytechnics as producers of economic growth, well-being and new employment is paramount. The State Council's Education Policy Report from the same year (Opetusministeriö, 2006:24, 10) notes that future challenges for Finnish society are the rapid changes in the international division of labour and in the open global economy, and thus, to be able to succeed, the level of know-how and productivity has to be improved in all areas of economic and business life. A little later, the report states (ibid, 15) that the rapid changes in working life and the increased demands of know-how, as well as advancement of innovation and development activities, entail close cooperation between the spheres of education and working life. In addition, the report argues (ibid, 19, trans. mine) that:

> Increasing human capital through education improves the absorption of new technologies and procedures and leads to increased productivity. A good general level of education is also necessary for the generation of domestic markets that utilise new technologies efficiently. A highly educated and skilled workforce that is capable of utilising and producing new technologies, has already been part of Finland's national know-how and growth of strategy for a long period of time.

In a similar fashion, in 2007, *Lisää liiketoimintaosaamista korkeakouluista* report (Opetusministeriö, 2007:38, 11) remarks that the importance of universities and polytechnics changes and increases as globalisation progresses, as the economy is increasingly based on knowledge and know-how. The report (ibid) concludes that higher education institutions are key producers of new knowledge, developers of innovation activities, moderators of new knowledge and educators of knowledgeable workforce. Along the same lines, the state's Science and Technology Council notes (Valtion tiede- ja teknologianeuvosto, 2008, 44, trans. mine) that:

> The population of Finland has a high level of education. When young adults enter working life, they have increasingly better knowledge, know-how and other basic skills. Through postgraduate, in-service training and adult education, these

capacities are developed further. This intellectual capital also has to be increased in the future to enhance citizens' abilities to undertake creative and innovative activities. In addition to quantitative development, it is essential to target actions at different levels, so that the compatibility of education and working life improves.

Concerning employment, skills, and know-how, in the Ministry of Education and Culture's *Kansallisen osaamisperustan vahvistaminen: Johtopäätöksiä* report (Opetus- ja kulttuuriministeriö, 2014:19, 11) it is stated that:

> Finland should continue to strive for high productivity and a high employment rate, through which good international competitiveness and individual well-being are to be accomplished. A strategy based on high level of education and know-how seems necessary to achieve this goal, because the skills required in citizens' working lives seem to continue to grow. In the world of rapid technological development, there is also a major social risk if the skills and know-how of the population does not enable the development of working tasks that demand high-level know-how, and thus limit economic growth.

Even more explicit accounts from the state's perspective regarding cooperation, interaction and connection between education and working life are to be found from the education policy documents concerning entrepreneurial education. The Development Plan for Education (Opetusministeriö, 2004:6, 16) argues that new entrepreneurship is needed to sustain the level of services of the welfare society, and that an entrepreneurial education that penetrates the whole education system, along with a positive attitude towards entrepreneurship, create the foundation for entrepreneurship. The report (ibid) concludes that entrepreneurship is supported by enhancing interaction between education and working life, improving the knowledge of teachers and study counsellors on entrepreneurship, as well as developing content and methods in teaching in levels of education.

In the Development Plan for Education (Opetusministeriö, 2008:9, 49) it is stated that the role of companies and entrepreneurship as providers of economic growth and employment increases, and that promoting entrepreneurship entails diversifying and expansion of entrepreneurial education, as well as consolidating entrepreneurial education. The report (ibid, 50, trans. mine) also states aims concerning higher education and entrepreneurship:

> The interaction between higher education institutions and working life has been strengthened. The aim is that, during their studies, students can already become oriented to their working tasks, and that the future skills required in working life can be adequately anticipated in the content of education, as the research and development projects between universities and working life create a foundation for this. Those who graduate from higher education institutions are activated to become entrepreneurs.

In 2009, in *Yrittäjäkasvatuksen suuntaviivat* report (trans: *The guidelines for entrepreneurial education*, Opetusministeriö, 2009:7, 23, trans. mine) the aims for higher education regarding entrepreneurial education are stated as follows:

> Higher education's role in promoting entrepreneurship involves strengthening entrepreneurial attitudes, the generation of potential innovations, supporting entrepreneurial activities that are founded on the skills and know-how acquired in higher education institutions, as well as promoting growth entrepreneurship. [...] In addition, the role of universities in supporting growth entrepreneurship, the internationalisation of business activities, and in knowledge and innovation transfer will strengthen.

Finally, and to conclude this chapter, *Osaamisella ja luovuudella hyvinvointia* (trans. *Well-being from know-how and creativity*) report (Opetus- ja kulttuuriministeriö, 2014:18, 11) notes that the vast changes that have occurred in demands regarding know-how, the ways of learning, and in learning environments (such as e-learning) have to be taken into consideration in the development of education. The report (ibid) lists that the increasingly important skills are analytical deduction, data acquisition and management, critical thinking, creative problem solving, entrepreneurial skills, as well as cooperation and communication skills.

Higher education as a factory-like institution vol. 2: competitiveness and innovations

Regarding competitiveness in particular, education is portrayed as a means to succeed in global economic competition (see e.g. Tutkimus ja innovaationeuvosto, 2010, 42), whereas the exploitation of research results is seen, among other concerns, as a means to expand the field of operations of higher educational institutions and academics (Valtion tiede- ja teknologianeuvosto, 2003, 36). In any sense, competitiveness and innovations, as the central targeted aims of Finnish education policy, are deeply interlinked, as they are seen as prerequisites for societal well-being and economic growth from the state's perspective. It is also important to note that the arguments concerning competitiveness and innovation are not only part of national rhetoric, but also inter- and transnational phenomena and trends as well, which is also noticeable in the education policy documents.

In *Yliopistot 2001* (Opetusministeriö, 2002, 4) report, it is noted that Finland's international competitiveness has been evaluated in a favourable fashion in numerous international assessments. The report states that the latest example of this is the World Economic Forum's account, which evaluated Finnish national competitiveness as number one in the world. According to the evaluation, strong areas of Finland were, among others, quality of education, level of research, and the cooperation of universities and companies. Thus, the Ministry of Education's report (ibid) states that universities are the cornerstone of Finnish competitiveness. The report (ibid) notes that, internationally, the importance of universities regarding development, well-being and competitiveness has been brought forward recently. The following part of the report's statement is also repeated in next year's university report (*Yliopistot 2002*, Opetusministeriö, 2003, 4). These reports state that the EU's heads of state have set an agenda for a dynamic, knowledge-based economic region, and education and research has central importance in its execution. The 2002 report (*Yliopistot 2001*, Opetusministeriö, 2002, 4) also notes that European Ministers of Education have, in the Bologna Process, set joint targets for European higher education, and Finland is well on board in this development. Along the same lines, the next year's report (*Yliopistot 2002*, Ministry of Education, 2003, 4) states, concerning the execution of the joint targets, that the level of research, development and innovation activities have been evaluated in European countries, and in this evaluation Finland is right at the top of Europe and universities have had an essential role in this.

The state's Science and Technology Council (Valtion tiede- ja teknologianeuvosto, 2003, 17) concludes that universities' central role as facilitators of innovations will inevitably increase more and more, and this will happen both in education and in research. The council (ibid) notes that the guiding principle, of the cooperation between universities and business life, is to see that high quality and relevant knowledge and know-how is utilised more widely by all parties involved than has traditionally been seen. The state's Science and Technology Council (ibid, 36, trans. mine) further remarks that:

> The development and intensification of interaction between research and business are concrete signs of expanding the field of operations of universities, research institutes and polytechnics. The promotion of research results and their utilisation is already a basic task for all research organisations. From the perspective of companies, the basis for cooperation is the in-depth know-how of research organisations. A skilled research community is, in addition to produced knowledge, a vital resource for business life.

In the Development Plan for Education (Opetusministeriö, 2004:6, 18), it is noted that the preconditions for innovation are improved by investing in research areas that are important for Finland and by securing new growth industries, as well as by developing the education of research. In addition, the guidelines for cooperation of business and education are clarified, and the conditions for utilisation of the results of research are to be improved. The State Council's Definition of Principle notes (Valtioneuvosto, 2005, 1) that joint projects between higher education institutions, research organisations and companies will be increased, and infrastructure and other cooperation will be intensified to develop the activities of the research system, as well as the promotion of activities based on research and technological innovations.

A demand concerning the internationalisation of higher education is also well represented throughout the period (2000-2015), and is also closely connected to innovations and especially to competitiveness. For instance, the State Council's Education Policy Report (Opetusministeriö, 2006:24, 63) remarks that the internationalisation of higher education institutions is one of the core targets of education policy along with the aspiration to raise the level of education and research, and to improve the national basis for innovation through international cooperation. In the *Osaava ja luova Suomi* (trans. Skilled and creative Finland, Opetus-ja kulttuuriministeriö, 2010:15, 12, trans. mine) report, on the other hand, it is noted that:

> The globalising operating field of education, research, and the generation of new knowledge requires active and open-minded actors in Finland. Increased social networks, openness of society, and cultural changes have altered the situation for the Finnish research, development and innovation system. The transformed global environment requires the adoption of a new kind of knowledge and understanding and its use. Nationally produced knowledge must therefore be of top quality and interesting to be of prominent interest internationally. Research environments have to attract experts of high-level to Finland based on their quality, long lasting funding, and open culture.

Likewise, the Research and Innovation Council (Tutkimus- ja innovaationeuvosto, 2014, 6) suggest that raising the level of education and research is the key for the sake of sustainable competitiveness, and thus higher educational institutions are to be reformed by eliminating redundancies and by intensifying cooperation among research institutions and businesses. The council continues (ibid, trans. mine) by arguing that:

> The restructuring of universities must be promoted without delay. Universities must profile themselves globally in a visible way. [...] At the same time, internationally attractive centres of excellence are to be formed, and public and private development projects are executed to serve these joint development activities.

As shown, in these excerpts, the focus and aims behind the internationalisation demands of higher education and research are in taking care of, and guaranteeing, national competitiveness (see also *Korkeakoulujen kansainvälistymistrategia*, Opetusministeriö, 2009:21). In this sense, these statements are in line with the overall perception of the state regarding the source of Finnish national competitiveness. In a similar vein, the *Osaava ja luova Suomi* (Opetus- ja kulttuuriministeriö, 2010:15, 10) report notes that the central asset for competition for Finland is its exceptionally high-level of know-how, high level of value added in production, and rapid diffusion of innovations into production and services internationally. The pivotal role in sustaining and developing competitiveness is a world-class level of education and know-how (ibid). A report examining the internationalisation of higher education (*Korkeakoulujen kansainvälistymistrategia* 2009-2015, Opetusministeriö, 2009:21, 4) states that:

> The sustainable core of Finland's national strategy for success is investment in knowledge and know-how. International comparisons and assessments have shown that the high-quality education and research system is a major strength and competitive advantage for us. Higher education institutions have contributed positively to the renewal of society and to the development of economy and productivity. In a global operational environment, the importance of higher education is emphasised. The competition is based more and more, in addition to market positions and capital, on an educated workforce and resources of research. Production of new knowledge and know-how and their versatile utilisation are also the basis for our success in the future.

The Development Plan for Education (Opetus- ja kulttuuriministeriö, 2012:1, 7) notes that a central aim for the government is to raise the competitiveness of Finnish know-how. The report states also (ibid, 12) that Finland has already long based its international competitiveness on a high-level of know-how, as well as in higher education and in strong professional competence, and based on these, in innovation capabilities and in the rapid application of innovations in production. The report remarks (ibid, 46) that the research, development and innovation activities of universities and polytechnics are utilised in the promotion of diversification of the economic structure, in the promotion of creative economies and in new growth industries, such as environment and energy technology, in the promotion of development of new materials and natural resource industries, and in the reform of society's service structure, and in the promotion of sustainable growth.

In addition, in *Osaamisella ja luovuudella hyvinvointia* report (Opetus- ja kulttuuriministeriö, 2014:18, 13) it is argued that:

> Cutting-edge science and knowledge are prerequisites for the emergence of innovative companies in Finland, and that these companies are successful, and seek the most valuable expertise in the value chain in Finland, and that society develops and prospers. [...] The universities and polytechnics have an important role in the creation of appealing research, employment, and innovation environments, and in the foundation of international intellectual atmosphere and connections.

The current government's 'Lead initiative' no. 5 (*Kärkihanke*) concerning education and know-how (Valtioneuvoston kanslia, 2015, 10-11) seeks to improve the cooperation between higher education institutions and the business world in order to commercialise innovations. The lead initiative's objective is, according to the Prime Minister's office, to ensure that the resources of science and research are utilised in a more efficient and more influential manner, and commercialisation proceeds and research brings new growth to Finland (ibid).

Finally, another prominent example regarding the symbiosis of higher education, innovations and competitiveness, and how this is manifested in Finnish education policy, is the foundation of Aalto University (a merger of three higher education institutions: Helsinki School of Economics, Helsinki University of Science, and University of Art and Design 2009-2010). In a Ministry of Education report (*Teknillisen korkeakoulun, Helsingin kauppakorkeakoulun ja Taideteollisen korkeakoulun yhdistyminen uudeksi yliopistoksi*, 2007:16, 9, trans. mine) it is argued that:

> Finland's competitiveness generally requires not only a higher education system of high quality but also individual universities, whose research and teaching are at an internationally advanced level in the key areas, or very close to this level. As the investments in the development of universities have increased significantly and will continue to increase, both in Europe and the growing Asian economies, concrete solutions must also be rapidly implemented in Finland.

Before its foundation, Aalto University was characterised by several phrases which informed its function and vision. These include, among others, innovation institute (ibid, 6, 56), cutting-edge university (ibid, 13), and innovation university (*Korkeakoulutuksen rakenteellisen kehittämisen suuntaviivat vuosille* 2008-2011, Opetusministeriö, 2008, 10; *Talouspoliittinen ministeriövaliokunta*, Opetusministeriö, 10.4. 2008, 1). According to the Ministry of Education report (*Teknillisen korkeakoulun, Helsingin kauppakorkeakoulun ja Taideteollisen korkeakoulun yhdistyminen uudeksi yliopistoksi*, Opetusministeriö, 2007:16, 10) the specific mission of the new university is, with the help of high-level research and teaching, to support the success of Finland in the international economy. Aalto University's mission, as of late 2015[33], states that:

> Aalto University works towards a better world through top-quality research, interdisciplinary collaboration, pioneering education, surpassing traditional boundaries, and enabling renewal. The national mission of the university is to support Finland's success and contribute to Finnish society, its

---

33   http://www.aalto.fi/en/about/strategy/, page visited 16.12.2015

internationalisation and competitiveness, and to promote the welfare of its people.

State's expectations regarding higher education are quite clear in terms of competitiveness and innovations. Higher education is expected to enhance national competiveness and facilitate innovations to foster economic growth. While it is clear that higher education cannot be reduced to a mere factory, it is reasonable to argue here that, from the state's perspective, certain factory-like outcomes are expected.

Higher education as a factory-like institution vol. 3: education as a commodity

In contrast to know-how and competitiveness demands concerning higher education, the third, and last, 'factory' chapter deals with a phenomenon in which higher education is not only seen as an instrument from the state's perspective but as a commodity to be developed, commodified, and to be sold in the 'international education market' to foster capital accumulation and economic growth. This tendency is noticeable in the education policy documents and in the state's education policy, especially from the mid-2000s onwards. It is also to be noted, that it is not only educational services, but also scientific research (research outputs) that are to be commercialised and commodified (see e.g. Kauppinen, 2014).

In the State Council's Education Policy Report (Opetusministeriö, 2006:24, 12) it is stated that the high quality of education and research are supported by internationalisation. The report argues (ibid) that education, and especially higher education, should be developed as a new international area of business for Finland. In contrast, in the *Osaava ja luova Suomi* report (Opetus- ja kulttuuriministeriö, 2010:15, 7, trans. mine), it is noted that:

> The internationalisation of companies and the increased movement of qualified labour give birth to an international

labour market that promotes the development of the European and global educational market, the specialisation of universities, differentiation, and even cross-border structural alliances and mergers. The importance of education and skills exports grows more and more significant.

The most significant statement concerning higher education as a commodity is, in principle, the State Council's definition regarding education exports (Valtioneuvoston periaatepäätös 29.4.2010). The first sentence of the report (1, trans. mine) argues that:

> Education exports are part of the world trade in services. In policy definitions, education exports are widely considered as a sector that unites a wide range of industries […]. Finland's strengths are the competitive education system, and an excellent reputation thanks to good PISA results. Finnish know-how is subject to a significant demand, which, so far, has not been fully met.

The State Council's policy definition continues (ibid, 1), by noting that trade in education services is a growing international market, and because of this, education exportation offers a great deal of opportunities for Finland. Consequently, the State Council states that Finland is one of the leading education-based economies and testifies to the quality of the education system, and that the proportion of education exports from the total exports of Finland will increase significantly until the year 2015 (ibid). The State Council argues that functioning domestic markets are to be cultivated in order to be able to promote Finnish education exports. This means, according to the State Council, a strongly public-financed Finnish education system, securing research and innovation environments in the field of education, as well as developing expertise in public procurements, for instance in education technology and concerning other services in the field (ibid).

The State Council's Policy Definition Report (2010, 1) also mentions that, as part of the education exports, the exports of other business areas are also to be strengthened along with commodification. To foster cooperation, a business cluster is to be developed, which actively seeks new business opportunities (ibid). In addition, in the first page of the policy definition, it is stated that higher educational institutions have a central role in education exports, because they possess great export potential and the needed expertise. The report also states that, if well executed, education exports will diversify degrees or parts of the degrees, increase know-how, and operate as an element in the promotion of the internationalisation of higher education (ibid).

State Council's policy definition report concerning education exports (2010, 3) notes that educational know-how is one of the future Finnish export clusters. The importance of educational know-how increases as a part of the industrial products and service products, and it thus supports other export sectors. Because of the active educational know-how cluster, Finnish export companies can offer solutions to their customers, in which education and educational know-how belong as natural components (ibid). The report notes also that the success in the international education market requires a careful commodification, and that greater know-how and resources are needed in this respect (ibid, 5). Moreover, the State Council's report's strategic definition of policy states (ibid, 6-7, trans. mine) that:

> Higher education institutions have a key role in the export of educational know-how. Regulation concerning in-company higher education (*tilauskoulutus*) will be further developed so that higher education institutions are able to participate more flexibly in the education business. The expansion of internationally oriented fee-based activities would increase the possibilities for the education exports and the operational

resources of higher education institutions. Higher education institutions are encouraged to be active and to take a major role as actors in the education export industry.

The Research and Innovation Council's report (Tutkimus ja innovaationeuvosto, 2010, 46) responds to State Council's policy definition in a similar manner, stating that the main export product in the world is higher education degree. Thus, the legislation concerning higher education has to be changed to support educational exports (ibid, 47). The demand to promote educational exports is also to be found in Prime Minister Katainen's government platform (Valtioneuvoston kanslia, 2011, 31) and in the Development Plan for Education (Opetusministeriö, 2012:1, 50). In addition, in Prime Minister Sipilä's government platform (2015, 17), it is mentioned that the aim for this term of office, among others, is to increase the internationalisation of education and research and to bring down the obstacles to education exports.

Consequently, education is not merely a factory-like institution from the state's perspective, but rather a factory-manufactured commodity to be sold in the international education market to grow the Finnish economy and spark Finnish trade and commerce. Similarly, the good international reputation of the Finnish education system is to be capitalised, while a share of the growing international education market is to be secured. In this way, education is not solely an instrument to serve the needs of the economy (employment, know-how, innovations) and competitiveness, but a business or a commodity among other commodities to foster economic growth.

Transnationalisation and competitiveness as a region

To bring together the themes of this empirical illustration, a broader restructuring regarding the overall capitalist socio-economic structure is brought forward and coupled with the state's perspectives on higher education in this chapter. The restructuring concerns the role of the nation state in the global capitalist socio-economic structure, and of course, higher education's role in it. It is shown how the objective of Finnish state is to create an attractive operational environment for transnational capital, and also to enhance Finnish competitiveness as a region in the global capitalist economy.

The state's Science and Technology Council report (Valtion tiede- ja teknologianeuvosto, 2003, 1) states that a central future challenge for economic and societal development is to keep Finland sufficiently attractive for business, employment, and as an environment in general. The report also notes (ibid) that determined ambition to develop innovations cannot limit itself to only the national environment and traditional international cooperation, but internationalisation has to occur throughout the innovation system. The Development Plan for Education (Opetusministeriö, 2004:6, 12-13, trans. mine) remarks that:

> Economic globalisation stands for ever-deepening global division of labour and increasing competition. This entails changes in the structures of working life, professions and know-how demands. The mobility of labour is expected to increase with globalisation. These changes will also have an impact on the education system. Production and services are less and less tied to place, when the key means of production, labour and capital move around freely. Companies are located in the countries and regions which offer them the best and most favourable operating conditions. The development offers Finland opportunities, but also threats. There is a danger of a strong differentiation of regions, as well as clearer and clearer division of winners and marginalised individuals. On the other hand, it has to be considered as an opportunity from Finland's perspective that Finland does not compete with cheap production costs in the international market, but rather with a high-level of know-how and stable social

conditions.

The State Council's decision in principle (Valtioneuvosto, 2005, 1), argues that the internationalisation of education, research and innovation activities is the most central development target for the entire research system, and which will also be advanced by legislative means. Another account from the State Council (Opetusministeriö, 2006:24, 19) states that economic growth made the transition to an innovation and know-how centred stage in the 1990s. In the global economy, regions and countries compete from the location of knowledge centres and from the production activities attached to these (ibid). The way the production activities demanding high-level of know-how will locate in the future, is greatly dependent on the demand for a highly educated workforce, as well as on the basic material and social structure of the national economy (ibid).

In its 2008 report (Valtion tiede- ja teknologianeuvosto, 2008, 13) the state's Science and Technology Council repeats that the question is about Finland being an attractive business, working location, and place to live. The report (ibid) also states that this requires a joint understanding of the development needs and means from both the public and private sector to transfer Finland's strengths to a real competitive advantage.

In this sense and from the state's perspective, the aim, according to a Ministry of Education report (Koulutus ja tiede Suomessa, 2008:24, 5 trans. mine), of the higher education reform is clear. It states that *'we want that each and every Finnish university is better yet place to study, to teach, and conduct research. The aim is that Finnish universities produce knowledge that Finnish companies need, instead of retrieving that knowledge from abroad.'* Another report from the Ministry of Education (Korkeakoulut 2007, Opetusministeriö, 2008:30, 8) argues that the higher education reform is also a part of a broader ongoing modernisation process of higher education within the framework of the EU. For the sake of Finland, in central countries with advanced science systems, universities and higher education institutions are no longer developed as parts of the state administration, but instead from the perspective of advancing university teaching, research and innovation activities (ibid).

Higher education reform is seen as a counter measure to a looming decline in Finnish competitiveness. For instance, a Ministry of Education report (*Korkeakoulujen kansainvälistymisstrategia 2009-2015*, 2009:21, 5) argues that the attractiveness of Finland as a working environment for industrial production and high-tech, as well as for experts, is inadequate. Consequently, Finland's attractiveness as a business, working, and living environment has to be strengthened (ibid, 9). The report also adds (ibid), that the internationalisation of education, research, and innovation system is at the core of society's renewal. Another Ministry of Education report (*Korkeakoulut 2009*, 2009:49, 8) repeats the same threat concerning Finnish declining competitiveness by stating that there is a danger that Finnish higher education institutions and, more broadly, Finland as a model country in innovation policy, will lose its position as an internationally interesting partner in cooperation. Thus, the report (ibid, 8-9) argues that the aim of the internationalisation strategy of higher education institutions is to create a strong and attractive higher education and research community in Finland, which promotes society's ability to operate in the open international environment, supports the balanced development of a multicultural society and takes responsibility for solving global problems.

Finally, concerning regional competitiveness, attractiveness and higher education, a Research and Innovation Council report (Tutkimus- ja innovaationeuvosto, 2010, 21) remarks that, so far, the technological development and the possibilities of globalisation have been successfully utilised in Finland. The report (ibid) notes that a core question is how Finland is able to create strengths and factors of attraction (*vetovoimatekijöitä*), through which Finland is able to improve its position as an international actor. The report (ibid, 22) states also that the EU's 2020 strategic vision is intelligent, sustainable and inclusive growth, and that Finland has to make content choices according to the EU strategy. In this respect, Development Plan for Education (Opetus- ja kulttuuriministeriö, 2012:1, 43, trans. mine) argues that:

> The competitiveness of regions depends on their success in the global market. Resources are to be gathered together in regional centres of excellence, to define common strategic objectives for cooperation, and to agree on the mutual division of labour. Impressiveness is generated by improving the quality of education and research, and by making use of research and innovation know-how in business and working life.

Another Ministry of Education and Culture report (*Osaamisella ja luovuudella hyvinvointia*, 2014:18, 13, trans. mine) states that:

> Large science nations and markets attract, in addition to fixed investments, the best experts as well as research and innovation activities. Research is, in many fields, genuinely global. Due to the small size of Finland, it is important that the higher education system is competitive and of a high quality as a whole. Finland has the potential to invest only in a few areas in which research is world-class. However, these peaks are necessary. They open up access to global networks and attract experts and investments to Finland.

As a final remark, Prime Minister Stubb writes in the Research and Innovation Council's report (Tutkimus- ja innovaationeuvosto, 2014, 3) that Finland is not considered as attractive; the volume of foreign direct investments and international mobility is low. The Prime Minister's statement is repeated later in the report (ibid, 10) when it is noted that in spite of a world-class innovation system, high-quality research environments and other strengths, Finland has not been able to attract foreign know-how or capital.

Higher education and ecological crisis – the Finnish context conclusion

As Ranson (1995) argues, the task of theory, in the case of state policy documents, is to explain why public policy is as it is in a particular political context. In this sense, the starting point of the empirical illustration – the so-called national innovation system – is useful in understanding the overall orientation and purpose of higher education in Finland. Accordingly, especially higher education, is seen from the state's perspective as an integral component of the national innovation system, which is, above all, committed to facilitating national competitiveness and conditions for capital accumulation. Overall, in the empirical illustration, it was highlighted how the Finnish state perceives higher education in an instrumental fashion. Among other things, higher education was perceived as a provider of employment, competitiveness, and innovations to foster economic growth, and as a commodity and a business opportunity to be capitalised upon in the international education market.

Nevertheless, the state's instrumental take concerning higher education is not necessarily a new way of expressing the purpose of higher education, but is, in fact, a historical phenomenon that has arguably prevailed ever since the 'union' of universities and nation states was formed (see e.g. Kwiek, 2000; 2001). The situation has been much the same in Finland, as education and higher education have historically been perceived as means to succeed in international competition (Välimaa, 2001; Heikkinen and Leino-Kaukiainen, 2010). Yet, it is also apparent that the overall restructuring of capitalism has brought changes in the relationship between the nation state and higher education, as higher education in neoliberal capitalism is increasingly seen as a key factor in terms of knowledge production and innovation, which has arguably led to the increasing integration of higher education and capitalist markets (see e.g. Slaughter and Leslie, 1997; Slaughter and Rhoades, 2004; Cantwell and Kauppinen, 2014).

Considering the historical developments of the past decades, existing academic research, and the theoretical argument put forward, there are strong grounds to argue that one of the main purposes of contemporary higher education is to reproduce capitalism. Likewise, by submitting and by following the overall outlines of the state's education policy, as it was illustrated, it is evident that higher education institutions in Finland – some more than others – contribute to the reproduction of capitalism. In the Finnish context, higher education institutions are expected to educate students to become part of the capitalist economy but also are expected to contribute in other ways to foster capital accumulation and conditions for capital accumulation (innovations, public-private partnerships, business opportunities).

First, based on the Finnish education policy documents, it is clear that the Finnish state has commitments to the reproduction of the capitalist workforce. In the first 'factory' chapter, I illustrated how the state expresses the purpose of higher education in regard to skills, know-how, and employment. It was shown that the Finnish's state seeks to enhance its competitiveness in the global economy by increasing cooperation, interaction, and connections between working life and higher education. As it was reasoned in the Finnish education policy documents, the importance of universities and polytechnics is paramount in regard to economic growth, well-being, and employment because the world economy is increasingly based on knowledge. In this way, higher education is utilised, from state's point of view, to foster economic growth (to create jobs, innovations, business opportunities). If from the perspective of capitalist rationale this aim is understandable, from the perspective of overburdened ecosystems and future generations of life, this kind of policy-making can be argued to be destructive and irresponsible.

Second, in the competitiveness and innovations 'factory' chapter, I illustrated, among other things, how the exploitation of research results is seen by the state as means to expand the scope of operations of higher education institutions and academics. As Kauppinen and Kaidesoja (2013, 7) have identified, the beginning of the new millennium marks a period in Finland when a qualitative shift towards academic capitalism occurred. This was, they (ibid) claim, because *'institutional conditions for academic entrepreneurship were significantly facilitated particularly [...] through establishing technology transfer offices and enacting new national legislation'.* In a sense, Aalto University can be considered to reflect the academic capitalist ethos of Finnish higher education in the 21st century, for instance, when it comes to technology transfer. Aalto Innovation Services is Aalto University's technology transfer office. It says on its website[34],

> Innovation Services manages the university's patent portfolio with the goal to commercialize research done at Aalto University. The commercialization process enables researchers and students to turn their inventions and business ideas into startup companies or licensing opportunities.

Aalto Innovation Services's commercial approach to the exploitation of research results is explicit. On the website, it says:

> Aalto University files about 30 patent applications annually. Technologies developed at Aalto University are used by a number of varying global companies.
>
> Aalto University's licensable and salable patent portfolio

---

34   http://innovation.aalto.fi/about-us/, page visited 14.3.2017

covers five main categories:

> Chemistry & Materials, Computer Science & ICT, Energy & Cleantech, Engineering & Electronics, Medical Devices & Life Science.

More generally, from the state's perspective, it was illustrated how higher education is expected to deliver certain predetermined outcomes concerning knowledge production and facilitation of innovations in search of economic growth. Consequently, higher education is both expected to contribute and already contributing to processes of capital accumulation and economic growth.

Third, higher education contributes to the reproduction of capitalism and ecological crisis by commodifying education to foster economic growth. In the 'factory' chapter 'education as commodity', I illustrated how the Finnish state seeks new growth opportunities from the growing international education market. In this case, higher education is not only seen as an instrument to improve national and regional competitiveness but as a commodity to be sold in the market to increase revenue from exports. Perhaps the connection between capitalism and higher education is the most explicit the particular case that education is perceived as a commodity among other commodities. From the perspective of the ecological crisis, the revenue from selling educational services (no matter how immaterial they are) is likely to be used to foster further capital accumulation and economic growth opportunities, and, therefore, Jevons paradox and the absolute contradiction – between expansive socio-economic structure and finite planet – takes hold again.

As an overall summary of the Finnish context, and based on the arguments of this section, it is evident that the Finnish state's education policy legitimises and supports the reproduction of capitalism. As Rekilä (2006), for instance, has argued, the state in Finland still has the greatest influence on the overall operations of universities, even above capitalist markets and academia itself. By following the state's policy guidelines for education, higher educational institutions in Finland support and legitimise the capitalist relations of production and contribute to the operations targeting economic growth and capital accumulation. Because of this, it is argued that contemporary higher education in Finland is operating in an increasingly unsustainable basis from an ecological standpoint.

7

REPRODUCTION REVISITED
Conclusions

Marx and Marxism are often accused of perceiving everything through production and economy. This is, however, an inaccurate accusation. Rather, it is capitalism that makes everything about production and the economy, not Marx and Marxism (Eagleton, 2012, 123). The development of neoliberal capitalism should be considered a testament to this claim, as the sphere of the capitalist economy and rationale keeps on expanding to, for instance, basic infrastructure, public healthcare and education. Capitalism is a mode of production, in a narrow sense, because in capitalism there is production mainly for the sake of production (ibid), as it is capital accumulation for the sake of capital accumulation, which stands in a contradictory relation to its biophysical surroundings. This is, above all, because many natural resources on planet Earth are finite or that there is a limit to their sustainable use, whereas capitalism is premised on the infinite (Magdoff and Foster, 2011; Moore, 2015).

In this book have attempted to describe how socio-ideological structures (such as institutional higher education) are integral in reproducing capitalism. To illustrate this, I have made an effort to update a theory of (complex) reproduction of capitalism by complementing Louis Althusser's (2014) original theory. I have brought together the old sparring partners, Gramsci and Althusser, and tried to complement their arguments concerning state, power and ideology with the help of Nicos Poulantzas. The theoretical dispute between Gramsci and Althusser remains significant but it is reconcilable in some ways. Accordingly, the main task of the theoretical elaboration in this book has been to argue that we need both Althusser's and Gramsci's accounts on power and ideology to understand the reproduction of capitalism in the 21st century. This is also why the work of Poulantzas has been essential for this task. I have presented that Gramsci needs Althusser and Althusser needs Gramsci, because, on the one hand, the capitalist state, dominated by the bourgeois class, has a significant role in steering education and education policy and mediating the dominant ideology, but on the other, the dominant ideology remains ever contested. The state's role in providing conditions for capital accumulation has to be taken into consideration as Poulantzas has argued, and moreover, how the state's role has changed to promote regional conditions for capital accumulation along with the transnationalisation of capital (Robinson, 2014). There has happened a convergence and integration of nation states into global field of accumulation, where different nation states try to produce attractive environments for transnational capital to operate.

As presented, the capitalist socio-economic structure is reproduced by interplay between the capitalist mode of production and the so-called socio-ideological structures (see figure 3 overleaf).

In the capitalist mode of production the logic of capital and the characteristics of capitalism, including debt, interest, return on investment, market competition, and profit maximisation, push the capitalist structure towards expansion and regeneration. In addition, I have presented how the socio-ideological structures, which are not necessarily directly linked to material production, including nation state and its institutions, capitalist elites (transnational and national) as dominant classes and transnational organisations, support and protect the functioning of the capitalist mode of production. The common denominator and the driving force for the entire capitalist socio-economic structure is the hegemony of capital. The imperative for continuous and endless capital accumulation is the one thing that both creates common interests for economic actors in capitalism, but also influences their actions and choices.

I also argued that higher education and higher education institutions within the capitalist socio-economic structure reproduce capitalism by educating students to become part of the capitalist economy, but also by contributing other ways to foster capital accumulation or the conditions for capital accumulation (innovations, public-private partnerships, business opportunities), as well as taking part in the capital circulation process. Likewise, by contributing these 'inputs', contemporary higher education simultaneously reproduces, legitimates and indoctrinates the hegemonic capitalist relations of production and the dominant class ideology. Nonetheless, it is important to note that higher education is not only a factory. It is unmistakably true that contemporary higher education has multiple agendas and aims; yet, I argue that one of the primary purposes of contemporary higher education is to reproduce capitalism.

To understand why this might be so, let us bring the remarks of Gramsci, Althusser and Poulantzas regarding state, power, ideology and state apparatuses together one more time. As Gramsci (1971, 244) argues, the state is the complex of practical and theoretical activities with which the ruling class not only legitimates and maintains dominance but also attempts to win the consent of those it rules. In Gramsci's interpretation, the hegemony of the dominant classes is constantly contested, but in any case, the state

CONCLUSIONS

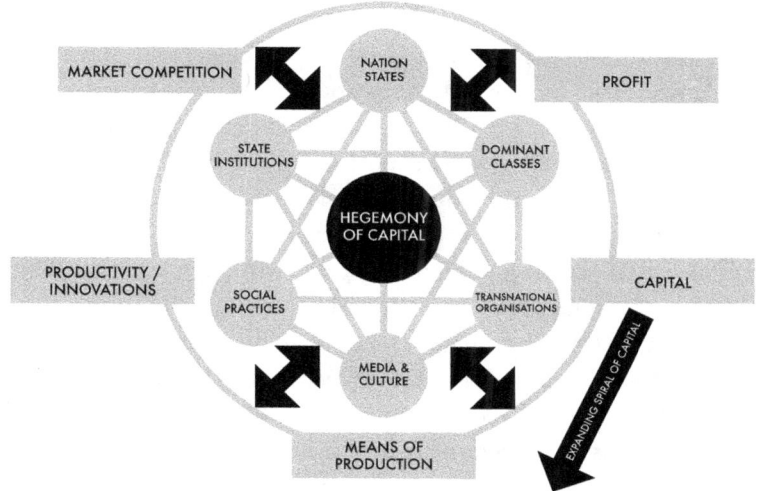

represents the dominant and prevailing ideology of the dominant classes. In this respect, the state is an organiser of the class hegemony, as Poulantzas (2000, 125-128) has argued. Althusser (2014) for his part, turned Gramsci's perception of the modern capitalist state into a more rigid presentation of state ideology and indoctrination, by presenting state institutions as means for the dominant classes to secure their domination. Here Poulantzas can be seen as a mediator. As Poulantzas (2000) argues, ideology involves material practices, but ideology is, at the same time, class-based, particularly concerning the dominating ideology, which is then passed on and reproduced in the state institutions. Regarding Althusser's perception of the capitalist state, Poulantzas rejects a simplistic conception of the state – an Althusserian state one could call it – that primarily concerns coercion and ideological indoctrination. On the contrary, Poulantzas emphasises the importance of the state as an organiser of class hegemony, but more importantly for the sake of the overall argument, its role in social and economic reproduction. Poulantzas' relational conception of the capitalist state offers, thus, a way of understanding how state institutions are determined by class struggle, and moreover, Poulantzas' take on the state does not deny class hegemony and its contested nature, or ideological indoctrination within state apparatuses, but puts them in a more dialectical framework, which also indicates, concerning the theory of reproduction, that there is room for both Gramsci's and Althusser's arguments.

The state is neither neutral or impartial. Although it is clear that the capitalist state does not simply mirror the 'needs of capital', it is at the same time clear that it indeed guarantees and supports the reproduction of capitalism through various material, repressive, as well as ideological means (Poulantzas, 2000; Althusser, 2014). Hence, and as an integral part of the state apparatus, education and higher education play an essential role in furthering the economic interests of the dominant classes (Carnoy, 1982; Dale, 1989), by providing students with certain ideology, skills, attitudes, and values (Althusser, 2014).

As Sotiris (2013) claims, the most recent restructuring of capitalism has brought higher education and capitalism closer together, as is also well established in the literature concerning academic capitalism (see e.g. Slaughter and Leslie, 1997; Slaughter and Rhoades, 2004; Cantwell and Kauppinen, 2014). Therefore, higher education can indeed be perceived as a hegemonic and ideological state apparatus. Consequently, from this perspective, higher education supports the reproduction of the capitalist class society and communicates the dominant class strategies, as well as fosters capital accumulation, and undermines the resistance of the subaltern classes (Sotiris, 2013).

Whereas it is true that we can generally grasp the essence of the present-day capitalist state and the class hegemony of the bourgeoisie through Gramsci's, Althusser's and Poulantzas' remarks, it is at the same time evident that the latest restructuring of capitalism, since the early 1970s, has also produced novel global power relations and hegemonies that arguably go beyond their analysis, at least to some extent, especially concerning the transnationalisation of capital and the restructuring of the global relations of production. For instance, considering the transformations of the modern world order, Robinson (2004; 2014) has argued that, as the world economy was suffering the economic crisis of the 1970s, capital went global by breaking free from territorially bound organised labour, and by developing new kinds of labour relations. One of the outcomes of this process has been that the leading groups among national capitalist classes interpenetrated across national borders through a wide repertoire of mechanisms and arrangements (Robinson, 2014). This up-and-coming transnational capitalist class operates across national borders in numerous countries, as its class power is anchored in global capitalist relations of production, particularly in its domination over the world's resources, i.e. the global means of production, as well as in global media and cultural industries (ibid).

Although it is true that Poulantzas (2000, 106) recognised the transnationalisation of capital and labour, he, meanwhile, insisted that the nation state is the primary agent to further the expansion of capital. Unmistakably, capital transcends national borders while shaping novel territories to its expansive purposes, but in this sense Poulantzas' argument concerning national imperialism (ibid, 106) regarding the movements of national capital seems to be incorrect in the contemporary global capitalist economy. As Robinson (2014) and Harvey (2014) have argued, it is not the modern nation state that has transnationalised capitalism, but the very logic of capital. More precisely, it is not a group of individuals within a single nation state that is holding the reins of the capitalist structure on a world scale, but as Robinson (2005) remarks, an emergent global capitalist historical bloc led by transnational capitalist class. In addition, as the movements of capital have globalised and transnationalised, global policy planning organisations have become vital elements for the transnational capitalist class to bring together transnational corporations, global governance institutions and policy planning organisations (Gill, 1995). In principle, international organisations, such as IMF, World Bank and WTO, work together with national states to reformulate global production processes, labour relations, and financial institutions to establish a global field of accumulation (Robinson, 2014, 7). The transnational capitalist class and its agents on their part make use of these international organisations, while these organisations organise the operations for the transnational capitalist class (ibid), an assertion that also can be considered to supplement the original analysis of Gramsci, Althusser and Poulantzas.

One of the prevailing contradictions in the global capitalist socio-economic structure seems to be that the nation state still possesses a great deal of political authority and legitimacy, especially in international forums (Robinson, 2014, 82). This is also to say that although the functions of the state have, in many ways, been restructured, the nation state is still a key institution especially concerning the reproduction of capitalism. Therefore, the most accurate way of describing the advancement of neoliberal globalisation, from the perspective of nation states, is to insist that it is the transnational capital controlling the state rather than the state controlling capital (Magdoff and Foster, 2011; Robinson, 2014).

From the perspective of the reproduction theory, it seems that the state's transformed role in the global capitalist structure has not changed its core functions regarding the reproduction of capitalism, that is, providing a suitable legal framework and infrastructure, and political and ideological setting, as well as a disciplined and skilful labour. In a greater fashion, the change has affected the economic order globally, as nation states are increasingly integrated into a global capitalist structure, steered by the movements and logic of transnational capital. In this global order, nation states are inevitably caught in the midst of neoliberal restructuring of global capitalism. Consequently, in the 21st century, the legitimacy and competitive position of a single nation state seems to depend on its ability to attract and maintain conditions for transnational capital accumulation (Robinson, 2014, 8-9). At the same time, competition has taken on novel forms, while companies are required, if not forced, to establish and expand to global, instead of national or regional markets. Hence, in addition to the competition between transnational corporations, there exists a conflict between national and transnational fractions of capital (ibid, 27-28). Moreover, parallel to the web of nation states, there exists another web of transnational state apparatuses. As Robinson (2014, 74) points out, on the one hand:

> global corporations could not reproduce their control if it were not for national state apparatuses that provide property rights, arbitration, and social control, and that open up national territories for transnational corporations.

But, on the other hand, the transnational capitalist class could not extend its hegemony to novel territories if, for instance, the:

> IMF did not impose structural adjustments on countries, if the World Bank did not make its lending conditional on the reform of labour laws to make workers flexible, if the WTO did not impose worldwide trade liberalisation, and so on' (ibid).

Concerning the restructuring of global relations of power, it is important to consider how compatible regional, national, and transnational fractions of capital are in reality. As noted, historically in Finland, one of the primary purposes of higher education has been to ensure national competitiveness (see Välimaa, 2012). However, from a transnational perspective, it seems that this aim is increasingly transcended by a trend to homogenise and integrate national economies into a global field of accumulation (Robinson, 2014, 133-134). From this perspective, the primary goal of Finnish higher education would no longer be to secure national competitiveness, but to advance the conditions of transnational capital accumulation, for instance as a regional unit in the EU in the global capitalist economy. As Robinson (2014, 27) has argued, there seems to exist some kind of a paradox between transnationality and nationality in terms of capital. However, if one, in this case, lets go of the idea of nationality, national identity, and national capital, it seems that the paradox somewhat disappears. This is to say that there does not exist a conflict between regional competitiveness (for example Finland as a region in the EU promoting its context for accumulation, while securing its position in global competition) and transnational capital, but an ongoing and seemingly endless competition regarding regional attractiveness concerning conditions and environments for accumulation. Thus, the competition of transnational capital would then increasingly occur between regions, rather than nations, as capital gradually loses its national origins.

The restructuring of Finnish higher education is closely tied to the overall neoliberal restructuring of capitalism, that is, to the requirements of transnational competition regarding investments, innovation, and favourable operating environments for capital accumulation. The aim of the state is to facilitate and organise favourable and attractive operating conditions for (transnational) capital, and the purpose of higher education, from the state's perspective, is to support this process. From this point of view, it also seems difficult to argue that a paradox exists between various fractions of capital, again keeping in mind that there exists an ongoing competition between economic actors and regions. Accordingly, Kauppinen (2013, 11) states that:

> when universities collaborate with the local economy, it does not exclude the possibility that they are simultaneously linked into transnational production networks, and vice versa. In this way, for instance, the transnationalisation of R&D may enforce fuzziness between local, national and transnational scales. This kind of collaboration makes it also problematic to claim that the interests of nationally and globally oriented capitalists would always be opposed to each other.

Disregarding the requirements of capital, an entirely different question concerning the restructuring of higher education and capitalisation of academia is linked to the overall purpose and orientation of higher education. As Kankaanpää (2013) and Lund (2015) have established, for instance, the overall purpose of higher education is perceived very differently among academics in Finland than from the state's perspective. Although it is true that the purpose of contemporary higher education is debated and remains contested, the literature concerning academic, capitalism (e.g. Slaughter and Leslie, 1997; Slaughter and Rhoades, 2004) has convincingly shown how academia, or some parts of academia, have moved closer to the capitalist markets during the last decades. Therefore, it seems that the social conflict over the overall purpose and orientation of higher education is, and has been, consistently won by capital and the agents of capital during the past decades, not only in Finland but transnationally as well.

Turn towards anti-capital in education

> While many faculty think of themselves as advancing the cutting edge of their field of inquiry, few recognize that their thinking is based on many of the same deep cultural assumptions that underlie the last two hundred or so years of forging the modern, industrially dependent and consumer-

oriented form of consciousness that is now being globalized and pushing the world toward ecological catastrophe. (Bowers, 2011, 2)

One of the aims in this book has been to portray the hegemony of capital in the capitalist socio-economic structure. The domination of capital is noticeably felt in many corners of social life, but nevertheless the impact is much more devastating in natural environments. This is no coincidence, because this is the way that capitalism ultimately functions: its hegemonic logic subordinates other social and environmental aims, as accumulation and circulation of capital become the primary societal goals (Marx, 1993; Wallerstein, 2003; Foster, 2009). Therefore, modern-day cries for ecologically and socially sustainable development are among many barriers for capital to overcome and to capitalise upon.

Thus, we have come to a somewhat demoralising conclusion. To live within the capitalist socio-economic structure, it indicates, in principle, that most of our habitual practices, individual choices, and societal structures are unsustainable from an ecological standpoint because of the amount of natural resources we (affluent Westerners) consume, and because of the absolute contradiction (see Foster, 2009, 15). This unsustainable way of being includes higher education because it is an important part of the destructive capitalist structure and its reproduction. As argued, one of the primary purposes of contemporary higher education is to contribute to the reproduction of capitalism by educating the workforce to become part of processes of capital accumulation and by producing outputs and opportunities for economic growth and expansive capital accumulation. Therefore, rather than mitigating the ecological crisis, higher education exacerbates it.

Nonetheless, it is important to note that higher education is by no means the main culprit for the 21st century global crises. For sure, education can be a force for good, and not of destruction.

CONCLUSIONS

Nevertheless, as long as the demands concerning ecological sustainability are not at the forefront of the state's educational policy, which they clearly are not in the case of Finland, as well as in educational activities, practices, and structures, there seems to be little hope for change. This statement relates of course to a wider discussion regarding the purpose, orientation, and politics of nation states and institutional education.

Either way, it is evident that for the sake of life and future human and non-human generations the current priority order in political decision-making, which favours economic growth and economic growth-related social aims over ecological sustainability, should be reversed. This is because without a biosphere that is capable of supporting life, everything else is essentially secondary, and thus, the material world is indeed primary (Jensen, 2006). This is irrespective of human needs, and the needs of whatever social, economic or educational structure. It is persuasively noted, for instance in ecocentric theorising, that nature as a whole is *'more important than humans, as humans are simply one animal species in the ecosystem'* (Ketola, 2008, 426).

Walter Benjamin famously denounces the myth of modernisation and progress in *Illuminations* (1968) referring to written history celebrating technological and economic development. Benjamin remarks that the ones who have been victorious have the privilege to write history, and according to the wishes of those who are in power. Therefore, for example modernity is, according to Benjamin, considered as 'progress'. As Khosravi (2011) notes, for those who have been conquered, suppressed and enslaved, this 'progress' has brought genocide, extinction, slavery, land grabbing, and refugee camps.

In spite of ongoing oppression, inequality, and the self-destructive path of human civilisation, the emergence of human ecological consciousness is a philosophically important occurrence, as has been noted by Naess (1989, 166) and Bowers (1993, 2). It remains to be seen whether the human-caused crisis in the life conditions of our planet can speed up the diffusion of this consciousness and help humans to choose a new path with new criteria for progress, prosperity and peaceful coexistence (see also Heikkurinen, 2017). Meanwhile, it is clear that this kind of reorientation is among the most far reaching in consequences than anything experienced before in human history, entailing profound changes in thinking and existence. In fact, the global ecological crisis seems to have given us an opportunity, if not forcing us industrious Westerners, to ask what it means to be human, and to redefine our relations to self, as well as to fellow humans and non-human beings. To be sure, it is apparent that this kind of reorientation is not likely to come about without a struggle. This is because we are, left with the heavy burden and questionable legacy of industrial capitalism and arrogant belief in technological advancements and Western superiority, while we are offered limited resources and social imaginaries to turn around the course of destruction. Regarding capitalism in particular, it should be clear by now that there is no cure for the logic of capital other than challenging the entire capitalist structure. Thus, *the choice* of our time is between subordination to the hegemony and rule of capital, and between anti-capital(ism). By subordinating to the hegemony of capital, we submit ourselves to a process where things move around more and more quickly, while our subordination is constantly intensified because capital simply cannot stand still (see Holloway, 2015). The other choice is between resistance, and individual and structural change, which is, indeed, *'why the environmental movement, when it goes beyond a merely cosmetic or ameliorative politics, must become anti-capital'* (Harvey, 2014, 252). This is because, as long as the definitive drive behind societal decision-making and structural reforms is capital accumulation and growth for growth's sake, instead of ecological sustainability, social equality and economic wealth redistribution, these reforms are doomed to fail as we have come to realise.

Therefore, instead of 'education for accumulation', (higher) education has to become anti-capital(ist) as well, while the condition of planetary ecosystems and natural habitats should frame not only educational, but all other future social reforms (Bowers, 1993, 2). In today's socio-political situation we are constantly drifting further away from a socially just and ecologically sustainable reforms (in education). The outlook of contemporary higher education is a testimony of this claim. As Anyon (2011, 12) argues, Marx (and Engels) would have agreed that today, in advanced capitalist societies, *'government, large scale media (where a few corporations own the main media outlets) and state education systems produce ideas and truths – the ideologies – that tend to be those who profit most from it.'* According to Marxist educational scholars, like Jean Anyon, it is highly unlikely that capitalist education can contribute to egalitarian society where humans are largely free from coercion and oppression. On the contrary, inequality and exploitation seem to be key elements in societies, if the imperatives of capital are to be pursued, while critical and historical consciousness, and sustainable ecological organisation are not (see Anyon, 1997, 2005; Bowers, 1993; 2011). Accordingly, it is because of these reasons why Marx and Engels (2002, 239) referred to the need to *'rescue education from the influence of the ruling class.'*

With this said, the most fundamental social antagonism concerning capitalism is not actually between wage-labourers and capitalists, but between capital and *anti-capital*; between those who exploit and take part in the exploitation, and those who are trying to get rid of the exploitative practices and structures marked by the hegemony of capital. From an ecological perspective, anti-capitalism in education, or in any other level of social organising, is not to be considered radical, but in fact plain common sense. Sadly, it is clear that the current mental mind-set deems anti-capitalism revolutionary. In contrast, capitalism is very destructive ecologically, but socially legitimate, at least for the time being. This is why I have attempted to portray capitalism the way it is: a radical utopia running against the foundations of life. Especially from this perspective, Karl Marx is truly an important thinker and historical figure. He famously pointed out that societal structures and institutions are not eternal, and argued instead that any historical structure can be transformed or replaced (Eagleton, 1999). Capitalism is a historical structure. It *can* be replaced. It *must* be replaced. It *will* be replaced.

REFERENCES

Aarrevaara, T., Dobson, I. R., and Camilla, E., 2009. Brave New World: Higher Education Reform in Finland. *Higher Education Management and Policy*, vol. 21, no. 2, 1–18.

Alasuutari, P., 1996. Theorizing in Qualitative Research: A Cultural Studies Perspective. *Qualitative Inquiry*, vol. 2, no. 4, 371-384.

Alasuutari, P. 2006. Suunnittelutaloudesta kilpailutalouteen. Miten murros oli ideologisesti mahdollinen? In *Uusi jako: Miten suomesta tuli kilpailukykyyhteiskunta?* Heiskala, R. and Luhtakallio, E. (eds.). Gaudeamus, Helsinki.

Allen, A., 2017. The Cynical Educator. MayflyBooks, Leicester. Available online at: http://mayflybooks.org/?page_id=131.

Althusser, L., 2005. *For Marx*. Orig: *Pour Marx* (1965). Translated by Brewster, B. Verso, Penguin, London.

Althusser, L., 2014. *On the Reproduction of Capitalism: Ideology and Ideological State Apparatuses*. Orig: *Sur la reproduction* (1995). Translated by Goshgarian G. M. Verso, London.

Althusser, L., and Balibar, E., 2009. *Reading Capital*. Orig: *Lire le capital* (1968). Translated by Brewster, B. Verso, Penguin, London.

Andersen, O., 2013. *Unintended Consequences of Renewable Energy*. Springer, London.

Anyon, J., 1979. Education, Social "Structure" and the Power of Individuals. *Theory and Research in Social Education*, vol. 7, no. 1, 49-59.

REFERENCES

Anyon, J., 1980. Social Class and the Hidden Curriculum of Work. *Journal of Education*, vol. 162, no. 1, 67-92.

Anyon, J., 1994. The Retreat of Marxism and Socialist Feminism: Postmodern and Poststructural Theories in Education. *Curriculum Inquiry*, vol. 24, no. 2, 115-133.

Anyon, J., 1997. *Ghetto Schooling: A Political Economy of Urban Educational Reform*. Teachers College Press, Teacher College Columbia University, New York and London.

Anyon, J., 2005. *Radical possibilities: public policy, urban education, and a new social movement*. Routledge, NY: New York.

Anyon, J., 2011. *Marx and Education*. Routledge, New York and London.

Apple, M. W., 1979. *Ideology and Curriculum*. Routledge and Kegan Paul, London.

Apple, M. W., 1981. Reproduction, Contestation, and Curriculum. *Interchange*, vol. 12, no. 2-3. 27-47.

Apple, M. W., 1982. *Education and Power*. Routledge and Kegan Paul, MA: Boston.

Apple, M. W., 2000. Can Critical Pedagogies Interrupt Rightist Policies? *Educational theory*, vol. 50, no. 2, 229-254.

Apple, M. W., 2006. *Educating the "Right" Way* (2nd edition). Routledge, NY: New York.

Apple, M. W., Au, W. and Gandin, L. A., 2009. Mapping Critical Education. In *The Routledge International Handbook of Critical Education*, Apple, M. W., Au, W. and Gandin, L. A. (eds.). Routledge, New York and London.

Apple, M. W. and Buras K. L., 2006. *The Subaltern Speak*. Routledge, NY: New York.

Arrighi, G., 2010. *The Long Twentieth Century: Money, Power and the Origins of Our Times*. Verso, London.

Au, W. and Apple, M. W., 2009. Rethinking Reproduction: Neo-Marxism in Critical Education Theory. In *The Routledge International Handbook of Critical Education*, Apple, M. W., Au, W. and Gandin, L. A. (eds.). Routledge, New York and London.

Balibar, E., 2014. Preface. In *On the Reproduction of Capitalism: Ideology and Ideological State Apparatuses*. Orig: *Sur la reproduction* (1995). Translated by Goshgarian G. M. Verso, London.

Bannon, B. E., 2014. *From Mastery to Mystery: A Phenomenological Foundation for an Environmental Ethic.* Ohio University Press, OH: Athens.

Barnett, R., 2000. *Realizing the University in an Age of Supercomplexity.* Open University Press, Ballmoor.

Barnosky, A. D amd Hadly, E. A., 2016. End Game: Tipping Point for Planet Earth? HarperCollins, NY: New York.

Barnosky, A. D., Hadly, E. A., Bascompte, J., Berlow, E. L., Brown, J. H., Fortelius, M., [...] Smith, A. B., 2012. Approaching a state shift in Earth's biosphere. *Nature* 486, 52–58.

Barnosky, A. D., Matzke, N., Tomiya, S., Wogan, G. O., Swartz, B., Quental, T. B., [...] Ferrer, E. A., 2011. Has the Earth's sixth mass extinction already arrived? *Nature* 471, 51–57.

Bateson, G., 1972. *Steps to an Ecology of Mind.* Ballantine Books, NY, New York.

Bateson, G., 2002. *Mind and Nature.* Hampton Press, NY: New York.

Beck, U., 1999. *Mitä on globalisaatio? Virhekäsityksiä ja poliittisia vastauksia.* Orig: *Was ist globalisierung? Irrtümer des Globalismus – Antworten auf Globalisierung* (1997). Vastapaino, Tampere.

Beerkens, H. J. J. G., 2004. *Global Opportunities and Institutional Embeddedness. Higher Education Consortia in Europe and Southeast Asia.* Retrieved from: https://www.utwente.nl/bms/cheps/phdportal/CHEPS%20Alumni%20and%20Their%20Theses/thesisbeerkens.pdf

Benjamin, W., 1968. *Illuminations.* Orig: *Illuminationen* (1955). Schocken Books, NY: New York.

Bennell, P. and Pearce, T., 2003. The internationalisation of higher education: exporting education to developing and transitional economies. *International Journal of Educational Development*, vol. 23, iss. 2, 215–232.

Benton, T., 1989. Marxism and Natural Limits: An Ecological Critique and Reconstruction. *New Left Review*, 178, 51-86,

Bidet, J., 2014. Introduction. In *On the Reproduction of Capitalism: Ideology and Ideological State Apparatuses.* Orig: *Sur la reproduction* (1995). Translated by Goshgarian G. M. Verso, London.

Bieler, A. and Morton, A. D., 2001. Introduction: Neo-Gramscian Perspectives in International Political Economy and the Relevance to European Integration. In *Social forces and the making of the New Europe: Restructuring European social*

REFERENCES

relations in the global political economy, Bieler, A. and Morton, A. D. (eds.). Palgrave McMillan, Basingstoke.

Bok, D., 2003. *Universities in the Marketplace: The Commercialization of Higher Education*. Princeton University Press, NJ: Princeton.

Boltanski, L. and Chiapello E., 2005. *The New Spirit of Capitalism*. Orig: *Le nouvel espirit du* capitalisme (1999). Translated by Elliott G. Verso, London.

Bourdieu, P., 1996. *The State Nobility*. Orig: *La Nobresse d'état: grande écoles et esprit de corps* (1989). Translated by Clough, L. C. Stanford University Press, CA: Redwood City.

Bourdieu, P. and Passeron, J., 1990. *Reproduction in Education, Society and Culture* (2nd edition). Orig: *La Reproduction. Éléments pour une théorie du système d'enseignement* (1970). Translated by Nice, R. Sage Publications, London.

Bowers, C. A., 1993. *Education, Cultural Myths, and the Ecological Crisis: Toward Deep Changes*. State University of New York Press, NY: Albany.

Bowers, C. A., 2011. *Perspectives on the Ideas of Gregory Bateson, Ecological Intelligence and Educational Reforms*. Eco-Justice Press, OR: Eugene.

Bowles, S. and Gintis, H., 1976. *Schooling in Capitalist America: Educational Reform and the Contradictions of Economic Life*. Basic Books, NY: New York.

Boyle, J., 2003. *The Second Enclosure Movement and the Construction of the Public Domain*. Retrieved from: https://scholarship.law.duke.edu/cgi/viewcontent.cgi?article=1273&context=lcp

Brand, U., 2013. State, context and correspondence. Contours of a historical-materialist policy analysis. Österreichische Zeitschrift für Politikwissenschaft (ÖZP), vol. 42, no. 4, 425-442.

Brenner, R., 2006. *The Economics of Global Turbulence*. Verso, London.

Brown, L. R., 2011. *World on the edge: How to prevent environmental and economic collapse*. WW Norton & Company, NY: New York.

Buci-Glucksmann, C., 1980. *Gramsci and State*. Orig: *Gramsci et l'État: Pour Une Théorie Materialiste de la Philosophie* (1975). Translated by Fernbach D. Lawrence and Wishart, London.

Burkett, P., 2003. The value problem in ecological economics: lessons from the Physiocrats and Marx. *Organization & Environment*, vol. 16, no. 2, 137-167.

Burton-Jones, A., 1999. *Knowledge Capitalism: Business, Work and Learning in the New Economy*. Oxford University Press, Oxford.

Böhm, S., Bharucha, Z. P., and Pretty, J., 2015. *Ecocultures: Blueprints for Sustainable Communities*. Routledge, Oxon and New York.

Calhoun, C., 2013. What Threatens Capitalism Now? In *Does Capitalism Have a Future?*, Wallerstein I., Collins, R., Mann, M., Derluguian, G. and Calhoun C. (eds.). Oxford University Press, Oxford.

Cantwell, B. and Kauppinen I. (eds.), 2014. *Academic Capitalism in the Age of Globalization*. John Hopkins University Press, MD: Baltimore.

Carnoy, M., 1982. Education, Economy and the State. In *Cultural and Economic Reproduction in Education*. Apple, M. W. (ed.). Routledge and Paul Kegan, MA: Boston.

Carnoy, M. and Levin, H. M., 1985. *Schooling and Work in the Democratic State*. Stanford University Press, CA: Redwood City.

Cole, M., 2008. *Marxism and Educational Theory: Origins and Issues*. Routledge, London and New York.

Collins, J., 2009. Social Reproduction in Classrooms and Schools. *Annual Review of Anthropology*, 38, 33-48.

Commoner, B., 1992. *Making Peace with the Planet*. The New Press, NY: New York.

Crutzen, P. J., 2002. Geology of mankind. *Nature* 415, 23–23.

Crutzen, P. J. and Steffen W., 2003. How long have we been in the Anthropocene Era? *Climatic Change*, 61, 251–257.

Crutzen, P. J., Stoermer, E.F., 2000. The Anthropocene. *Global Change Newsletter* 41, 17–18.

Dale, R., 1989. *The State and Education Policy*. Open University Press, London.

Daly, H., 1991. *Steady-State Economics* (2nd edition). Island Press, Washington D.C.

Daly, H. E., 1996. *Beyond Growth*. Beacon Press, MA: Boston.

Darder, A., 1991. *Culture and Power in the Classroom*. Bergin and Garvey, CT: Westport.

Davis, M., 2007. *Planet of Slums*. Verso, London.

Deem, R., Hillyard, S. and Reed M., 2007. *Knowledge, Higher Education, and the New Managerialism. The Changing Management of UK Universities*. Oxford University Press, Oxford.

REFERENCES

Deleuze G., and Guattari F. 2004. *Anti-Œdipus: Capitalism and Schizophrenia.* Orig: Capitalisme et schizophrénie. L'anti-Œdipe (1972). Translated by Hurley R., Seem, M. and Lane, H. Continuum, NY: New York.

Diamond, J., 2005. *Collapse: How Societies Choose to Fail or Succeed.* Viking Press, NY: New York.

Diáz, S., Fargione, J., Chapin, F. S. III and Tilman, D., 2006. Biodiversity Loss Threatens Human Well-Being. *PLoS Biology*, vol. 4, no. 8, e277.

Diefenbach, K., Farris, S., Kirn, G. and Thomas P. D., 2013. *Encountering Althusser: Politics and Materialism in Contemporary Radical Thought.* Bloomsbury Academic, London.

du Gay, P., 2000. Enterprise and its Future: A Response to Fournier and Grey. *Organization*, vol. 7, no. 1, 165-183.

Duménil, G., and Lévy, D., 2004. *Capital Resurgent. Roots of the Neoliberal Revolution.* Harvard University Press, MA: Cambridge.

Eagleton, T., 1999. Marx. *Great Philosophers Series*, Routledge, London.

Eagleton, T., 2012. *Miksi Marx oli oikeassa?* Orig: *Why Marx Was Right?* (2011). Translated by Stenman, P. Like Kustannus, Helsinki.

European Commission, 2000. *Presidential conclusions: Lisbon European Council 23 and 24 March 2000.* Retrieved from: http://www.europarl.e uropa.eu/summits /lis1_en.htm

European Commission, 2006. *Delivering on the modernization agenda for universities: education, research and innovation.* Retrieved from: http://eurlex.europa.eu/LexUriServ/LexUriServ.do?uri=COM:2006:0208:FIN:en:PDF

Eräsaari, L., 2002. *Julkinen tila ja valtion yhtiöittäminen.* Gaudeamus, Helsinki.

Fassbinder, S. D., 2008. Capitalist Discipline and Ecological Discipline. *Green Theory and Praxis: The Journal of Ecopedagogy*, vol. 4, no. 2, 87-101.

Fassbinder, S. D., Nocella, A. J. II and Kahn, R., 2012. *Greening the Academy – Ecopedagogy through Liberal Arts.* Sense Publishers, Rotterdam.

Foster, J. B., 2000. *Marx's Ecology: Materialism and Nature.* Monthly Review Press, NY: New York.

Foster, J. B., 2001. Ecology against Capitalism, *Monthly Review*, vol. 51, no. 5, 1-15.

Foster, J.B., 2002. Marx's ecology in historical perspective. *International Socialism Journal*, iss. 96, 71-86.

Foster, J. B., 2009. *Ecological Revolution – Making Peace with the Planet*. Monthly Review Press, NY: New York.

Foster, J. B., York, R. and Clark B., 2010. *The Ecological Rift: Capitalism's War on Earth*. Monthly Review Press, NY: New York.

Freeman, R., 2006. *The Great Doubling: The Challenge of the New Global Labor Market*. Retrieved from: http://eml.berkeley.edu/~webfac/eichengreen/e183sp07/greatdoub.pdf

Freire, P., 1996. *Pedagogy of the Oppressed*. Orig: *Pedagogia do Oprimido* (1968). Penguin Books, London.

Georgescu-Roegen, N., 1975. Energy and Economic Myths. *Southern Economic Journal*, vol. 41, No. 3, 347-381.

Georgescu-Roegen, N., 1999. *The Entropy Law and the Economic Process* (1971). iUniverse, NE: Lincoln.

Gibson-Graham, J. K., 2006. *A Postcapitalist Politics*. University of Minnesota Press, MN: Minneapolis.

Gill, S., 1995. Globalization, Market Civilization and Disciplinary Neoliberalism. *Journal of International Studies*, vol. 24, no. 3, 399-423.

Giroux, H., 1980. Beyond the Correspondence Theory. *Curriculum Inquiry*, vol. 10, no. 3, 225-247.

Giroux, H., 1981. *Ideology, Culture, and the Process of Schooling*. Temple University Press, PA: Philadelphia.

Giroux, H., 1983. Theories of Reproduction and Resistance in the New Sociology of Education: A Critical Analysis. *Harvard Educational Review*, vol. 53, no. 3, 257-293.

Giroux, H., 1983a. *Theory and Resistance in Education: A Pedagogy for the Opposition*. Bergin & Garvey Publishers, MA: South Hadley.

Giroux, H., 2014. *Neoliberalism's War on Higher Education*. Haymarket Books, IL: Chicago.

Glade, C. and Ekins, P., 2015. The geographical distribution of fossil fuels unused when limiting global warming to 2°C. *Nature*, 517, 187-190.

Gottesman, I., 2016. *The Critical Turn in Education: From Marxist Critique to Postructuralist Feminism to Critical Theories of Race*. Routledge, New York and London.

REFERENCES

Gould, K. A., Pellow, D. N. and Schnaiberg A., 2008. *Treadmill of Production: Injustice and Unsustainability in the Global Economy*. Paradigm Publishers, DE: Colorado.

Graeber, D., 2014. *Debt: The First 5000 Years*. Melville House, London.

Graeber, D., 2015. *The Utopia of Rules – On Technology, Stupidity, and the Secret Joys of Bureaucracy*. Melville House Publishing, London.

Gramsci, A., 1971. *Selections from the Prison Notebooks*. Edited and translated by Hoare Q. and Nowell-Smith G. International Publishers, NY: New York.

Green, A., Rikowski, G. and Raduntz H., 2007. *Renewing Dialogues in Marxism and Education: Openings*. Palgrave Macmillan, NY: New York.

Grigorov, S. K., 2012. *International Handbook of Ecopedagogy for Students, Educators and Parents. A Project for a New Civilization*. Bulgarian Centre for Sustainable Local Development and Ecopedagogy, Sofia. Retrieved from:http://bcslde.org/wp-content/uploads/2012/01/International-Handbook-of-Ecopedagogy-for-Students-Educators-and-Parents.-A-Project-for-a-New-Eco-Sustainable-Civilization.pdf

Hall, S., 2006. The Rediscovery of 'Ideology': Return of the Repressed in Media Studies. In *Cultural Theory and Popular Culture: A Reader* (3rd edition). Storey, J. (ed.). Pearson Education Limited, Dorchester.

Hamilton, C., 2013. *Earthmasters: The Dawn of the Age of Climate Engineering*. Yale University Press, CT: New Haven.

Hamilton, C., Bonneuil C., and Gemenne F., 2015. *The Anthropocene and the Global Environmental Crisis*. Routledge, New York and London.

Harris, J., 2009. Statist Globalization in China, Russia and the Gulf States. *Perspectives on Global Development and Technology*, iss. 8, 139-163.

Harvey, D., 2005. *A Brief History of Neoliberalism*. Oxford University Press, NY: New York.

Harvey, D., 2011. *The Enigma of Capital and the Crises of Capitalism*. Oxford University Press, NY: New York.

Harvey, D., 2014. *Seventeen Contradictions and the End of Capitalism*. Oxford University Press, NY: New York.

Heikkinen A. and Leino-Kaukiainen, P., 2011. Johdanto. In *Valistus ja koulunpenkki: Kasvatus ja koulutus Suomessa 1860-luvulta 1960-luvulle*, Heikkinen A. and Leino-Kaukiainen, P. (eds.). Suomalaisen kirjallisuuden seura, Helsinki.

Heikkurinen, P., 2016. Degrowth by Means of Technology? A Treatise for an Ethos of Releasement. *Journal of Cleaner Production*, online first doi: 10.1016/j.jclepro.2016.07.070

Heikkurinen, P., 2017. *Sustainability and Peaceful Coexistence for the Anthropocene*. Routledge, New York and London.

Heikkurinen, P., Rinkinen, J., Järvensivu, T., Wilén, K. and Ruuska, T., 2016. Organising in the Anthropocene: an ontological outline for ecocentric theorising. *Journal of Cleaner Production*, vol. 113, 705-714.

Heinberg, R., 2005. *The Party's Over*. New Society Publishers, BC: Gabriola Island.

Heiskala, R. and Luhtakallio, E., 2006. Johdanto: Suunnittelutaloudesta kilpailukyky-yhteiskuntaan. In *Uusi jako. Miten Suomesta tuli kilpailukyky-yhteiskunta?*. Heiskala, R. and Luhtakallio, E (eds.). Gaudeamus, Helsinki.

Heiskanen, J., 2001, Ihmisen vieraantuminen luonnosta – Karl Marxin vieraantumisteorian unohdettu puoli. In *Marx ja ekologia*, Heiskanen J. (ed.). Kustannusyhtiö TA-Tieto & Demokraattinen sivistysliitto.

Heiskanen, J., 2010. *Nuoren Marxin luonnonfilosofia ja sen ekologiset seuraukset*. Demokraattinen sivistysliitto, Karl Marx –seura, Helsinki.

Heiskanen, J., 2015. *Karl Marx filosofina*. Demokraattinen sivistysliitto, Karl Marx - seura, Helsinki.

Heiskanen, J., 2016. Karl Marxin materialistinen historiankäsitys. Kyllä vain: monilinjaisuutta ja indeterminismiä. In *Historian teoria: lingvistisestä käänteestä mahdolliseen historiaan*, Väyrynen, K. and Pulkkinen, J. (eds.). Vastapaino, Tampere.

Herrmann, U., 2015. *Pääoman voitto – Kasvun, rahan ja kriisien historia*. Orig: *Der Sieg des Kapitals – Wie der Reichtum in die Welt kam: Die Geschichte von Wachstum, Geld und Krisen* (2013). Translated by Janatuinen M. Into Kustannus, Print Best, Estonia.

Holloway, J., 2015. No, No, No. *ROAR*, iss. 0, 10-31.

Horkheimer, M. and Adorno, T. W., 2008. *Valistuksen dialektiikka: filosofisia sirpaleita*. Orig: *Dialektik der Aufklärung. Philosophische Fragmente* (1944). Translated by Pietilä, V. Vastapaino, Tampere.

Hornborg, A., 2013. *Global Ecology and Unequal Exchange: Fetishism in a Zero-Sum World*. Routledge, London.

REFERENCES

Hornborg, A., 2014. Ecological economics, Marxism, and technological progress: Some explorations of the conceptual foundations of theories of ecologically unequal exchange. *Ecological Economics*, 105, 11-18.

Iivarinen V., 2011. *Raha – Mitä se todella on ja mitä sen tulisi olla?* Into Kustannus, Helsinki.

Ikonen, R., 2011. Korkeasti koulutetun ihmisen ihanne. In *Valistus ja koulunpenkki: Kasvatus ja koulutus Suomessa 1860-luvulta 1960-luvulle*, Heikkinen A. and Leino-Kaukiainen, P. (eds.). Suomalaisen kirjallisuuden seura, Helsinki.

IPCC (Intergovernmental Panel on Climate Change), 2014. *5th Assessment Report. Climate change 2014: Impacts, Adaption, and Vulnerability.*

Jackson, T., 2009. *Prosperity without Growth: Economics for a Finite Planet.* Earthscan, London.

Jalava, M., 2011. Kansanopetuksen suuri murros ja 1860-luvun väittely kansakoulusta. In *Valistus ja koulunpenkki: Kasvatus ja koulutus Suomessa 1860-luvulta 1960-luvulle*, Heikkinen A. and Leino-Kaukiainen, P. (eds.). Suomalaisen kirjallisuuden seura, Helsinki.

Jensen, D., 2006. *Endgame, vol. 1: The Problem of Civilization.* Seven Stories Press, NY: New York.

Jensen, D. and McBay, A., 2009. *What We Leave Behind.* Seven Stories Press, NY: New York.

Jessop, B., 2008. A Cultural Political Economy of Competitiveness and its Implications for Higher Education. In *Education and the Knowledge-based Economy in Europe*, Jessop B., Fairclough, N. and Wodak, R. (eds). Sense, Rotterdam and Taipei.

Jevons, W. S., 1865. On the Coal Question: An Enquiry Concerning the Progress of the Nation, and the Probable Exhaustion of Our Coal-Mines. MacMillan and Co. London. Retrieved from: https://books.google.fi/books?id=gAAKAAAAIAAJ&printsec=frontcover&hl=fi&source=gbs_ge_summary_r&cad=0#v=onepage&q&f=false

Jónasson, J. T., 2005. Counterpoint from an educationalist. In Managing University Autonomy: University autonomy and the institutional balancing of teaching and research. Bononia University Press, Bologna.

Jones, D. S., 2013. Masters of the Universe. Hayek, Friedman and the Birth of Neoliberal Politics. Princeton University Press, NJ: Princeton.

Jones, G. S. 2016. Karl Marx: Greatness and Illusions. The Belknap Press of Harvard University Press, MA: Cambridge.

Julkunen, R., 2006. Kuka vastaa? Hyvinvointivaltion rajat ja julkinen vastuu. Stakes, Helsinki.

Järvensivu, P., 2016. Rajattomasti rahaa niukkuudessa. Like, Helsinki.

Kahn, R. V., 2010. Critical Pedagogy, Ecoliterary & Planetary Crisis: The Ecopedagogy Movement. Peter Land, NY: New York.

Kallunki, J., Koriseva, S. and Saarela H., 2015. Suomalaista yliopistopolitiikkaa ohjaavat perustelut tuloksellisuuden aikakaudella. Kasvatus & Aika, vol. 9, no. 3, 117-133.

Kankaanpää, J., 2013. Kohti yritysmäistä hyöty-yliopistoa. Valtiovallan tahto Suomessa vuosina 1985-2006 ja kokemukset kolmessa yliopistossa. University of Turku, Doctoral Dissertation. Turun yliopiston julkaisuja, Painosalama, Turku.

Kantola, A., 2002. Markkinakuri ja managerivalta. Poliittinen hallinta Suomen 1990-luvun talouskriisissä. Loki-Kirjat, Helsinki.

Kauko, J., 2011. Korkeakoulupolitiikan dynamiikat Suomessa. University of Helsinki, Doctoral Dissertation, Unigrafia, Helsinki.

Kauppinen, I., 2012. Towards transnational academic capitalism. Higher Education, vol. 64, iss. 4, 543-556.

Kauppinen, I., 2013. Academic capitalism and the informational fraction of the transnational capitalist class. Globalisation, Societies and Education, vol. 11, no. 1, 1-22.

Kauppinen, I., 2014. Different Meanings of 'Knowledge as Commodity' in the Context of Higher Education. Critical Sociology, vol. 40, no. 3, 393-409.

Kauppinen, I., 2014a. A moral economy of patents: case of Finnish research universities' patent policies. Studies in Higher Education, vol. 39, No. 10, 1732-1749.

Kauppinen, I. and Cantwell B., 2014. The Global Enterprise of Higher Education. In Academic Capitalism in the Age of Globalization, Cantwell B. and Kauppinen I. (eds.). John Hopkins University Press, MD: Baltimore.

Kauppinen, I. and Cantwell B., 2014a. Transnationalization of Academic Capitalism through Global Production Networks. In Academic Capitalism in

REFERENCES

the Age of Globalization, Cantwell B. and Kauppinen I. (eds.). John Hopkins University Press, MD: Baltimore.

Kauppinen I., and Kaidesoja, T., 2013. A Shift Towards Academic Capitalism in Finland. Higher Education Policy, vol. 1, no. 9, 1-19.

Kelsh, D. and Hill, D., 2006. The Culturalization of Class and the Occluding of Class Consciousness. Journal for Critical Education Policy Studies, vol. 4, no. 1, 1-47. Retrieved from: http://www.jceps.com/wp-content/uplo ads /PDFs/04-01-1.pdf

Ketola, T., 2008. A holistic corporate responsibility model: Integrating values, discourses and actions. Journal of Business Ethics, vol. 80, iss. 3, 419–435.

Kettunen, P., 2008. Globalisaatio ja kansallinen me. Kansallisen katseen historiallinen kritiikki, Vastapaino, Tampere.

Kettunen, P., 2010. Esipuhe. In Huoneentaulun maailma: Kasvatus ja koulutus Suomessa keskiajalta 1860-luvulle, Hanska, J. and Vainio-Korhonen, K. (eds.). Suomalaisen kirjallisuuden seura, Helsinki.

Kettunen, P. and Simola, H., 2012. Johdanto. In Tiedon ja osaamisen Suomi: kasvatus ja koulutus Suomessa 1960-luvulta 2000-luvulle, Kettunen, P. and Simola, H. (eds.). Suomalaisen Kirjallisuuden Seura, Helsinki.

Kettunen, P., Jalava, M. and Simola, H., 2013. Tasa-arvon ihanteesta erinomaisuuden eetokseen. In Tiedon ja osaamisen Suomi: kasvatus ja koulutus Suomessa 1960-luvulta 2000-luvulle, Kettunen, P. and Simola, H. (eds.). Suomalaisen Kirjallisuuden Seura, Helsinki.

Khalanyane, T., 2010. State, schooling and society: Contemporary debates. Educational Research and Reviews, vol. 5, no. 12, 742-747.

Khosravi, S., 2011. 'Illegal' Traveller: An Auto-Ethnography of Borders. Palgrave-Macmillan, London.

Klare, M., 2008. Rising Powers, Shrinking Planet. Henry Holt, NY: New York.

Klein, N., 2014. This Changes Everything: Capitalism vs. The Climate. Simon & Schuster, NY: New York.

Kohn, A., 1992. No Contest: The Case against Competition. Houghton Mifflin Company, NY: New York.

Koivisto, J. and Oittinen, V., 2011. Saatteeksi. In MEGA-Marx: johdatus uuteen Marxiin, Koivisto, J. and Oittinen, V. (eds.). Vastapaino, Tampere.

Kolakowski, L., 2008. Main currents of Marxism: the founders, the golden age, the breakdown. Orig: Główne nurty marksizmu (1978). Translated by Falla, P. S. W. W. Norton & Company, London.

Krätke, M., 2011. Poliittisen taloustieteen uudistaminen ei onnistu ilman Marxia. Translated by Poser, L. and Koivisto, J. In MEGA-Marx: johdatus uuteen Marxiin, Koivisto J. and Oittinen V. (eds.), Vastapaino, Tampere.

Kuisma, M., 2013. Suomen poliittinen taloushistoria 1000-2000. Siltala, Helsinki.

Kumar, R., 2012. Neoliberal Education and Imagining Strategies of Resistance: An Introduction. In Education and the Reproduction of Capital: Neoliberal Knowledge and Counterstrategies, Kumar, R. (ed.). Palgrave MacMillan, NY: New York.

Kwiek, M., 2000. The Nation-State, Globalization and the Modern Institution of the University. Theoria: A Journal of Social and Political Theory, 96, 74–99.

Kwiek, M., 2001. Globalization and Higher Education. Higher Education in Europe, vol. 26, no. 1, 27–38.

Lahtinen, M., 2015. Louis Althusser – Marxin filosofiasta filosofiaan marxismille. In 1900-luvun ranskalainen yhteiskuntafilosofia, Pyykkönen M., and Kauppinen I. (eds.). Gaudeamus Helsinki University Press, Helsinki.

Latouche, S., 2010. Jäähyväiset kasvulle. Orig: Petit traité de la décroissance sereine (2007). Translated by Ollila, M. Into Kustannus, Vantaa.

Lears, T. J. J., 1985. The Concept of Cultural Hegemony: Problems and Possibilities. The American Historical Review, vol. 90, no. 3, 567-593.

Leino-Kaukiainen, P. and Heikkinen A., 2011. Yhteiskunta ja koulutus. In Valistus ja koulunpenkki: Kasvatus ja koulutus Suomessa 1860-luvulta 1960-luvulle, Heikkinen A. and Leino-Kaukiainen, P. (eds.). Suomalaisen kirjallisuuden seura, Helsinki.

Lorek, S. and Spangenberg, J. H., 2014. Sustainable consumption within a sustainable economy – beyond green growth and green economies. Journal of Cleaner Production, 63, 33−44.

Lund, R., 2015. Doing the Ideal Academic: Gender, Excellence and Changing Academia. Doctoral Dissertation, Aalto University publication series, Unigrafia, Helsinki.

Magdoff, F. and Foster J. B., 2011. What Every Environmentalist Needs to

REFERENCES

Know about Capitalism. Monthly Review Press, NY: New York.

Malm, A., 2016. Fossil Capital: The Rise of Steam Power and the Roots of Global Warming. Verso, NY: New York.

Malm, A., 2018. The Progress of This Storm: Nature and Society in a Warming World. Verso, London and New York.

Marx, K., 1970. A Contribution to the Critique of Political Economy. Orig: Kritik der Politischen Ökonomie (1859). Translated by Ryazanskaya, S. W. International Publishers, NY: New York.

Marx, K., 1973. Capital: A Critique of Political Economy, Volume 1: The Process of Capitalist Production. Orig: Das Kapital: Kritik der politischen Ökonomie, Buch 1: Der Produktionsprocess des Kapitals (1867). Translated by Moore, S. and Aveling, E. International Publishers, NY: New York.

Marx, K., 1973a. Capital: A Critique of Political Economy, Volume 2: The Process of Circulation of Capital. Orig: Das Kapital: Kritik der politischen Ökonomie, Buch 2: Der Circulationsprocess des Kapitals (1893). International Publishers, NY: New York.

Marx, K., 1981. Capital: A Critique of Political Economy, Volume 3: The Process of Capitalist Production as a Whole. Orig: Das Kapital: Kritik der politischen Ökonomie, Buch 3: Der Gesamtprozess der kapitalistischen Produktion (1894). Translated by Fernbach, D. Penguin Classics in association with New Left Review, London.

Marx, K., 1993. Grundrisse: Foundations of the Critique of Political Economy. Orig: Grundrisse der Kritik der Politischen Ökonomie (Rohentwurf) (1857-1858). Translated by Nicolaus, M. Penguin Books, London.

Marx, K., 2011. Economic & Philosophic Manuscripts of 1844. Orig: Ökonomisch-philosophische Manuskripte aus dem Jahre 1844. Translated by Milligran M. Martino Publishing, CT: Masnfield Centre.

Marx, K. and Engels, F., 1965. Selected Correspondence. Progress Publishers, Moscow.

Marx, K. and Engels, F., 1979. Collected Works, vol. 11. Progress Publishers, Moscow) in collaboration with Lawrence and Wishart, London, and International Publishers, NY: New York.

Marx, K. and Engels, F., 1998. The German Ideology. Orig: Die Deutsche Ideologie (1846). Translator unknown. Prometheus Books, NY: New York.

Marx, K. and Engels, F., 2002. The Communist Manifesto. Orig: Manifest der Kommunistischen Partei (1848). Translated by: Moore, S. Penguin Classics, London.

McLaren, P., 1988. Culture or Canon? Critical Pedagogy and the Politics of Literacy. Harvard Educational Review, vol. 58, no. 2, 213-234.

McLaren, P., 2013. Seeds of Resistance: Towards a Revolutionary Critical Pedagogy. Socialist Studies, vol. 9, no. 1, 84-108.

McLaren, P. and Houston, D., 2005. Revolutionary Ecologies: Ecosocialism and Critical Pedagogy. In Capitalists and Conquerors: a Critical Pedagogy Against Empire, McLaren, P. (ed.). Rowman and Littlefield, MD: Lanham.

McLellan, D., 1990. Karl Marx: elämä ja teokset. Orig: Karl Marx: His Life and Thought (1973). Translated by Tiusanen, A. Love kirjat, Helsinki.

McLellan, D., 2007. Marxism After Marx. Palgrave MacMillan, NY: New York.

McSherry, C., 2001. Who Owns Academic Work? Battling for Control of Intellectual Property. Harvard University Press, MA: Cambridge.

Meadows, D., Meadows, D., Randers, J. and Behrens, W., 1972. The Limits to Growth. New American Library, NY: New York.

Meadows, D., Meadows, D. and Randers, J., 2002. The Limits to Growth: the 30-Year Update. Chelsea Green Publishing, VT: White River Junction.

Moore, J. W., 2007. Ecology and the Rise of Capitalism. Philosophical Dissertation, University of California, Berkeley.

Moore, J. W., 2015. Capitalism in the Web of Life. Ecology and the Accumulation of Capital. Verso, NY: New York.

Morgan, D. R., 2009. World on fire: two scenarios of the destruction of human civilization and possible extinction of the human race. Futures, vol. 41, iss. 10, 683-693.

Morrow, R, A. and Torres C. A., 1995. Social Theory and Education: A Critique of Theories of Social and Cultural Reproduction. State University of New York Press, NY: Albany.

Mowery, D., C., Richard, N., R., Bhaven S., N. and Arvids, Z., A., 2004. Ivory Tower and Industrial Innovation: University-Industry Technology Transfer Before and After the Bayh-Doyle Act in the United States. Stanford Business Books, CA: Redwood City.

Mumford, L., 1967. The Myth of the Machine: Technics and Human

REFERENCES

Development. Harvest/HBJ Publishers, NY: New York.

Mumford, L., 1970. The Myth of the Machine: The Pentagon of Power. Harvest/HBJ Publishers, NY: New York.

Mäkinen J. and Kourula, A., 2014. Globalization, National Politics and Corporate Responsibility. In Limits to Globalization: National Borders Still Matter, Tainio R., Meriläinen S., Mäkinen J. and Laihonen M. (eds.). Copenhagen Business School Press, Copenhagen.

Naess, A., 1973. The shallow and the deep, long-range ecology movement. A summary. Inquiry: An Interdisciplinary Journal of Philosophy, 16, 95–100.

Naess, A., 1989. Ecology, community and lifestyle. Orig: Økologi, samfunn og livsstil utkast til en økosofi (1974). Translated by Rothenberg, D. Cambridge University Press, Cambridge.

Neave, G., 2000. Introduction. Universities' Responsibilities to Society: An Historical Exploration of an Enduring Issue. In The Universities' Responsibilities to Society: International Perspectives, Neave, G. (ed.). Pergamon Press for International Association of Universities, Oxford.

Nevala, A., 1999. Korkeakoulutuksen kasvu, lohkoutuminen ja eriarvoisuus Suomessa. Suomalaisen kirjallisuuden seura, Helsinki.

Nevala, A., Rinne, R., 2012. Korkeakoulutuksen muodonmuutos. In Tiedon ja osaamisen Suomi: kasvatus ja koulutus Suomessa 1960-luvulta 2000-luvulle, Kettunen, P. and Simola, H. (eds.). Suomalaisen Kirjallisuuden Seura, Helsinki.

Niiniluoto, I., 2015. Yliopistot ja ammattikorkeakoulut yhteiskunnallisina vaikuttajina: yhteenveto. In Vastuullinen ja vaikuttava: Tulokulmia korkeakoulujen yhteiskunnalliseen vaikuttavuuteen. Opetus ja kulttuuriministeriön julkaisuja 2015: 13.

Nixon, J., 2004. Education for the Good Society: the integrity of academic practice. London review of Education, vol. 2, no. 3, 245-252.

O'Connor, J., 1998. Natural Causes: Essays in Ecological Marxism. Guilford Press, NY: New York.

OECD, 2007. Innovation and Growth: Rationale for an Innovation Strategy. Retrieved from: http://www.oecd.org/sti/inno/39374789.pdf

OECD, 2011. Resource Productivity in the G8 and the OECD. A Report in the Framework of the Kobe 3R Action Plan. Retrieved from: http://www.oecd.org/env/waste/47944428.pdf.

Olssen, M. and Peters, M., 2005. Neoliberalism, higher education and the knowledge economy: from the free market to knowledge capitalism. Journal of Education Policy, 20(3), 313-345.

Ortiz, I., Burke, S., Berrada, M. and Cortes, H., 2013. The World Protests 2006-2013. Initiative for Policy Dialogue. Friedrich-Ebert-Stiftung, Columbia University, New York.

Oxfam, 2017. An Economy for the 1%. It's time to build a human economy that benefits everyone, not just the privileged few. Retrieved from: https://www.oxfam.org/sites/www.oxfam.org/files/fileattachments/bp-economy-for-99-percent-160117-en.pdf

Patomäki, H., 2007. Uusliberalismi Suomessa: Lyhyt historia ja tulevaisuuden vaihtoehdot. WSOY, Dark Oy, Vantaa.

Perelman, M., 2000. The Invention of Capitalism. Classical Political Economy and the Secret History of Primitive Accumulation. Duke University Press, London.

Piketty, T., 2014. Capital in the Twenty-first Century. Orig: Le capital au XXI siècle (2013). Translated by Goldhammer, A. The Belknap Press of Harvard University Press, MA: Cambridge.

Polanyi, K., 1968. The Great Transformation (1944). Beacon Press, MA: Boston.

Poulantzas, N., 1975. Classes in Contemporary Capitalism. Orig: Classes sociales dans le capitalisme aujourd'hui (1973). Translated by Fernbach D. New Left Books, London.

Poulantzas, N., 1978. Political Power and Social Classes. Orig: Pouvoir politique et classes sociales de l'état capitaliste (1968). Translated by O'Hagan, T. New Left Books, London.

Poulantzas, N., 2000. State, Power, Socialism. Orig: L'Etat, le Pouvoir, le Socialisme (1978). Translated by Camiller, P. Verso, London.

Pollin, R., 2003. Contours of Descent. Verso, London.

Prieto, P. A. and Hall C. A. S., 2013. Spain's Photovoltaic Revolution: The Energy Return on Investment. Springer, NY: New York.

Pusser, B., Kemper, K., Margison, S. and Ordorika, I. (eds.), 2012. Universities in the Public Sphere: Knowledge Creation and State Building in the Era of Globalization. Routledge, New York.

Pylkkö, P., 2011. Marxin viherpäivityksen vakavasta uskottavuusvajeesta – Jukka

REFERENCES

Heiskasen Marx-tulkinnan tarkastelua. Kustantamo Uuni, retrieved from: www.uunikustannus.fi/marx.pdf

Ranson, S., 1995. Theorising Education Policy. Journal of Education Policy, vol. 10, no. 4, 427-448.

Ray, L. and Sayer, A, 1999. Culture and Economy After the Cultural Turn. Sage Publications, London.

Ranciére, J., 1999. Disagreement: Politics and Philosophy. University of Minnesota Press, MN: Minneapolis.

Rehmann, J., 2014. Theories of Ideology: The Powers of Alienation and Subjection. Haymarket Books, IL: Chicago.

Rekilä, E., 2006. Kenen yliopisto? Tutkimus yliopistojen valtionohjauksesta, markkinaohjautuvuudesta ja itseohjautuvuudesta suomalaisessa yliopistojärjestelmässä. Doctoral dissertation, University of Vaasa, Vaasa.

Resch, R. P., 1992. Althusser and the Renewal of Marxist Social Theory. University of California Press, CA: Berkeley.

Rhoades, G., 2005. Capitalism, Academic Style, and Shared Governance. Academe, vol. 91, no. 3, 38-42.

Rikowski, G., 2000. That Other Great Class of Commodities: Repositioning Marxist Educational Theory. British Educational Research Association conference paper, Cardiff University, 7-10 September. Retrieved from: https://www.academia.edu/6055571/That_Other_Great_Class_of_Commodities_Repositioning_Marxist_Educational_Theory

Rinne, R., 2004. Searching for the Rainbow: Changing the Course of Finnish Higher Education. In Reforming Higher Education in the Nordic Countries – Studies of Change in Denmark, Finland, Iceland, Norway and Sweden, Fägerlind, I. and Strömqvist, G. (eds.). UNESCO and International Institute for Educational Planning.

Rinne, R., 2010. The Nordic University Model from a Comparative and Historical Perspective. In Restructuring the Truth of Schooling – Essays on Discursive Practices in the Sociology and Politics of Education. A Festschrift for Hannu Simola. Research in Educational Sciences 48. FERA, Turku.

Robinson, W. I., 2004. A Theory of Global Capitalism: Production, Class, and State in a Transnational World. The John Hopkins University Press, London.

Robinson, W. I., 2005. Gramsci and Globalisation: From Nation-State to Transnational Hegemony. Critical Review of International Social and Political Philosophy, vol. 8, no. 4, 559-574.

Robinson, W. I., 2014. Global Capitalism and the Crisis of Humanity. Cambridge University Press, NY: New York.

Rockström, J., Steffen W., Noone, K., Persson Å., Chapin S.F.III, [...], and Foley J.A., 2009. A safe operating space for humanity. Nature, 461, 472–475.

Ross, E. W. and Gibson, R., 2007. Introduction. In Neoliberalism and Education Reform, Ross, E. W. and Gibson, R. (eds.). Hampton Pres, NJ: Cresskill.

Rothkopf, D., 2008. Superclass: The Global Power Elite and the World They Are Making. Farrar, Strauss and Giroux, NY: New York.

Saad-Filho, A., 2003. Introduction. In Anti-capitalism: A Marxist Introduction. Saad-Filho, A. (ed.). Pluto Press, London.

Salminen, A. and Vadén, T., 2015. Energy and Experience: An Essay in Naftology. Retrieved from: http://www.mcmprime.com/files/Energy-and-Experience.pdf

Sarkar, S., 2012. The Crises of Capitalism: A Different Study of Political Economy. Counterpoint, CA: Berkeley.

Sennet, R., 1998. The Corrosion of Character: The Personal Consequences of Work in the New Capitalism. W. W. Norton and Company, NY: New York.

Severino, E., 2016. The Essence of Nihilism. Orig: Essenza del nichilismo (1982). Translated by Donis, G. Testoni, I. and Carrera A. (eds). Verso, London and New York.

Shaikh, A., 2005. The Economic Mythology of Neoliberalism. In Neoliberalism: A Critical Reader. Saado-Filho, R. and Johnston, D. (eds.). Pluto Press, London.

Sievers, B., 2008. The Psychotic University. Ephemera, vol. 8, no. 3, 238-257.

Sklair, L., 2001. The Transnational Capitalist Class. Basil Blackwell, Oxford.

Sklair, L., 2002. Globalization. Oxford University Press, Oxford.

Sklair, L., 2008. The transnational capitalist class. Soundings. Cited in Kauppinen I., 2013. Academic capitalism and the informational fraction of the transnational capitalist class. Globalisation, Societies and Education, vol. 11, no. 1, 1-22.

REFERENCES

Slaughter, S. and Cantwell B., 2012. Transatlantic moves to the market: the United States and the European Union. Higher Education, vol. 63, iss. 5, 583-606.

Slaughter, S. and Leslie L. L., 1997. Academic Capitalism. Politics, Policies, and the Entrepreneurial University. John Hopkins University Press, MD: Baltimore.

Slaughter, S. and Rhoades, G., 2004. Academic Capitalism and the New Economy. Markets, State, and Higher Education. John Hopkins University Press, MD: Baltimore.

Smith, A., 1976. An inquiry into the nature and causes of the wealth of nations (1776). Campbell, R. H. and Skinner, A. S (eds.) Oxford University Press, NY: New York.

Soper, K., 1995. What is Nature: Culture, Politics and the Non-Human. Blackwell Publishers, Oxford.

Sotiris, P., 2012. Theorizing the Entrepreneurial University: Open questions and possible answers. Journal for Critical Education Policy Studies, vol. 10, no. 1, 112-126.

Sotiris, P., 2013. Higher Education and Class: production or reproduction? Journal for Critical Education Policy Studies, vol. 11, no. 1, 95-143.

Sotiris, P., 2014. Neither an Instrument nor a Fortress. Poulantzas's Theory of the State and his Dialogue with Gramsci. Historical Materialism, vol. 22, iss. 2, 135-157.

Spash, C. L., 2012. New foundations for ecological economics. Ecological Economics, 77, 36–47.

Standing, G., 2011. The Precariat: The New Dangerous Class. Bloomsbury Academic, London.

Steffen, W., Richardson, K., Rockström, J., Cornell, S.E., Fetzer, I., Bennett, E.M., [...], and Sörlin, S., 2015. Planetary boundaries: Guiding human development on a changing planet. Science, 347, 1259855.

Stiglitz, J., 2012. The Price of Inequality: How Today's Divided Society Endangers Our Future. W. W. Norton & Company, London.

Struna, J., 2009. Toward a Theory of Global Proletarian Fractions. Perspectives on Global Development and Technology, vol. 8, iss. 2, 230-260.

Sweezy, P. M., 1989. Capitalism and the Environment, Monthly Review, vol. 41, no. 2, 1-10.

Tainter, J. A., 2015. The Collapse of Complex Societies. Cambridge University Press, Cambridge.

Tawney, R. H., 1912. The Agrarian Problem in the 16th Century. Longmans, Green and Co, London.

Taylor, G., 1995. Socialism and Education: Marx on Education, Industry and the Fall of Capitalism. General Educator: Journal of the Nafte General Education Supplement, Iss. 35, 19-22.

Therborn, G., 2007. After Dialectics. Radical Social Theory in a Post-Communist World. New Left Review, 43, 63-114.

Thomas, P. D., 2010. The Gramscian Moment: Philosophy, Hegemony and Marxism. Haymarket Books, IL: Chicago.

Thomas, P. D., 2013. Althusser's last encounter: Gramsci. In Encountering Althusser: Politics and Materialism in Contemporary Radical Thought, Diefenbach, K., Farris, S., Kirn, G. and Thomas P. D. (eds.). Bloomsbury Academic, London.

Tomperi, T., 2009. Akateeminen kysymys: yliopistolain kritiikki ja kiista uudesta yliopistosta. Vastapaino, Tampere.

Torres, C. A. and Rhoads, R. A., 2006. Introduction: Globalization and Higher Education in the Americas. In The University, State, and Market: The Political Economy of Globalization in the Americas, Rhoads, R. A. and Torres (eds.). Stanford University Press, CA: Redwood City.

Trainer, T., 2013. Can the world run on renewable energy? A revised negative case. Humanomics, vol. 29, Iss. 2, 88-104.

Uljas, P., 2012. Hyvinvointivaltion läpimurto. Into Kustannus, Helsinki.

Ulvila, M. and Wilen, K., 2017. Engaging with the Plutocene: moving towards degrowth and postcapitalist futures. In Sustainability and Peaceful Coexistence for the Anthropocene, Heikkurinen, P. (ed). Routledge, New York and London.

Unterhalter, E. and Carpenter, V., 2010. Introduction: Whose Interests are We Serving? Global Inequalities and Higher Education. In Global Inequalities and Higher Education: Whose interests are we serving?, Unterhalter, E., and Carpenter, V. (eds.). Palgrave Macmillan, Hampshire.

REFERENCES

Vadén, T., 2009. EROEI-fantasia eli kysymyksiä tulevaisuuden filosofeille. Niin & Näin, 4/09, 46-54.

Wake, D. B. and Vredenburg, V. T., 2008. Are we in the midst of the sixth mass extinction? A view from the world of amphibians. PNAS, 105, 11466-11473.

Wallerstein, I., 2003. Historical Capitalism and Capitalist Civilization (1983). Verso, London.

Wallerstein, I., 2013. Structural Crisis, or Why Capitalists May No Longer Find Capitalism Re-warding. In Does Capitalism Have a Future?, Wallerstein I., Collins, R., Mann, M., Derluguian, G. and Calhoun C. (eds.). Oxford University Press, NY: New York.

Ward, S., C., 2012. Neoliberalism and the Global Restructuring of Knowledge and Education. Routledge, New York and London.

Ward, J.D., Sutton P.C., Werner, A.D., Costanza, R., Mohr, S.H. and Simmons C.T., 2016. Is Decoupling GDP Growth from Environmental Impact Possible? PLoS One, vol. 11, no. 10, e0164733.

Weber, M.. 1958. The Protestant Ethic and the Spirit of Capitalism. Orig: Die protestantische Ethik und der Geist des Kapitalismus (1904-1905). Scribner's Press, NY: New York.

Weiler, K., 1994. Freire and Feminist Pedagogy of Difference. Harward Educational Review, vol. 61, no. 4, 449-474.

Victor, P. A., 2008. Managing without Growth: Slower by Design, Not Disaster. Edward Elgar, Chelteham.

Wiedmann, T., Schandl, H., Lenzen, M., Moran, D., Suh, S., West, J. and Kanemoto, K., 2015. The material footprint of nations. PNAS, vol. 112, no. 20, 6271-6276.

Vitali, S., Glattfielder, J. & Battison, S., 2011. The Network of Global Corporate Control. PLOS ONE, retrieved from: http://journals.plos.org/plosone/article?id=10.1371/journal. pone.0025995

Williams, R., 1973. Base and Superstructure in Marxist Cultural Theory. New Left Review, 82, 3-16.

Willis, P., 1983. Cultural Production and Theories of Reproduction. In Race, Class and Education, Barton, L. and Walker S. (eds.). Groom-Helm, London.

Wood, E. M., 2002. The Origin of Capitalism. A Longer View. Verso, London.

Wood, E. M., 2003. Globalisation and the State: Where is the Power of Capital?

In Anti-capitalism: A Marxist Introduction, Saad-Filho, A. (ed.). Pluto Press, London.

Wood, E. M., 2005. Pääoman imperiumi. Orig: Empire of Capital (2003). Translated by Koivisto J. Vastapaino, Tampere.

WWF, 2014. Living Planet Report 2014: Species and spaces, peoples and places. Retrieved from: http://ba04e385e36eeed47f9cabbcd57a2a90674a4bcb7fab6c619 8d0.r88.cf1.rackcdn.com/Living_Planet_Report_2014.pdf

Wright, E. O., 1987. The Intellectual Saga of Althusserian Marxism. A review of Benton, T., The Rise and Fall of Structure Marxism: Althusser and His Influence. Contemporary Sociology, vol. 16, no. 1, 14-15.

Wrigley, E. A., 2010. Energy and the English Industrial Revolution. Cambridge University Press, Cambridge.

Välimaa, J. 2001. A Historical Introduction to Finnish Higher Education. In Finnish Higher Education in Transition: Perspectives on Massification and Globalisation, Välimaa, J. (ed.). Institute for Educational Research, University of Jyväskylä, Jyväskylä.

Välimaa, J., 2012. The corporatization of national universities in Finland. In Universities in the Public Sphere: Knowledge Creation and State Building in the Era of Globalization, Pusser, B., Kemper, K., Margison, S. and Ordorika, I. (eds.). Routledge, NY: New York.

Välimää, J. and Hoffman, D., 2008. Knowledge society discourse and higher education. Higher Education, vol. 56, iss. 3, 265-285.

Yliaska, V., 2014. Tehokkuuden toiveuni – Uuden julkisjohtamisen historia Suomessa 1970-luvulta 1990-luvulle. Into Kustannus, Helsinki.

Young, M., and Whitty, G., 1977. Society, State and Schooling: Readings on the possibilities for radical education. Falmer, London.

Young, M., and Whitty, G., 1977a. Introduction. In Society, State and Schooling: Readings on the possibilities for radical education, Young, M., and Whitty, G., (eds.). Falmer, London.

Zencey, E., 2013. Energy as Master Resource. In State of the World 2013: Is Sustainability Still Possible? The Worldwatch Institute, Washington D.C.

REFERENCES

State policy documents (documents available online)

2000

Katsaus 2000: Tiedon ja osaamisen haasteet. Valtion tiede- ja teknologianeuvosto, Helsinki.

2001

Management by result in higher education. Opetusministeriö.

2002

Education for sustainable development in Finland. Loukola, M., Isoaho S. and Lindström K. (eds.). Opetusministeriö.

Yliopistot 2001. Patosalmi, I. and Korpi, J. (eds.). Opetusministeriö.

2003

Osaaminen, innovaatiot ja kansainvälistyminen. Valtion tiede- ja teknologianeuvosto, Helsinki.

Pääministeri Matti Vanhasen hallituksen ohjelma 24.6.2003. Valtioneuvoston kanslia.

Yliopistot 2002. Patosalmi, I. and Korpi, J. (eds.). Opetusministeriö.

2004

Koulutus ja tutkimus 2003-2008: Kehittämissuunnitelma. Opetusministeriön julkaisuja 2004:6.

Management and Steering of Higher Education in Finland. Publications of the Ministry of Education, Finland 2004:20. Helsinki.

2005

Valtioneuvoston periaatepäätös julkisen tutkimusjärjestelmän rakenteellisesta kehittämisestä. Valtioneuvosto, 7.4.2005.

Yliopistot 2004: Vuosikertomus. Patosalmi, I. and Halonen T. (eds.). Opetusministeriön julkaisuja 2005:12.

2006

Koulutus ja tiede Suomessa. Opetusministeriön julkaisuja 2006:8.

Valtioneuvoston koulutuspoliittinen selonteko eduskunnalle. Opetusministeriön julkaisuja 2006:24.

Yliopistot 2004: Vuosikertomus. Halonen T., Mäkeläinen, U. and Vuorinen, B. (eds.). Opetusministeriön julkaisuja 2006:30.

2007

Lisää liiketoimintaosaamista korkeakouluista: Liiketoimintaosaamisen selvitysryhmän raportti. Opetusministeriön työryhmämuistioita ja selvityksiä 2007:38.

Pääministeri Matti Vanhasen II hallituksen ohjelma, 19.4.2007. Valtioneuvoston kanslia.

Teknillisen korkeakoulun, Helsingin kauppakorkeakoulun ja Taideteollisen korkeakoulun yhdistyminen uudeksi yliopistoksi. Opetusministeriön työryhmämuistioita ja selvityksiä 2007:16.

Towards Sustainable Development in Higher Education – Reflections. Kaivola, T. and Rohweder, L. (eds.). Publications of the Ministry of Education 2007:6.

Yliopistojen taloudellisen ja hallinnollisen aseman uudistaminen. Jääskinen, N. and Rantanen J. (eds.). Opetusministeriön työryhmämuistioita ja selvityksiä 2007:2.

Yliopistot 2006: Vuosikertomus. Haapamäki, J., Mäkeläinen, U., Hiltunen, K. and Nokkala, T. (eds.). Opetusministeriön julkaisuja 2007:17.

2008

Korkeakoulujen rakeenteellisen kehittämisen suuntaviivat vuosille 2008-2011. Opetusministeriö 7.3.2008.

Korkeakoulut 2007: Vuosikertomus. Haapamäki, J., Mäkeläinen, U. and Piiroinen, K. (eds.). Opetusministeriön julkaisuja 2008:30.

Koulutus ja tiede Suomessa. Opetusministeriön julkaisuja 2008:24.

Koulutus ja tutkimus 2007-2012: Kehittämissuunnitelma. Opetusministeriön julkaisuja 2008:9.

Laki 1043/2008. Valtioneuvoston asetus tutkimus- ja innovaationeuvostosta.

Linjaus 2008. Tiede- ja teknologianeuvosto, Helsinki.

Talouspoliittinen ministeriövaliokunta koskien yliopistojen säätiöittämismahdollisuutta. Opetusministeriö 10.4.2008.

REFERENCES

2009

Korkeakoulujen kansainvälistymisstrategia 2009–2015. Opetusministeriön julkaisuja 2009:21.

Korkeakoulut 2009: Yliopistot ja ammattikorkeakoulut korkeakoulupolitiikan toteuttajina. Haapamäki, J., Mäkeläinen, U. Nokkonen, I. and Piiroinen, K. (eds.). Opetusministeriön julkaisuja 2009:49.

Laki 558/2009. Yliopistolaki.

Yliopistojen ohjaus ja rahoitus vuodesta 2010 alkaen. Opetusministeriö, Luonnos 3.3.2009.

Yrittäjyyskasvatuksen suuntaviivat. Opetusministeriön julkaisuja 2009:7.

2010

Kiinnostuksesta kysynnäksi ja tuotteiksi – Suomen koulutusviennin strategiset linjaukset. Valtioneuvoston periaatepäätös 29.4.2010.

Osaava ja luova Suomi: Opetus- ja kulttuuriministeriön tulevaisuuskatsaus. Opetus- ja kulttuuriministeriön julkaisuja 2010:15.

Tutkimus- ja innovaatiopoliittinen linjaus 2011–2015. Tutkimus ja innovaationeuvosto.

2011

Pääministeri Jyrki Kataisen hallituksen ohjelma, 22.6.2011. Valtioneuvoston kanslia.

Korkeakoulut 2011- yliopistot ja ammattikorkeakoulut. Haapamäki, J., Kumpulainen, J., Piiroinen, K. and Halonen, T. (eds.). Opetus- ja kulttuuriministeriön julkaisuja 2011:10.

Tasapainoiseen työllisyyskehitykseen 2025: Ehdotus koulutustarjonnan tavoitteiksi vuodelle 2016. Opetus- ja kulttuuriministeriön työryhmämuistioita ja selvityksiä 2011:16.

2012

Koulutus ja tutkimus 2011-2016: Kehittämissuunnitelma. Opetus- ja kulttuuriministeriön julkaisu-ja 2012:1.

Yliopistolakiuudistuksen vaikutusten arviointi. Niinikoski, M., Lunabba, J., Raivio, T., Lehti, R. and Pessala, P. (eds.). Opetus- ja kulttuuriministeriön julkaisuja 2012:21.

2013

Yliopistojen tieteellinen ja taiteellinen toiminta sekä yhteiskunnallinen vaikuttavuus vuonna 2011: Yhteenveto yliopistoilta kerätyistä julkaisutiedoista. Opetus- ja kulttuuriministeriön julkaisuja 2013:4.

2014

Kansallisen osaamisperustan vahvistaminen: Johtopäätöksiä. Opetus- ja kulttuuriministeriön julkaisuja 2014:19.

Osaamisella ja luovuudella hyvinvointia: Opetus- ja kulttuuriministeriön tulevaisuuskatsaus 2014. Opetus- ja kulttuuriministeriön julkaisuja 2014:18.

Laki 932/2014. Ammattikorkeakoululaki.

Suomalaisten koulutusrakenne ja sen kehittyminen kansainvälisessä vertailussa. Kalenius, A. (ed.). Opetus- ja kulttuuriministeriön julkaisuja 2014:17.

Uudistava Suomi: tutkimus- ja innovaatio politiikan suunta 2015–2020. Tutkimus ja innovaationeuvosto.

2015

Kärkihanke: Osaaminen ja koulutus, 4.9.2015. Grahn-Laasonen, S. and Rehn O. Valtioneuvoston kanslia.

Opetus- ja kulttuuriministeri Sanni Grahn-Laasosen avoin kirje yliopistojen ja ammattikorkeakoulujen johdolle 27.10.2015. Opetus- ja kulttuuriministeriö, verkkouutinen, 27.10.2015.

Ratkaisujen Suomi: Pääministeri Juha Sipilän hallituksen strateginen ohjelma 29.5.2015. Hallituksen julkaisusarja, 10/2015.

Suomi osaamisen kasvu-uralle: Ehdotus tutkintotavoitteista 2020-luvulle. Opetus- ja kulttuuriministeriön työryhmämuistioita ja selvityksiä 2015:14.

Vastuullinen ja vaikuttava: Tulokulmia korkeakoulujen yhteiskunnalliseen vaikuttavuuteen. Opetus- ja kulttuuriministeriön julkaisuja 2015:13.